*Anti-Imperialism in
the United States*

Anti-Imperialism in the United States:
The Great Debate, 1890-1920

E. BERKELEY TOMPKINS

UNIVERSITY OF PENNSYLVANIA PRESS

Philadelphia

ISBN: 0-8122-7595-0
Manufactured in the United States of America

To S. K. T.

ACKNOWLEDGMENTS

I WOULD like to take this opportunity to thank the institutions, organizations, and individuals who aided me, both directly and indirectly, in this work.

For the use of their facilities and collections and for courtesies extended I wish to thank the directors and staffs of the following institutions: Sterling Library, Yale University, Widener Library, Harvard University, University of Pennsylvania Library, Free Library of Philadelphia, Library of Congress, Carnegie Library (Pittsburgh, Pa.), the Boston Athenaeum, Massachusetts Historical Society, Pennsylvania Historical Society, Hoover Institution Library, Stanford University Library.

For financial aid I am most grateful to the Samuel S. Fels Fund.

For permission to reprint certain material which appeared earlier in my articles in the *Pacific Historical Review* and *The Historian,* I wish to thank the editors of these journals.

For inspiration, encouragement, advice and criticism over a period of years I am indebted in various ways to Roy F. Nichols, F. Hilary Conroy, and Murray G. Murphey of the University of Pennsylvania; George W. Pierson and Howard R. Lamar of Yale University; David M. Potter of Stanford University; Richard E. Welch of Lafayette College; Albert E. Stone of Emory University; and most especially and deeply to Thomas C. Cochran of the University of Pennsylvania and Thomas A. Bailey of Stanford University.

Finally I wish to thank Sally, who endured.

E. B. T.

Contents

CHAPTER 1

Introduction

The final decade of the nineteenth century was one of the most significant transitional periods in American history. Nowhere is this more evident than in the field of American foreign affairs. Within the space of a few years the government abandoned the principles of traditional foreign policy which had guided the nation since its inception.

These turbulent years witnessed the emergence of an American imperialist rationale; and the United States, which a century earlier had been born out of a reaction against imperial domination, became, itself, an imperial power. Such a dramatic change, filled with momentous consequences, elicited a strong adverse reaction. This reaction—anti-imperialism—developed concomitantly with the growth of imperialist sentiment in the United States. Although the tangible symbols of America's insular empire—Hawaii, the Philippines, Samoa, Guam, and Puerto Rico—were not acquired until the last two years of the century, the ideological struggle between the imperialists and anti-imperialists considerably antedated the Spanish-American War period, and lingered on, although diminished in intensity, for many years afterward.

Much of the controversy between the imperialists and anti-imperialists in the United States in the late nineteenth and early twentieth centuries manifested itself in the form of a greatly extended and vigorously contested debate, with charges and countercharges, presentations and rebuttals filling the pages of the nation's journals and echoing in the halls of Congress and councils of state. As the title indicates, the anti-imperialist side of this debate is highlighted here. While the book spans the period between the genesis of the debate in 1890 and the demise of the Anti-Imperialist League in 1920, the decade between 1892 and 1902 is stressed, since these were the years in which the topic was of vital national concern.

The book is based on a wide range of materials, including many previously untapped sources, and provides the first comprehensive study of American anti-imperialism. It examines in a basically chronological context the issues, events, ideas, and organizations that were a part of the complex phenomenon of American anti-imperialism and emphasizes the thought and writings of the leading anti-imperialists in relation to changing incidents and circumstances.

The term "imperialism," as anyone living during the current cold war is well aware, means different things to different people. Therefore, lest contemporary concepts and propaganda confuse the reader, it should be pointed out here that it was the actual political domination of one people by another that the American anti-imperialists at the turn of the century primarily opposed.

The anti-imperialists contended not only that the problems of administering a colonial empire were myriad, complicated, and often highly distasteful, but also that imperialism, per se, represented a flagrant violation of the fundamental principles upon which the government of the United States was based. They emphasized that the United States had stood as the champion of liberty, democracy, equality, and self-government throughout the world and that imperialism, by its very nature, was a denial of the universal validity of these tenets.

Although the imperialists claimed that our annexation of insular possessions was merely an extension of our heritage of territorial expansion, the anti-imperialists felt that there was a definite dichotomy between the earlier type of continental expansion and the imperialism of the end of the nineteenth century. They pointed out that previous territorial acquisitions by the United States had all been upon the North American continent, and that all except Alaska were contiguous to the nation's then existing boundaries. If they had been populated at all, it was very sparsely; and it had not been necessary to swell the nation's military forces and alter traditional policies in dealing with them, as was the case with the eventual acquisitions of the 1890's. Also, there had always been the expectation, which in every case was subsequently justified, that these areas would be settled by Americans and eventually become self-governing and equal states of the Union.

The anti-imperialists, if perhaps regretting the aggressive character of some of our earlier acquisitions, largely accepted this former continental expansion as "natural." They believed, however, that the United States had reached the limit of its "normal" growth and that the people's attention should be devoted to developing the vast extent of territory which the nation already possessed. The imperialists, on the other hand, not only accepted this earlier expansion, but exulted in it, and felt that it should be emulated on a global scale.

Earlier there had been cursory feints in the direction of acquiring insular possessions. Even before the Civil War, covetous eyes were cast upon Cuba, Hawaii, and Santo Domingo. However, at mid-century the most urgent problem became not one of how to extend the national domain, but rather, how to keep the existing territory from being rent in twain. The Union was eventually preserved only by a long internecine conflict, which left the people of the nation physically ennervated, emotionally exhausted, financially burdened, and in no mood to undertake risky foreign ventures.

Although the strongly pro-imperialist Secretary of State, William H. Seward, was abetted by Presidents Johnson and Grant, he could not bring to fruition any of his manifold schemes for overseas expansion. Seward, in contemplating the frustration of his dream of matching his Alaskan coup by extending American hegemony to lands overseas, lamented that "public attention . . . continues to be fastened upon the domestic questions which have grown out of our late Civil War. The public mind refuses to dismiss these questions even so far as to entertain the higher, but more remote, questions of national extension." [1]

The nation underwent a vast transformation in the following two decades. By 1890 the physical and psychological wounds had largely healed. The nation was further drawn together by a vast network of transcontinental railroads and telegraph lines. The United States had changed economically from a predominantly agricultural nation intent upon the development of a virgin continent to a predominantly industrial one seeking to become the world's leading manufacturing and commercial power. The output of the country's mines and factories grew extraordinarily, and the need for wider markets was felt. This led many people to believe that the United States really had no choice but to expand overseas and obtain colonial markets. Thus Charles A. Conant remarked that "the irresistible tendency to expansion . . . seems again in operation demanding new outlets for American capital and new opportunities for American enterprises." [2]

Another potent influence upon the creation of imperialist sentiment in the United States was the example provided by European imperialism. This was noted and deplored by the anti-imperialists who felt strongly that the United States should not adopt the international policies of effete monarchies, which the leaders of this country had long criticized. Nevertheless, the rapid growth of the empires of European nations, especially those of Great Britain, Germany, and France, profoundly affected American public opinion. Thus Henry Cabot Lodge, one of the nation's foremost imperialists, commented significantly:

The modern movement is all toward the concentration of people and territory into great nations and large dominions. The great nations are rapidly absorbing for their future expansion and their present defense all the waste places of the earth. It is a movement which makes for civilization and the advancement

---

1. Frederick W. Seward, *Seward at Washington* (New York, 1891), Vol. II, p. 383.
2. Charles A. Conant, "The Economic Basis of Imperialism," *North American Review,* Vol. CLXVII (September, 1898), p. 326.

of the race. As one of the great nations of the world, the United States must not fall out of the line of march.[3]

Lodge's remark about "the advancement of the race" illustrates another factor which conditioned American imperialist ideology—the evolutionary theory of Charles Darwin, Herbert Spencer, and their interpreters, commentators, and supporters. The idea of a struggle for existence in the world of nature which resulted in the survival of the fittest was enthusiastically accepted, adapted, and utilized by the prophets of the new Manifest Destiny at the end of the century. The exponents of American imperialism applied the biological concepts to society and worked out pseudo-scientific theories to support and justify their own imperialistic doctrines. It was argued that since the survival of the fittest was the law of nature and the way of progress, the superior races and nations were merely obeying primordial and inexorable dictates in dominating the "lesser breeds."

The operation of these general factors—extraordinary industrial growth, the example of European imperialism, and the influence of Social Darwinism—combined with others which we shall subsequently examine, by 1890 had done much to induce the American people to look more favorably upon imperialism as a policy for the United States. In the final decade of the century imperialism was a miasma in the air. The surge of events in this period was to cause abstract imperial theory in the United States to be put into actual practice. Then the anti-imperialists were to feel that they were battling to save the very life of the nation as a democratic republic.

Arthur O'Shaughnessy wrote that "each age is a dream that is dying or one that is coming to birth." For the imperialists the age that the 1890's ushered in was one replete with dreams of imperial dominion. For the anti-imperialists, the ensuing decades would be a disturbing phantasmagoria which they would do their utmost to dispel.

---

3. Henry Cabot Lodge, "Our Blundering Foreign Policy," *The Forum,* Vol. XIX (March, 1895), p. 17.

CHAPTER 2

The Anxious Years

The anti-imperialists believed strongly in traditional American foreign policy and felt that the precepts enunciated in Washington's farewell address and Jefferson's first inaugural should continue to be the nation's guide in foreign affairs. They doubted the validity of sweeping predictions of the course of cosmic destiny. They questioned the inherent value of a burgeoning military establishment and decried chauvinism and jingoism. They felt imperialism in any of its protean forms was anathema. For them the final tumultuous decade of the nineteenth century was an anxious period indeed.

The anxiety of the opponents of imperialism was engendered by events and trends and attitudes which were, themselves, the products of a troubled transitional era. At the very commencement of the decade, Benjamin Flower, the perspicacious editor of *The Arena,* remarked: "To the serious observer . . . he who is in touch with the people, the mental attitude is unmistakable. A startled, uneasy, anxious condition of thought is abroad. The pulse of the people is becoming quick, nervous, ferverish." [1] In this electric atmosphere the exciting words and deeds of the imperialists were more welcome than the sober admonitions of the anti-imperialists. The preachers of "the strenuous life," much to the dismay of the anti-imperialists, were being applauded by an increasingly wider audience.

Toward the end of the century it would be the activists in

---

1. B. O. Flower, *The Arena,* Vol. III (December, 1890), pp. 124-125.

the political arena—Lodge, Roosevelt, Platt, Beveridge—who would be in the imperialist vanguard and who would be the devil's advocates whom the anti-imperialists scorned. But the way was prepared for these later imperialist leaders by earlier theorists.

One of the most prominent of the imperialist torchbearers whose views dismayed the anti-imperialists of the early 1890's was historian John Fiske. This popular lecturer, who was one of the most influential American intellectuals of his day, provided a succinct statement of imperialist thought in a widely disseminated essay entitled "Manifest Destiny." [2] It was very well received, not only by Fiske's young friends and fellow Harvard men Theodore Roosevelt and Henry Cabot Lodge, but also by the general public.

Fiske was profoundly influenced by the evolutionary theories of Charles Darwin and Herbert Spencer and combined these new ideas with the older doctrines of Manifest Destiny. Using the whole of previous human history as a background, he predicted in soaring rhetoric a future of great territorial expansion for the United States. Although claiming to be an objective historian and philosopher ("My course . . . is determined by historical or philosophical rather than by patriotic interest." [3]) he expounded a dynamic, chauvinistic theory of American Anglo-Saxon racial superiority and imperial destiny.

Fiske predicted a population explosion that would increase the number of Americans by several hundred millions. One can see the effect that his writing was to have; for Samuel L. Parrish, in an imperialistic article written years later, commented: "So philosophical an historian and conservative observer of events as Mr. John Fiske in his essay on 'Manifest Destiny' puts the number of Americans in the twentieth century between five and

---

2. Originally conceived as a lecture, which was repeated scores of times before large audiences, it was published in 1885 in *Harper's New Monthly Magazine,* and subsequently appeared in a book the same year.

3. John Fiske, "Manifest Destiny," *American Political Ideas* (New York, 1885), p. 103.

six hundred millions." [4] The rationale of these men was that the predicted population pressure, which was indeed at times a factor in European imperialism, would force the United States to expand abroad.

Fiske asserted that the twentieth century would see the United States as master of "a political aggregation immeasurably surpassing in power and dimensions any empire that has yet existed," and that "the time will come . . . when it will be possible . . . to speak of the United States as stretching from pole to pole." [5]

Fiske gave a strong stimulus to imperialistic thinking in the United States in the early 1890's and thereafter. He also, perhaps even more significantly, provided his countrymen—in his resuscitation of the phrase "Manifest Destiny"—with a convenient euphemism for imperialism—a word which had a pejorative connotation for many Americans. "Manifest Destiny" seemed to convey the idea of mere compliance with the dictates of Providence (another favorite imperialist shibboleth) or evolutionary or cosmic trends, instead of carrying the implications of aggressive and selfish imperialism. It was, therefore, increasingly invoked in the 1890's, as it had been in the 1840's, to justify American territorial expansion. This type of sophistry was not indigenous to the United States. John R. Seeley, probably the foremost contemporary chronicler of British imperialism,[6] noted a similar phenomenon in England and remarked that "when a metaphor comes to be regarded as an argument, what an irresistible argument it always seems." [7]

---

4. Samuel L. Parrish, "American Expansion Considered as Historical Evolution," *American Journal of the Social Sciences,* Vol. XXXVII (December, 1899), p. 106.

5. Fiske, *op. cit.,* pp. 139, 151.

6. Seeley is perhaps best known for his memorable and amusing, if not necessarily accurate, statement concerning British Imperialism: "We seem, as it were, to have conquered and peopled half the world in a fit of absence of mind." *Expansion of England* (Boston, 1886), p. 8.

7. *Ibid.,* p. 296.

This mellifluous phrase became a *bête-noire* for the anti-imperialists early in the 1890's. Its reiteration, such as in the Republican platform of 1892, which called for "the achievement of the Manifest Destiny of the Republic in its broadest sense," [8] profoundly disturbed men in all walks of life who feared the consequences of the adoption of an imperial policy by the United States. Carl Schurz, the talented and versatile German-American who served his adopted land so ably (as Major General in the Union Army, Minister to Spain, U.S. Senator, Secretary of the Interior, etc.), and who was such a strong and devoted anti-imperialist,[9] complained that "whenever there is a project on foot to annex foreign territory to this Republic, the cry of 'Manifest Destiny' is raised to produce the impression that all opposition to such a project is a struggle against fate." [10] Businessman Norris Gage declared that the claim that "aggressive expansion is our 'Manifest Destiny' and hence cannot be resisted is unworthy of the name of an argument. It is an apology only . . . a convenient catch phrase" used for purposes of rationalization and to beguile the unthinking.[11] George T. Curtis, a noted scholar, contended, moreover, that "the phrase 'Manifest Destiny' was never a favorite with considerate people; nor has the sentiment which it expresses given the world at large a pleasant idea of our national character." [12] Congressman Champ

---

8. Kirk H. Porter, *National Party Platforms* (New York, 1924), p. 175.

9. Schurz was a vice-president of the original Anti-Imperialist League, an officer of the New York and American Anti-Imperialist Leagues, and perhaps the leading publicist of the anti-imperialist cause. His pronouncements on the subject—in speeches, letters, pamphlets, editorials, and articles—are unusually cogent and astoundingly prolific.

10. Carl Schurz, "Manifest Destiny," *Harper's Magazine,* Vol. LCXXXVII (October, 1893), p. 737.

11. Norris Gage, "National Growth versus Foreign Conquest," address before the Economic League of Ashtabula, Ohio (pamphlet).

12. George T. Curtis, "Can Hawaii Be Constitutionally Annexed to the U.S.," *North American Review,* Vol. CLVI (March, 1893), p. 285.

Clark more bluntly condemned it as "the specious plea of every robber and freebooter since the world began." [13]

A related phenomenon which, like the resuscitated doctrine of Manifest Destiny, caused the anti-imperialists of the early nineties and thereafter great anxiety was what might be termed evangelical imperialism. This was the doctrine, so often emphasized at the end of the century in the phrase, "The White Man's Burden," which proclaimed that the more civilized and enlightened nations had a mission to perform by taking over the backward peoples of the earth. If "the lesser breeds without the law" were plundered and decimated, it was, of course, regrettable; but the imperialists implied that it was all in the interest of religion and the progress of civilization. The anti-imperialists considered this philosophy contemptible, hypocritical, and a travesty upon the tenets of Christianity. However, in the final decade of the nineteenth century, evangelical, or missionary, imperialism became increasingly popular in the United States.

Perhaps the most important single stimulus to this type of thinking was a slender volume written by a Congregational minister, Josiah Strong. In 1885, while Secretary of the American Home Mission Society, Strong wrote *Our Country: Its Possible Future and Its Present Crisis*. The book was very widely read, eventually selling more than 175,000 copies. Strong's philosophy, as evinced by this work, was a potpourri of evangelical Protestantism, vigorous nationalism, Social Darwinism, intense racialism, and American expansionism.

Strong praised his countrymen's "money making power" and "colonizing genius." This juxtaposition must have especially disturbed the anti-imperialists, many of whom claimed that the imperialists' moral maxims were simply a cloak for selfish aggrandizement. Strong, however, like a good Calvinist, believed that the nation's increasing affluence was simply another sign of a Chosen People who were destined to rule the earth. "Is it manifest," he asked rhetorically, "that the Anglo-Saxon holds in his hands the destinies of mankind for ages to come? Is it evident that the United States is to be the home of this race,

---

13. *Congressional Record,* 55th Congress, 2nd Session, p. 5794.

the principal seat of his power, the great center of his influence?" Unlike many contemporary clergymen, he was an advocate of evolution, and he believed that a sort of Nietzschean *Herrenvolk* was rising in the United States, which was destined to "impress its institutions on mankind" and "spread itself over the earth." He exhorted his countrymen to realize their position, their duty, their destiny. "Men of this generation," he declaimed, "from this pyramid top of opportunity on which God has set us, we look down on forty centuries! We stretch our hand into the future with power to mold the destinies of unborn millions." [14]

To the members of a host of church groups and missionary societies this was a dazzling and almost irresistible vision. They came to believe strongly, and undoubtedly sincerely, in the "imperialism of righteousness;" and it was not too difficult to transpose this into a belief in the righteousness of imperialism.

This phenomenon was a particularly difficult one for the anti-imperialists to counter, since the layman might feel diffident about opposing the clergy. The most effective response on the part of the anti-imperialists, therefore, was to marshal the forces of the articulate minority of eminent American Protestant clergymen in the nineties who opposed imperialism. This was eventually done most succinctly in a series of three *Anti-Imperialist Broadsides* which presented "The Moral and Religious Aspects of the So-Called Imperial Policy—Discussed by Representative Clergymen of Many Denominations." [15] These were replete with refutations of theories of missionary imperialism which had their genesis in Josiah Strong's writing.

Charles H. Parkhurst, a Presbyterian minister and well-

---

14. Josiah Strong, *Our Country: Its Possible Future and Its Present Crisis* (New York, 1885), pp. 179, 175, 180.

Strong was, perhaps, echoing in reverse Napoleon's remark to his troops in Egypt. The French empire builder actually displayed more humility than the American clergyman; for his statement was: "Soldiers, from the summit of yonder pyramids forty centuries look down upon you." Napoleon's implication was that history and the world would judge their conduct. Strong, however, reverses the image, placing the United States at the top of the pyramid as ruler and judge of all.

15. *Anti-Imperialist Broadside No. 5* (Washington; no date).

known reformer of the era, who was one of the original vice presidents of the Anti-Imperialist League, commented upon the "phenomenal . . . epidemic of Calvinism which has broken out among the expansionists. There is such an overwhelming conviction of divine destiny among them." Parkhurst observed mordantly that "religious people with an axe to grind have always apologized for what was queer, tricky, and cruel in their dealings with others by referring it to divine determination; it relieves the strain unspeakably to make God take the brunt of it." Finally, remarking upon the phenomenon which became increasingly prevalent among the Protestant sects in the years following Strong's pioneering publication, Parkhurst fumed: "One hardly knows what to say of the earnestness with which in certain Christian journals and Christian pulpits expansion is put forth as a means of extending the Kingdom of Christ. It is a novel idea that the reign of Jesus is to be widened in the world under the protection of shells and dynamite." [16] The Reverend William H. P. Faunce, a prominent Baptist cleric, echoed Parkhurst when he remarked that "the Kingdom of Heaven is to come as a grain of mustard seed, not as a thirteen-inch shell." [17]

Faunce's statement, in addition to decrying the imperialists' perversion of the missionary impulse, illustrates another of the principal factors which made the early 1890's anxious years for the anti-imperialists; for the thirteen-inch shells which he mentions were carried aboard newly constructed warships, which were part of the greatly expanded U.S. Navy. The growth of the U.S. fleet (the United States moved from twelfth to third place among the naval powers of the world in the last two decades

---

16. *Anti-Imperialist Broadside No. 6* (Washington; no date).
17. *Ibid.*
The vigorous support given to imperialism by American missionary groups also came in for contemporary commentary. Thus, the *Boston Herald* stated: "It is worthy of notice that the most active of those in this country interested in missionary efforts are also the strongest advocates of an extension of the influence and authority of the United States over what have in the past been foreign countries." —in *Anti-Imperialist Broadside No. 7* (Washington; no date).

of the century), and its change in character from a purely defensive force to an offensive one, went hand-in-hand with the development of an aggressive, and eventually imperialistic, foreign policy.

The Nation, which under the vigorous editorship of E. L. Godkin was a consistently anti-imperialist journal, in July, 1889 carried a report on a significant foreign policy statement made by Edward J. Phelps, former U.S. Minister to Great Britain, in the Phi Beta Kappa address at Harvard University. Phelps said that the United States should have a much more forceful foreign policy, and that "to enforce such a policy, a navy should be created that would leave nothing to fear from any other naval power." *The Nation*'s editor commented: "These opinions, coming from such a source, cannot be put aside as inconsequential. They will receive cordial approbation from the political leaders and party workers now in the ascendency in the White House and in Congress. The building of a great navy is already on their cards." [18]

The validity of this last statement was borne out, much to the displeasure of anti-imperialists like Godkin, when the militant members of the Navy Policy Board, recently created by Secretary of the Navy Benjamin F. Tracy, issued a report in 1890 recommending the creation of a vastly more powerful Navy. The Naval Act of 1890 which followed, although it did not go so far as the Policy Board suggested, did give approval to a multi-ocean fleet capable of engaging potential enemies on the high seas.

Another related matter which must have profoundly disturbed the basically anti-militaristic anti-imperialists was the ever-growing number of articles calling for a much more extensive military establishment, especially a large, modern offensive Navy.[19] There was one man—Alfred Thayer Mahan—who was particularly responsible for this phenomenon and who, thus, became one of the anti-imperialists' arch foes.

18. *The Nation,* Vol. XLIX, No. 1254 (July 11, 1889), p. 24.
19. A list of these articles during the years in question runs to scores of titles.

In 1886, a year after the publication of Fiske's and Strong's thought-provoking works, Mahan, a career naval officer, was made head of the Naval War College at Newport. While serving in this capacity, he gave a series of lectures which were collected and published in 1890 as *The Influence of Sea Power upon History*. This book soon became world-famous and acted as a powerful stimulus to navalism and imperialism in the United States. Mahan propounded in this monumental work the thesis which he was to expand and reiterate in voluminous writings for the next two decades. This theory was, in essence, that sea power was the most potent determining factor in the strength of a nation, and that without naval strength no nation could acquire the fullest measure of security, influence, and importance in world affairs. While documenting his thesis historically, he wrote, as Theodore Roosevelt observed in a contemporary review, "with especial heed to the circumstances of the United States at the present time, [stressing that] our greatest need is the need of a large fighting fleet." [20]

Although many men at the time praised the captain's "originality," one of his more perspicacious contemporaries, the Philadelphia ship builder Charles H. Cramp, pointed out that Mahan's theme was certainly not new, and that the principal value of his writing was the "new force" which he had given to "old and well known facts." Cramp observed correctly that the true importance of his works was the stimulus they gave to "universal public opinion as to the absolute necessity of adequate naval strength to every maritime power which aspires to commercial rank and profit." [21]

The anti-imperialists claimed that this reasoning was both dangerous and fallacious. They pointed out that the nation had grown tremendously and prospered greatly while possessing neither the large navy nor the overseas bases which the Captain advocated. Mahan, undaunted by the vociferous but sporadic

---

20. *Atlantic Monthly*, Vol. LXVI (October, 1890), pp. 564, 567.

21. Charles H. Cramp, "The Sea Power of the United States," *North American Review*, Vol. CLIX (August, 1894), pp. 137, 148.

opposition of the anti-imperialists, fired off an impressive broad-side of books, articles,[22] and letters which diffused his chauvinistic ideas throughout the nation. He hoped in this way to act as an expansionist mystagogue and initiate the American people into the ancient rites of imperialism. He wished to inculcate a new attitude more in keeping with the international *Zeitgeist*—imperialism.[23]

Mahan did his best to advance, as the anti-imperialists did their utmost to retard, the growing feeling in the United States that overseas expansion should be the sequel to our earlier westward movement. Strongly influenced by Social Darwinism, he attempted to demonstrate the inherent logic and almost biological regularity of our former national growth. "In our infancy," he wrote, "we bordered upon the Atlantic only; our youth carried our boundary to the Gulf of Mexico; today maturity sees us upon the Pacific. Have we no right or call to progress in any direction? Are there for us beyond the sea horizon none of those essential interests . . . which impose a policy and confer rights?" [24] These questions for Mahan and his fellow American imperialists were, of course, rhetorical. They believed that contemporary conditions urged the United States not to be "bound and swathed in the traditions of our own eighteenth century," [25] but rather to fulfill its Manifest Destiny amid the tumult of the international arena.

---

22. These appeared in *The Forum, Harper's, North American Review, Collier's, Century, Scribner's, World's Week, Atlantic Monthly, The Independent,* and many other periodicals.

23. A measure of his eventual influence in this regard is the commentary of the noted British journalist Frederick Greenwood: "Mahan's teaching [is] as oil to the flame of colonial expansion everywhere leaping into life. Everywhere a new-sprung ambition to go forth and possess and enjoy [finds] its sanction in the philosophy of history enobled by the glory of conquest. . . ." *Blackwood's Edinburgh Magazine,* Vol. CLXIII (April, 1898), p. 565.

24. A. T. Mahan, "Hawaii and Our Future Sea Power," *Forum,* Vol. XV (March, 1898), p. 2.

25. Mahan, "A Twentieth Century Outlook," *Harper's Monthly* (September, 1897), reprinted in *The Interest of America in Sea*

A gradual, but vaguely discernible, alteration of public opinion in the direction which Mahan desired was occurring in the United States as early as 1890. The Captain noted with approval in December of that year that "indications are not wanting of an approaching change in the thoughts and policy of Americans as to their relations with the world outside their own borders." He felt that "the interesting and significant feature of this changing attitude is the turning of the eyes outward, instead of inward only to seek the welfare of the nation." [26] Albert Shaw, the influential editor of *Review of Reviews,* writing soon after Mahan, made the same point. "The American nation," he said, "for twenty-five years has turned its gaze inward, intent upon the development of a continent. . . . The times have changed somewhat; and there are unmistakable marks of a strong disposition to return to the sea." [27]

A significant motivation for this change in outlook was the theoretical closing of the frontier. Until 1890, the American people had been content to fulfill their expansion within the continental boundaries of North America. The existence of a huge mass of unsettled virgin land in the West had seemed to be sufficient area in which to transact the destiny of the United States. To a certain extent the frontier had acted as a "safety valve" to drain off the boundless energy and expansionist spirit of the American people.

Power (Boston, 1898), p. 255. This remark points up a very real dichotomy; for the anti-imperialists were quite proud to be "swathed" in the traditions, precepts, and principles of the nation's founding fathers and saw no good reason for departing from them.

26. Mahan, "The U.S. Looking Outward," *Atlantic Monthly,* Vol. LXVI (Dec., 1890), pp. 816, 817.

27. Albert Shaw, editorial, *Review of Reviews,* Vol. IV (Sept., 1891), p. 125.

Shaw, of course, like Mahan, approved strongly of the trend. Later in the period he was to write: "It is a great mistake to assume that our country has no more history to make, that acquisitions, developments, and bold projects belong wholly to the past, while henceforth we must fossilize."—*Review of Reviews,* Vol. VX (May, 1897), p. 528.

Jefferson had voiced the belief in the early years of the nineteenth century that it would take centuries to occupy even the territory which had been gained by the Louisiana Purchase in 1803. However, by 1890 energetic Americans, aided by the huge influx of European immigrants, had spread over the United States to such an extent that the Census Bureau could announce that, for all practical purposes, the frontier had ceased to exist. The bulletin of the Superintendent of the Census for 1890 contained the statement that:

> Up to and including 1880 the country had a frontier of settlement, but at present the unsettled area has been so broken into isolated bodies of settlement that there can hardly be said to be a frontier line. In the discussion of its extent, its westward movement, etc., it cannot therefore, any longer have a place in the census report.[28]

Frederick Jackson Turner and others have explored and debated the polydimensional significance of this report in voluminous writings. Our only concern with it here is its relation to American imperialism and anti-imperialism in the 1890's. Its importance in this respect is that it helped to inculcate the belief that the United States, having supposedly "filled" its possessions on this continent, must expand abroad. Professor Ray A. Billington, a staunch defender of the "frontier theory" of American history, has stated that "for the man in the street, there was a direct connection between the Census Bureau's announcement of 1890 and the need for overseas possessions. With opportunity drawing to a close within the nation's borders, he reasoned, the government's duty was to provide areas for exploitation elsewhere." [29]

Although probably only the most thoughtful and observant Americans were aware of this report in 1890, its import was increasingly conveyed to the larger public via newspaper edi-

---

28. Cited by Frederick Jackson Turner, *The Frontier in American History* (New York, 1920), p. 1.
29. Ray A. Billington, *Westward Expansion* (New York, 1949), p. 754.

torials, magazine articles, and speeches. Thus A. Lawrence Lowell, President of Harvard, remarked in an article in *The Atlantic Monthly* in the late 1890's: "The conditions that made possible the expansion of our people westward at a furious and constantly accelerated pace are surely, and not very slowly, coming to an end." [30] Ulysses D. Eddy observed in June, 1891, that "hitherto this nation has been busy subduing a virgin continent;" [31] and a more assertive writer later echoed this view when he stated that "the subjugation of a continent was sufficient to keep the American people busy at home for a century . . . but now that the continent is subdued, we are looking for fresh worlds to conquer. . . ." [32]

The change in national attitude in the final decade of the century, to which the theoretical closing of the frontier contributed, was hastened by what Mahan recognized in 1890 as "a restlessness in the world at large." [33] This significant feeling of uneasiness was a reaction to the great material changes and intellectual ferment of the late nineteenth century, as were the writings of Fiske, Strong, and Mahan themselves.

Many men in the early 1890's were affected by a sense of foreboding. The signs of the times were ominous, not least because they presaged a departure from the foreign policy that had guided the nation for over a century. The anti-imperialists believed strongly in the tried and true American foreign policy as it "was originally outlined by Washington in his farewell address." [34] They pointed out that "the traditional policy handed

---

30. A. Lawrence Lowell, "The Colonial Expansion of the United States," *The Atlantic Monthly*, Vol. LXXXIII (Feb., 1899), pp. 146-147.

31. U. D. Eddy, "Our Chances for Commercial Supremacy," *The Forum*, Vol. XI (June, 1891), p. 419.

32. James Howard Bridge, editorial, *The Overland Monthly*, Vol. XXXI, Second Series (August, 1898), pp. 177-178. Also see Bridge's "A Fresh View of Manifest Destiny," *The Overland Monthly*, Vol. XXXI, Second Series (February, 1898), pp. 115-119.

33. Mahan, "The U.S. Looking Outward," *loc. cit.*

34. Theodore Woolsey, "An Inquiry Concerning Our Foreign Relations," *Yale Review*, Vol. I (August, 1892), p. 162.

down from George Washington—and he left us nothing better, nothing which time has more fully approved—was opposed to [overseas] acquisitions." [35]

One can readily appreciate why men holding such views would be so anxious about the welfare of the nation when confronted with the trend toward imperialism. They heard premonitory rumblings on many sides which seemed to portend a possible imperialist earthquake. Even in the early 1890's, those in agreement with the views of Fiske, Strong, and Mahan were pointing to specific places on the globe where they felt the American Flag should be placed.

Diplomat Henry S. Sanford [36] writing in *The Forum* of June, 1890, stated that "The scramble in Africa for 'protectorates' and possessions, and for the extension of 'spheres of influence' and action, by the commercial powers of Europe, is the event of the century." He insisted that the United States should not be left behind, but should take an active part in the division of the Dark Continent. He demanded: "Are we to avail ourselves of the opportunity at our hand, or shall nations reputed less enterprising than we alone reap benefits from it?" [37]

General Thomas Jordan [38] sought a prize nearer home. In an article, published in July, 1891, entitled "Why We Need

---

35. *The Nation,* Vol. LVII (December 21, 1893), p. 457.

36. In his lengthy diplomatic career, which began in 1847, Sanford served in a number of European posts, including St. Petersburg, Frankfurt, Paris, and Brussels. He first became interested in African colonial affairs while serving as U.S. Minister to Belgium (1861-1869), and he was an important member of the International Association for the Exploration and Civilization of Central Africa, to which he was appointed in 1876 by King Leopold II.

37. Henry S. Sanford, "American Interests in Africa," *The Forum,* vol. IX (June, 1890), pp. 409, 429.

38. Jordan, an 1836 graduate of West Point where he was the roommate of William T. Sherman, distinguished himself in the Mexican War and later as Beauregard's chief of staff in the Civil War. Long interested in Cuba, he went so far as to command an insurgent army there in 1869, at which time Spain reportedly placed a price of $100,000 on his head.

Cuba," [39] he attempted to demonstrate the necessity and desirability of immediate American annexation of the "Pearl of the Antilles." William L. Merry seconded Jordan, and, along with many of his contemporaries, called for American ownership of a Nicaraguan canal.[40] He noted anti-imperialist objections to such plans. "It has been contended by some," he said, "that it is a dangerous policy for the United States to acquire realty and interests abroad which may require protection, but the policy which was applicable to the thirteen federated colonies does not apply to a growing nation of over 60 millions, seeking a market abroad for its products and manufactures." He also attempted to parry the anti-imperialists' objections on constitutional grounds. "We also hear occasionally," he said, "that it may be unconstitutional to acquire property abroad. . . . Dr. Johnson once wrote that 'patriotism is the last refuge of a scoundrel,' and, in imitation of this saying, we might add that 'constitutionality is the last refuge of an obstructionist.' " [41]

The anti-imperialists anxiously inquired in what manner were these areas abroad to be obtained. Those men who believed strongly in the nation's imperial destiny blandly replied that they would be acquired by whatever method was most suitable; peacefully, it was hoped, but if not, by war. "War," wrote Rear Admiral S. B. Luce [42] in 1891, "is one of the great

---

39. *The Forum,* vol. XI (July, 1898), pp. 559-567.

40. Merry—a sea-captain, merchant, and diplomat—was a vigorous supporter of Mahan's theories for a powerful navy and overseas bases, but was especially active between 1890 and 1895 as the foremost exponent of a Nicaraguan Canal. He was appointed Minister to Nicaragua, Costa Rica, and El Salvador by McKinley in 1897 and continued to represent the United States in that area until shortly before his death in 1911.

41. William L. Merry, "The Nicaraguan Canal: Its Political Aspects," *The Forum,* Vol. XII (February, 1892), pp. 724, 725.

42. Luce, who contributed very importantly to building the modern American Navy, while serving as the first president of the Naval War College, brought Mahan to that institution, thus launching the influential phase of the latter's career.

agencies by which human progress is effected." Luce was an interesting precursor of that better known advocate of the strenuous life and martial virtues, Theodore Roosevelt; and his thought and writings, like those of his colleague, Alfred Thayer Mahan, undoubtedly influenced Roosevelt. Luce stated emphatically his belief that war "stimulates natural growth, solves otherwise insoluble problems of domestic and political economy, and purges a nation of its humors." In words that were to be echoed throughout the world by the strident voice of Theodore Roosevelt, Luce proclaimed that "war arouses all the latent energies of a people, stimulates them to the highest exertion, and develops their mental and material resources." The call of Darwinism, deity, duty, destiny—all the imperialist rationalizations—appear in Luce's bellicose philosophy. "So in the economy of nature," he asserted, "or the providence of God, war is sent . . . for the forming of national character, the shaping of a people's destiny, and the spreading of civilization." Paraphrasing Bishop Berkeley, Luce declared:

> The course of empire still holds its accustomed way. With the United States as the dominant power of the western world, lies the obligation of contributing her share to the further extension of civilization, to the spreading of the gospel, and conveying to less favored nations the most enlightened views of civil government. . . . The time will come . . . when the nation in its manhood will "put away childish things," assume its own high responsibilities, and organize its forces for practical use.[43]

The increasing dissemination and acceptance of such aggressive views in the early 1890's contributed greatly to the anxiety of those who opposed war, foreign entanglements, and imperialism. The anti-imperialists thought that they discerned an ultimately egocentric motivation in men like Luce. Norris Gage observed that "the powerful diplomatic, army and navy circles, with a growing influence little understood by the public, now as

---

43. S. B. Luce, "The Benefits of War," *North American Review,* Vol. CLIII (December, 1891), pp. 672, 673, 675.

in all ages, are in favor of any policy which will stimulate foreign intrigue and promote war, thus adding to their power and prestige and enhancing the value of their services." [44] The anti-imperialists were even more disturbed by the realization that a growing proportion of the public was beginning to view their cherished traditional beliefs about foreign policy and the role of the United States as "childish things" which were no longer acceptable, but which should be replaced by the more "mature" and sophisticated concepts of imperialism.

The anti-imperialists of the early 90's had already recently witnessed what they considered to be a distressing departure from traditional American foreign policy in the case of Samoa. Increasing American involvement in the affairs of the tiny insular kingdom eventually resulted under the pro-imperialist Secretary of State James G. Blaine in American entry into a tripartite condominium (with Great Britain and Germany) for control of the islands. The treaty effecting this arrangement drew the United States into an agreement which was incompatible with former American attitudes and policies in foreign affairs, and was a prelude to later and larger involvements in imperialist ventures.

The treaty was signed June 14, 1889, and was debated in the Senate early in 1890. There was a strong anti-imperialist minority who opposed ratification; but since no records were kept of the debates either in the Committee on Foreign Relations or in the traditionally clandestine executive session of the Senate, we cannot know exactly what points were made.

It is possible, however, to obtain some clue to the motivation, other than the purely partisan one (a Democratic minority opposing a Republican majority measure), of the opposition to the treaty in the Senate from certain other sources. For example, the independent *New York Herald* revealed what were the two principal objections to the treaty when it pointed out that it involved the United States "in agreements with European govern-

---

44. Gage, *op. cit.*, p. 5.

ments which are contrary to the fixed policy of this country," and expressed concern that it might serve as a precedent.[45]

There was also some fear that involvement in the condominium, especially with the expansionist Blaine serving as Secretary of State, might lead to an attempt at outright annexation. Count Arco, the German Minister to the United States, had discussed this earlier with Carl Schurz. Schurz informed Arco that the "traditional policy of the country was most decidedly adverse to such distant annexations." Although personally disturbed by the trend of events, he expressed confidence that this policy "was too deeply rooted in public opinion to be disregarded. The conservative and cautious spirit of the American people in this respect was," he observed, "clearly demonstrated by the refusal to accept St. Thomas and Santo Domingo when these countries were offered to the United States." [46]

Times and attitudes, however, change; and overseas expansion, which had been rejected in the 1860's and 1870's, by 1890 was considerably more popular. It is, however, not too surprising that with a substantial Republican majority in the Senate the opposition to Blaine's Samoan treaty was overcome and the measure approved by the Senate on February 21, 1890.

There are several other reasons why sufficient anti-imperialist sentiment could not be generated to cause a split in party ranks which would have put the Samoan treaty in jeopardy. First, theoretically the Samoans retained sovereignty in the islands, although it was the slightest shadow of autonomy. Even this shadow, however, could soothe troubled Senatorial consciences. Second, we were accepting a protectorate, rather than annexation as we would do in 1899. Third, many men probably agreed with the sentiments expressed by the editor of the

---

45. The editor of the *Herald,* like many anti-imperialists, felt that "we should have maintained that policy of independence from complications with European governments which has been our consistent policy from the foundation of the Union."—*Public Opinion,* Vol. VIII, No. 17 (February 1, 1890), p. 403.

46. Schurz Papers, Library of Congress.

Cincinnati *Volksblatt,* who wrote late in January, 1890, that the treaty "occasioned far more noise and commotion than was at all justified by its relative importance." [47]

The condominium, nevertheless, was to cause increased "noise and commotion" as its failure to solve the Samoan problem became more evident. It was later more widely castigated as an egregious departure from the American tradition of independence and nonentanglement in the affairs and arrangements of other governments; but this was not until the abortive attempt to annex Hawaii in 1893 had made imperialism a definite *cause célèbre.*

At this juncture the significance of American involvement in Samoa was twofold. It served as a harbinger of things to come and revealed an interesting shift in attitude on the part of many people toward international power politics and overseas expansion. This latter point was noted at the time by certain perceptive commentators such as Ulysses D. Eddy, who wrote in June, 1891: "The course of the United States in the Samoan matter, in throwing down the gauntlet to powerful Germany, created a profound impression in Europe where it is rightly regarded as the indication of a changed attitude." [48]

It was this changed, or rather changing (for the phenomenon in 1891 was still in a dynamic phase), attitude which especially disturbed those who were opposed to American imperialism. The very terms in which Eddy chose to couch his remarks were indicative of an increasingly chauvinistic and belligerent attitude toward other nations in our conduct of foreign affairs. To speak of "throwing down the gauntlet" implied a desire, which was becoming increasingly prevalent in the United States, to put on the national armor and go forth to joust in the international arena with the Old World powers for territorial prizes.

The anti-imperialists felt that this tendency could have highly undesirable consequences. Professor Theodore S. Wool-

---

47. *Public Opinion, op cit.,* p. 404.
48. Eddy, *op. cit.,* p. 421.

sey, a noted contemporary authority on American foreign affairs, in August, 1892 presented a particularly cogent critique of the prevailing trend, which constitutes an excellent summary of the anti-imperialist position in the anxious years.

Woolsey felt that our traditional foreign policy, originally outlined by Washington in his farewell address, had proven to be a wise and successful one. He questioned whether certain recent events and governmental pronouncements indicated a change in this valuable and time-honored course. Like other anti-imperialists, he was alarmed by "the enlarged view of our rights of sovereignty to which we are fast accustoming our people and in which we are training our navy," and by the tendency of the Harrison administration "to stretch its claims of jurisdiction unduly." He asked what all this meant and would entail. His reply to his own query emphasizes several basic arguments which were to be reiterated by the anti-imperialists on myriad occasions throughout the ensuing decade:

> It means a departure from the old and safe policy of the fathers . . . courting rather than avoiding foreign entanglements . . . one collision after another, each with its sulphurous war cloud about it [49] . . . the violation of former precedents, setting up new ones in their stead which may prove awkward, even dangerous. It will make this country hated and distrusted by its natural friends.[50]

Woolsey pointed out that if the United States took an extreme position, it must be prepared to maintain it. This, in turn, would lead to changes which the anti-imperialists abhorred. "We shall," he said, "need a larger army; a navy of the first rank; and increase of taxation to pay for these; a reversal of our military and

---

49. The imperialists—men like Luce, Mahan, and Roosevelt—actually welcomed such collisions as evidence of the inevitable Darwinian struggle, as an antidote to slothful ease, as representative of the strenuous life, as beneficial for the "race," etc.

50. Woolsey, *op. cit.,* p. 173.
Perhaps he anticipated the Latin American fear of the "Yankee Peril" and the "colossus of the North" engendered by the "Panama incident" and other events of the early twentieth century.

naval policy to maintain them." These changes, furthermore, would lead to an undesirable "admixture of foreign influences and foreign questions in our domestic politics."

Woolsey voiced a widespread fear of the anti-imperialists—that of establishing undesirable precedents that would lead the nation continually farther afield from its traditional policy. "The tendency," he warned, "is not one which will stand still. It must be checked at once or grow greater." He foresaw clearly what was to occur a decade later under the Roosevelt Corollary to the Monroe Doctrine. He cogently observed that if the nation allowed itself to embark upon such a dreaded "sea of adventure" as the imperialists desired, even the Monroe Doctrine, "a doctrine of non-interference on the part of European states in this continent, would be changed into a license to interfere on our part." What would be the end result of the adoption of an aggressive foreign policy by the United States? Woolsey and other anti-imperialists saw only a "burden of responsibilities, heavy cost, and empty glory." [51]

As the years of the final, momentous decade of the nineteenth century passed, the warnings of Professor Woolsey and his fellow anti-imperialists would be heeded less and less. The seed of imperialism had been planted in American soil, and there were many able and influential ultranationalists like Mahan, Lodge, Roosevelt, Shaw, and Beveridge, who were eager to devote their efforts to the nurture of this exotic growth. The anti-imperialists in these early years of the 1890's felt that "therefore there is room for apprehension and anxiety; but the excessive chauvinism which mars the American character, otherwise clear-sighted and admirable, sees nothing of it." [52]

---

51. *Ibid.*, p. 174.

52. Rhett S. Roman, "American Chauvinism," *North American Review,* Vol. CLV (December, 1892), p. 759.

CHAPTER 3

"First Fruit" Left Withering

Rhett Roman published his provocative article, in which he deplored what he felt to be a national myopia, in December of 1892. Within a month a literally revolutionary inicident occurred which was to provide the focal point of the imperialist—anti-imperialist debate for the ensuing half decade. The event which initiated the controversy over imperialism was the comic opera coup d'état by which the Hawaiian queen, Liliuokalani, was deposed and the islands which comprised her kingdom were offered to the United States for annexation.

Liliuokalani was overthrown by a small group of determined men composed primarily of large property holders, virtually all of whom were Americans either by birth or by recent extraction. Their motivation was, reduced to its simplest terms, the desire to protect their vested interests. These interests, although basically economic, were also social and political. These men by 1890 had grown to be the wealthiest, most powerful and influential element in the islands. Their wealth was based primarily upon control of the Hawaiian sugar industry and related enterprises. By a treaty of reciprocity negotiated with the United States in 1875 and renewed in 1884 Hawaiian sugar was admitted duty-free. This arrangement proved immensely profitable to the Hawaiian planters, who controlled vast plantations worked by imported, low-cost Oriental contract labor.

Two events of the early '90's, however, dealt severe blows to the wealth and position of the Hawaiian-American plutocracy. The first shock was the passage of the McKinley tariff of 1890, which put sugar on the free list and provided a bounty of two cents per pound for domestic producers. Hawaiian sugar consequently was undersold and lost much of its market, thereby causing a depression in the whole Hawaiian sugar-based economy. The troubles of the American element were compounded in 1891 by the accession to the Hawaiian throne of the highly autocratic and xenophobic Queen Liliuokalani. The new monarch disliked the foreign element, believed firmly in "Hawaii for the Hawaiians," and intended to rule by personal fiat, rather than by constitutional methods.

The planter plutocracy was seriously disturbed by the new state of political and economic affairs. Stated simply, the most expedient solution to this dilemma seemed to be to depose the queen and request annexation by the United States. These Machiavellian moves would give them local political control at the same time that Hawaii was brought under the aegis of U.S. tariff walls and the sugar bounty, thus restoring the islands' shaken economy and the personal wealth of the planters.

Interest in annexation was by no means one-sided. The islands had been an object of U.S. attention ever since the 1820's, when American whaling and merchant ships had begun to make them a regular port of call. The mariners, who sought water, fresh fruit, and willing *wahines,* were soon followed by New England missionaries in search of souls. The entrepreneurial pursuits of the missionaries' descendants provided the basis for increasing economic ties with the United States.

When Britain and France made feints, in 1842 and 1849 respectively, toward acquisition of the islands, the U.S. government lodged strenuous protests and stated that it could not view with indifference the transfer of sovereignty of the islands to another power. This solicitude, in the heady aura of Manifest Destiny in the late 1840's and early 1850's, was transmuted into an active desire on the part of American expansionists for annexation of the islands.

A treaty of annexation to the United States was actually negotiated and signed under Secretary of State William L. Marcy in 1854; but traditional American suspicion of the merits of overseas expansion, combined with dissatisfaction with provisions concerning statehood for the islands and exorbitant stipends for the royal family, prevented ratification. A decade later the islands became one of the principal objects of the insatiable expansionism of Secretary of State William H. Seward. Seward's efforts in this area, like those of Marcy, were in vain. However, American interest in the islands, as is evinced by the reciprocity treaties of 1875 and 1884, remained strong.

The gentlemen who headed the State Department in the early 1890's, James G. Blaine and John W. Foster, strongly favored American annexation of Hawaii, and labored assiduously, if discreetly, to bring it about. One of Blaine's most significant moves in this direction was his appointment as Minister to Hawaii of his erstwhile colleague on the Kennebec *Journal,* John L. Stevens. Stevens' penchant for imperialist ventures had been derived not only from Blaine, but from the master himself. "I followed Mr. Seward for twenty-five years," Stevens said, "I am a believer in his philosophy as to the future of America in the Pacific." [1] One is not surprised, therefore, when he reads Stevens' message to Blaine of February 8, 1892: "I shall deem it my official duty to give a more elaborate statement of facts and reasons why a 'new departure' by the United States as to Hawaii is rapidly becoming a necessity. . . . Annexation must be the future remedy." [2]

Later in the same year (November 20, 1892), we find Stevens, true to his word, writing to Secretary of State Foster [3] and elaborating on the reasons why the United States should annex Hawaii. "Destiny and the vast future interests of the U.S. in the Pacific," he wrote, "clearly indicate who, at no distant day, must be responsible for the government of these islands." [4]

In addition to being thoroughly in favor of American annexa-

---

1. *Senate Report 227,* 53rd Congress, 2nd Session, p. 551.
2. *Senate Executive Document 77,* 52nd Congress, 2nd Session, p. 177.
3. Foster had replaced Blaine in June.
4. *United States Foreign Relations, 1894* (Washington, 1895), Appendix II, pp. 181 ff.

tion, Stevens seems to have possessed a propensity for intrigue. Thus he conspired with the men who overthrew Queen Liliuokalani. He later denied any complicity in the revolution, but the facts of the situation, as well as the testimony of several of the prominent revolutionaries proved otherwise. For example, one of the principal conspirators, Frederic Wunderberg, testified that "without the previous assurance of support from the American Minister, and the actual presence of the U.S. troops, no [revolutionary] movement would have been attempted, and if attempted, would have been a dismal failure. . . ." [5]

The revolution, abetted by Stevens, took place on January 16, 1893. It was precipitated by the attempt of Liliuokalani two days earlier to set aside the constitution of 1887, which had largely been dictated by the white elite, and to rule by royal fiat. Stevens landed 160 Marines from the cruiser *Boston,* which was stationed in the harbor at Honolulu, and whose commander, Captain Wiltse, was also very sympathetic to the scheme of annexation. They were supposedly put ashore for the purpose of protecting American life and property, which actually was in no danger. The real reason for the Marines' presence was to intimidate the queen, which they did quite effectively.

The anti-imperialists denounced this maneuver often and vehemently. Eugene Chamberlain in an article pointedly titled "The Invasion of Hawaii" observed that American troops were landed against the "protest of a friendly power" and strategically deployed in a manner helpful to the revolutionary cause. He cited the significant testimony of Captain Wiltse's superior officer, Admiral Skerrett, that "the American troops were well located if designed to promote the movement for the Provisional Government, and very improperly located if only intended to protect American citizens in person and property." Chamberlain also, like many other commentators, called attention to the fact that the Queen's "surrender was in terms 'to the superior force of the United States' and 'until such time as the Government of the

---

5. *House Executive Document 47,* 53rd Congress, 2nd Session, p. 577.

United States shall, upon the facts being presented to it, undo the action of its representative'. . . ." [6]

The representative in question seems to have had little fear on this score, and on the following day, although without official permission from the State Department, recognized the revolutionary regime. A commission from the Provisional Government, thereupon, set out almost immediately for Washington to arrange a treaty of annexation. This "Hawaiian" commission (which consisted of four Americans and one Englishman, giving a fair idea of the representation of the natives in the Provisional Government) arrived in San Francisco on January 28 aboard the steamer *Claudine*, bringing the first account of the revolution to be received by the outside world.

The startling news precipitated in earnest the great debate over American imperialism. Discussion of Hawaiian annexation became the center of national attention overnight. The pages of the nation's newspapers were filled with the controversial subject. Many, like *The New York Times*, reserved judgment; others, like the *Cincinnati Commercial Gazette* and the *Springfield Republican* (later one of the nation's leading anti-imperialist papers) emphasized deliberation, while some took sides almost immediately.

Many newspapers throughout the country displayed strong opposition to imperialism in general and to Hawaiian annexation in particular. The *Chicago Herald* observed that the "appeal to American patriotism, ambition, and cupidity will be strong and will be pressed with earnestness," but concluded emphatically that "the Sandwich Islands would not be a desirable acquisition." [7] The *New York Evening Post,* one of the most consistently and

---

6. Eugene Tyler Chamberlain, "The Invasion of Hawaii," *North American Review,* Vol. CLVII (December, 1893), pp. 734, 735.

Stevens, however, in spite of very strong evidence and testimony to the contrary, stoutly maintained that "neither by force, threats, or intimidation, did the U.S. officials oppose the fallen queen, or aid the Provisional Government. . . ."—"A Plea for Annexation," *North American Review,* CLVII (Dec., 1893), p. 740.

7. *The New York Times* press survey Feb. 2, 1893.

vigorously anti-imperialist newspapers in the nation throughout the decade, recalled the rejection of President Grant's policy of overseas expansion and questioned whether there had been "any marked change in the public mind since that time as to the acquisition of distant islands." [8]

The *Hartford Courant* did not feel that there had been and commented that "some of the objections to annexing those Pacific islands have substance and should be weighed accordingly." [9] A frequently stated objection concerned the character of the people, and both the *Washington Evening Star* and *New York Voice*, among others, were critical of the prospect of annexing "a turbulent and motley population." [10] Another point which the *Voice* and other journals raised was that the natives "would resent annexation as tyrannical subjugation." The imperialists' argument (later often repeated in regard to the Filipinos, Puerto Ricans, and Cubans) that the natives were incapable of self-government was quickly countered by anti-imperialists like M. M. Trumbull, who wrote in *The Open Court* that this "has always been the excuse of strong governments for the oppression of the weak." [11]

Many anti-imperialists characterized the Provisional Government as nothing more than a self-aggrandizing, plutocratic clique, which desired to trade the Hawaiians' right to self-government for the U.S. sugar bounty. The *N.Y. Evening Post* called the recent coup d'état a "revolution of sugar and for sugar." [12] *The Nation,* another steadfastly anti-imperialist journal throughout the ensuing two decades, extended the paraphrase, calling it "a revolution of sugar, by sugar, and for sugar," [13] while the *New York Herald* complained that "there is more sugar than statesmanship and more jingoism than patriotism in the hasty [annexation] movement." [14]

---

8.   Jan. 31, 1893.
9.   *N.Y. Times* press survey Feb. 5, 1893.
10.   *Literary Digest,* 1893, Vol. VI (Feb. 4 and 9), pp. 389, 412.
11.   *Ibid.,* Feb. 18, 1893, p. 445.
12.   Feb. 22, 1893.
13.   Vol. LVI (March 9, 1893), p. 170.
14.   Feb. 24, 1893.

It should, perhaps, be noted here that the relationship of sugar, per se, to the Hawaiian revolution and the desire for annexation was not quite so direct and all pervasive as the fulminations of the anti-imperialists would have one believe. It was actually rather complex. It was not merely a question of the problems of one industry, but of the viability of the islands' entire economy. Also, the sugar industry was intimately connected with the Hawaiian racial problem. The white planters, who had brought in Oriental contract laborers in great numbers, feared that they might eventually be overwhelmed by this Frankenstein monster of their own creation, unless a strong white supremacist government ruled the islands. Adding to the subtleties of the matter, which the anti-imperialists obscured, was the fact that a few large planters opposed American annexation on the ground that union with the United States would lead to restrictive legislation which would cut off the cheap labor supply. For example, Claus Spreckels, whom the anti-imperialists often erroneously accused of being one of the Machiavellian figures behind the annexation movement, was strongly opposed to it on the grounds just mentioned and had publicly said so. [15]

Sugar was an important factor in the revolution and movement for annexation, but its role was not as simple and consistent as the anti-imperialists maintained. However, their interest in the question was more polemical than anything else, and they made the most of the "sugar conspiracy."

The anti-imperialists, in addition to dwelling on the saccharine quality of the annexation movement, refuted the arguments of imperialist strategists who claimed that the islands would be a great military asset. The *Pittsburgh Chronicle-Telegraph* of February 3 asserted that "so far from Hawaii adding to the military or naval strength of the country, the very reverse is the case." The *Buffalo Courier* concurred, and, referring to what the anti-imperialists felt had been an earlier grave blunder in this

---

15. See Claus Spreckels, "The Future of the Sandwich Islands," *North American Review,* Vol. CLII (March, 1891), pp. 287-298, especially p. 291.

area, advised the nation not to enter "entangling alliances in Hawaii as the Harrison Administration has put us into with England and Germany in the case of Samoa." [16]

The most frequently expressed anti-imperialist counsel was that the United States should simply leave Hawaii alone to work out its own destiny. A more elaborate and demonstrative variant of this, engendered by the imperialists' claim that if the United States did not take the islands some European power would, was the solution suggested by the *Boston Advertiser* on January 31: "All that is needed is . . . to warn Great Britain and the rest of Europe that the independence of Hawaii must on no account be assailed; that self-government shall be maintained in those islands in the future as in the past." The *Advertiser*'s contention that this was the "policy of honor and safety, in keeping with the principles laid by the founders of our Republic, consistent with all our best traditions, and whose wisdom the experience of years has demonstrated" contains the very essence of the anti-imperialist position throughout the ensuing two decades.

While the debate was continuing in the press, Congress took up discussion of the matter. The division of Congressional opinion was largely along party lines. *The New York Times* commented: "With a change of Administration, it is altogether probable that there would remain the same feeling of advocacy of annexation on the Republican side of the Senate that there has always been. If there is opposition anywhere, it may be looked for on the Democratic rather than the Republican side." [17] However, as on any important and emotionally charged issue—and this was both—there were mavericks who crossed party lines. For example, Senator Morgan (Democrat) of Alabama was one of the strongest supporters of annexation and Senator Pettigrew (Republican) of South Dakota was one of its arch foes.

On January 30 Senator Chandler of New Hampshire introduced a resolution calling for formal Senate consideration of annexation, and closed his remarks by saying that "the time has

---

16. *The New York Times* press survey Feb. 2, 1893.
17. *The New York Times,* Jan. 29, 1893.

come when the United States should acquire the Hawaiian Islands." This opinion was quickly countered by Senators Donelson Caffery and George Gray, who were to be two of the outstanding opponents of imperialism throughout the decade. Senator Gray hastened to point out that a great many Americans had "grave doubts of the advisability of the United States taking possession of a country two thousand miles distant from its coast." [18]

Meanwhile, the man who can be credited with providing the whole affair with much of its impetus, John L. Stevens, continued assiduously to cultivate the annexationist field. On February 1, Stevens, although acting without formal authorization from Washington, hoisted the Stars and Stripes above the government buildings in Honolulu and proclaimed Hawaii a U.S. protectorate. On the same day, which to say the least was a busy one for a gentleman from Maine in the soporific climate of Hawaii, he sent his famous advice to the State Department. "The Hawaiian pear," he said, "is now fully ripe and this is the golden hour for the United States to pluck it." [19]

The fruit analogy seemed to have a mystical appeal for the imperialists. However, the apple was more popular as a Hawaiian symbol, although horticulturally perhaps even less apt than Mr. Stevens' pear. The *Philadelphia Times* wrote: "The apple will fall into our lap when it is ripe, and we do not want it prematurely." [20] The *Times'* neighboring paper, the *Philadelphia Press,* agreed with Stevens that it was harvest time: "The apple is ripe. Let it be picked." [21] The *New York Independent* felt that even the exertion of picking was unnecessary: "The ripe apple falls into our hands, and we would be very foolish if we should throw it away." [22] The anti-imperialists, being perhaps better stu-

---

18. *Ibid.,* Jan. 31, 1893.

19. *Senate Executive Document 76,* 52nd Congress, 2nd Session, p. 49.

20. The *New York Times* press survey, *op. cit.,* February 5, 1893.

21. *Ibid.*

22. *Literary Digest, op. cit.,* February 4, 1893.

dents of Genesis than their ideological foes, disagreed and continued to regard the apple as forbidden fruit.

The anti-imperialists, however, were not in the ascendancy in Congress at this juncture. A poll taken of members of the House early in February revealed 83 in favor of annexation, 46 opposed, and 77 undecided.[23] The Senate also seemed considerably more receptive to the idea of annexation than the nation at large, and the Administration thought that it might be able to railroad through an annexation treaty before the anti-imperialists had an opportunity to rally their forces.

A treaty of annexation was, therefore, hastily drawn up by Secretary of State John Foster and the Hawaiian commissioners and signed on February 14. It was then sent with some accompanying papers to the Senate the following day. In submitting it for Senate approval, President Harrison stated that "prompt action upon this treaty is very desirable." [24]

An interesting letter from Secretary of State Foster to President Harrison dated the same day (February 15) also accompanied the treaty. In it Foster stated that "the change of government in the Hawaiian Islands . . . was entirely unexpected so far as this Government was concerned." [25] This statement would seem to allow for only three possibilities: 1) Foster never read the many dispatches on the subject which his Minister (i.e. Stevens) sent to the State Department. 2) He had an exceedingly (and conveniently) bad memory. 3) He was simply not telling the truth. These three possibilities would seem to yield three logical, if distressing, alternative conclusions. Foster was: 1) derelict in his duty, 2) incompetent, 3) lacking in integrity. No matter how one interprets it, Foster's letter is disturbing. The President's request for haste in ratifying the treaty only served

---

23. *New York Herald,* February 6, 1893.

As the debate progressed, most of those listed as undecided at this stage came out against annexation.

24. *Senate Executive Document 76,* 52nd Congress, 2nd Session, p. 1.

25. *Ibid.,* p. 3.

to increase the aura of chicanery which surrounded the annexation scheme and strengthened the hand of the anti-imperialist
opposition.

The treaty, reduced to its bare essentials, called for cession
of the Hawaiian Islands to the United States; in return the United
States agreed to assume the Hawaiian debt up to 3.25 million,
pay Queen Liliuokalani $20,000 per annum for life, and give a
lump sum of $150,000 to Princess Kaiulani.[26] The Administra-
tion forces in the Senate worked smoothly and quite expeditiously
in handling the treaty. It was given immediately (February 15)
to the Committee on Foreign Relations, which reported favorably
on it only two days later.

The Senate itself could not be so easily manipulated as the
Committee on Foreign Relations. Many of the Senators resented
the bulldozing tactics being employed by the Harrison Administration. The charge of precipitancy was leveled against the Administration with increasing frequency and telling effect. *The
Brooklyn Citizen* stated:

> We shall not look for any of that hurry in this business by
> which the persons who, in defiance of law, overthrew the Gov-
> ernment of Hawaii, and with their aiders and abettors of the
> press here, hoped to overwhelm all opposition of common sense
> by a flood of wretched sentiment about "Manifest Destiny." We
> shall take time to think about it, and we shall want to know
> in what way we are to be benefited by annexing Hawaii, before
> considering the request even of its people and of its lawful
> Government for annexation.[27]

The *Citizen*'s editorial pointed up two other issues which disturbed many men in the Senate and elsewhere. First, there was
the question of the legitimacy of the Provisional Government.
Second, even if that government were to be accepted as the de
jure, rather than simply the de facto, governing body of Hawaii,
there still remained the vital matter of whether a majority of the

---

26. See *ibid.*, pp. 6-9, for the full text of the treaty.
27. *Literary Digest,* February 4, 1893, p. 390.

Hawaiian people favored annexation. In any case, when injudicious haste was added to these and other troubling uncertainties, many people were profoundly disturbed.[28]

Criticism of the treaty of annexation and of the Administration's relationship to the whole affair mounted steadily in the waning days of Harrison's occupancy of the White House. *The Nation* noted sarcastically: "The filibustering message and treaty submitted to the Senate on Thursday by the President in the Hawaiian matter deserve to be framed and exhibited at the World's Fair." [29] The *New York World* claimed that the whole affair was an "administration plot" and that the President had been in it from the beginning." [30] Although Harrison himself was not actually involved in any diabolical "plot," neither was he a reluctant expansionist at this juncture, as has been suggested by one historian.[31] He was in fact quite anxious to annex Hawaii at this time, but by the third week of February anti-imperialist opposition to the treaty in the Senate had begun to solidify. *The New York Times* reported on February 18 that opposition to annexation had grown to the extent that it was being predicted that "ratification of the treaty is not possible."

The anti-imperialist forces in the Senate meanwhle were receiving valuable editorial support from coast to coast. Pragmatic considerations were stressed, and many newspapers, like the *New York Herald* and the *San Francisco Newsletter*, pointed out that annexation would yield only "new obligations and responsibilities without any additional advantages." [32] The initial enthusiasm for annexation was waning and the editor of the *Newsletter*, like

---

28. Newspapers throughout the nation (e.g. the *Chicago Herald, New York Times, Boston Herald,* etc.) echoed the *Pittsburgh Post's* criticism that "indecent haste has characterized the whole business."

29. Editorial—"Hail Columbia!," *The Nation,* Vol. CLVI (February 23, 1893), p. 136.

30. *Literary Digest, op. cit.* (February 18, 1893), p. 445.

31. George W. Baker, "Benjamin Harrison and Hawaiian Annexation: A Reinterpretation," *Pacific Historical Review* (August, 1964).

32. *New York Herald,* February 26, 1893.

many others, felt confident that "the sober second thought of our people will not approve of the planters' scheme." [33]

This confidence proved justified; for in the face of the determined opposition of Senators Caffery, White, Pugh, Pettigrew, Gray, Blackburn, Vilas, Daniel, Berry et al, the administration forces in the Senate realized that they could not collect the necessary two-thirds majority in the short interval that remained before Cleveland took office.

As the time for Cleveland's inauguration drew near, people began to speculate about what course he would pursue in regard to Hawaii. The strongly pro-imperialist *New York Sun* asserted that "Cleveland's luck . . . is the opportunity of annexing the Hawaiian Islands." [34] The more perceptive *Pittsburgh Chronicle-Telegraph* recalled with approval (in spite of the fact that it was a Republican paper) Cleveland's statement in his first annual message (December, 1885) that he was opposed to "a policy of acquisition of new and distant territory." [35] It was correctly assumed that this might offer a valuable clue to the President-elect's attitude toward Hawaiian annexation.

The pronounced and consistent anti-imperialism of Cleveland and the two most important members of his incoming cabinet—Secretary of State Walter Q. Gresham and Secretary of the Treasury John G. Carlisle [36]—undoubtedly did much to lend moral support to the opponents of the treaty of annexation in the Senate. Gresham's opinion on the issue may have been partly

---

33. *Literary Digest,* Vol. VI (March 4, 1893), p. 500.

34. February 28, 1893.

35. Cleveland's full statement was: "Maintaining, as I do, the tenets of a line of precedents from Washington's day which proscribe entangling alliances with foreign states, I do not favor a policy of acquisition of new or distant territory, or the incorporation of remote interests with our own."—James D. Richardson (Ed.), *A Compilation of the Messages and Papers of the Presidents, 1789-1897,* (Washington, 1899), Vol. VIII, p. 500.

36. Both Cleveland and Carlisle were among the original officers of the Anti-Imperialist League, and Gresham undoubtedly would have also been, had he not died before the founding of the League.

motivated by his hostility to President Harrison, who was a former rival of his in the Republican party, especially at the National Convention in Minneapolis the previous June. In any case, he opposed any hasty annexation scheme and so informed Cleveland. He also told him that he believed that a special commission should be appointed to ascertain all the facts before any action was taken. Carl Schurz [37] and several publications (e.g., *The N.Y. Times* of February 17) made the same suggestion.

Cleveland's acceptance of this advice was certainly consistent with his desire for high standards of governmental conduct and his previously stated view that the nation should scrupulously avoid "any departure from that foreign policy commended by the history and traditions . . . of our Republic." [38] He moved swiftly and forcefully. On March 9, only a few days after taking office, he requested the Senate to return the treaty to him for reexamination. Two days later he appointed James H. Blount, former Chairman of the Committee on Foreign Affairs, as "Special Commissioner" to investigate the entire Hawaiian imbroglio.

Blount was widely respected, and even Cleveland's opponents admitted that he was qualified for the job given to him. Blount was later to become a very staunch and outspoken anti-imperialist and in 1906 was elected a vice president of the Anti-Imperialist League.[39] However, at the time of his appointment as Special Commissioner, he was generally considered to be unbiased on the question, and certainly appears to have conducted the entire investigation with scrupulous impartiality.

The popular reaction to Cleveland's withdrawal of the treaty

---

37. Schurz sent Cleveland copies of his anti-imperialist articles and urged him in several letters to eschew "all acquisitions of territory outside of the continent." Cleveland replied on March 19, saying that he had read the articles "with great satisfaction and was especially pleased with the one on Hawaiian annexation."—Schurz Papers.

38. First Inaugural Address. Richardson, *op. cit.,* p. 30.

39. *Report of the Eighth Annual Meeting of the Anti-Imperialist League* (Boston, 1906), p. 15.

Another indication of recognition of his long service to the cause was a testimonial luncheon given in his honor by the Anti-Imperialist League at the 20th Century Club in Boston on October 22, 1906.

from the Senate was a mixed one. Those in favor of annexation were, of course, disappointed and tended to deprecate the President's action. The anti-imperialists, on the other hand, were naturally pleased and applauded Cleveland's vigorous handling of the matter. The *Brooklyn Eagle* probably came closest to expressing the national consensus when it commented that "in withdrawing the treaty he has exerted a clear executive right, and at the same time has wisely afforded ample time for deliberation upon a difficult and delicate subject." [40]

Blount in his first significant official move terminated the protectorate instituted by Stevens and ordered the re-embarkation of the American Marines and the lowering of the flag from the Hawaiian Government Building. This caused immediate and widespread furor in the imperialist camp. A vigorous hue and cry was raised over the supposed indignity to "Old Glory." "The programme is a shameful one," scolded the *Chicago Tribune*, "and the most shameful part of it, which will wound most deeply the patriotic feelings of the citizens of this country, in the hauling down of the American flag." [41]

The lowering of the flag anywhere after it had once been raised was to remain a bone of contention between imperialists and anti-imperialists for decades to come. The imperialists felt that wherever the flag had been run up, apparently almost regardless of circumstances, there it should stay. To lower it, or even to suggest that it be lowered, was viewed as a highly unpatriotic, perhaps even seditious act. The issue initially discussed here in the spring of 1893 would be embellished and reiterated almost ad nauseam in the case of the Philippines in later years. In the instance under consideration, the anti-imperialists immediately replied to the objections of their antagonists. Many newspapers (e.g. the *New York Evening Post, New York World,* and *Philadelphia Record*) and several prominent national magazines expressed the belief that "there is a widespread feeling that raising the American flag as if it were a piratical ensign is not an

---

40. *Literary Digest,* Vol. VI (March, 1893), p. 554.
41. *Ibid.* (April, 1893), p. 695.

act of pure patriotism, and that the best thing to do with the flag when it has been raised in that way is to haul it down." [42]

By mid-March the anti-imperialists were breathing easier. Support for the acquisition of Hawaii was growing weaker. The *New York Voice* reported that the "tide of public sentiment has changed visibly and rapidly within the last few weeks, running more and more strongly against the idea of annexation. . . ." [43] The anti-imperialists might, thus, even have begun to feel a bit complacent, and thought, with the year "at the spring," the treaty removed from the Senate, Blount on his way to Hawaii, Gresham at the State Department, and Cleveland in the White House, that all was right with the world.

However, just when it looked as if the imperialist forces were being routed, Captain Mahan published a highly influential article entitled "Hawaii and Our Future Sea-Power." This article was widely disseminated, highly praised by the imperialists, duly noted and rebutted by many anti-imperialists, quoted frequently in Congress, and even reprinted as part of the Morgan Committee Report. [44]

Mahan offered many reasons why the United States should abandon its traditional foreign policy and make Hawaii a precedent-setting, initial overseas possession. "The Hawaiian group," he asserted, "possesses unique importance—not from its intrinsic commercial value, but from its favorable position for maritime and military control." He insisted that the possible construction

---

42. See *New York Evening Post* (April 14), *New York World* (April 15), *Philadelphia Record* (April 15), *Literary Digest* (April 22), and *The Nation* (source of quotation) Vol. LVI (May 11, 1893), p. 338.

43. March 18, 1893, *Literary Digest*, p. 55.

44. Report of the Senate Committee on Foreign Relations, John T. Morgan, Chairman, re affairs in the Hawaiian Islands—*Senate Report 227*, 53rd Congress, 2nd Session (Washington, 1894), pp. 113-121.

Mahan, himself, also reissued the article as Chapter II, pp. 31-49 of his *The Interest of America in Sea Power, Present and Future* (Boston, 1898).

of an isthmian canal would make possession of the islands even more desirable.

Although he obviously favored the acquisition of the Hawaiian Islands, it was not this, per se, which intrigued Mahan. It was rather the whole process of expansion and imperialism, of which Hawaii was to be but a facet—albeit a highly significant one, which fascinated the Captain. He repeatedly emphasized the fond and fundamental hope of the imperialists that "the annexation of Hawaii would be no mere sporadic effort . . . but a first-fruit and a token that the nation in its evolution has aroused itself to the necessity of carrying its life . . . beyond the borders that have heretofore sufficed for its activities." [45]

This idea of Hawaii as the "first fruit" is precisely what the anti-imperialists most dreaded and abhorred. This was the ultimate fear that lay behind and motivated the sundry objections to Hawaiian annexation. Objectors pointed out that it would set a very dangerous precedent. "When once the greedy appetite for more territory is excited," George Curtis warned, "it will go on, and will grow by what it feeds on." [46]

Many people agreed that the imperialists would probably view the islands as merely an appetizer. "If we annex Hawaii now," the *New York Herald* predicted, "it won't be long before some cranks will want to annex [other] South Sea Islands, or get a slice of the coast of Africa." [47] The anti-imperialists solemnly admonished the nation to realize that if it set forth "on the road to territorial conquest, there is no knowing where we may end." [48]

Thus it was feared that the result of sampling this "first fruit"

---

45. Alfred Thayer Mahan, "Hawaii and Our Future Sea Power," *Forum,* Vol. XV (March, 1893), pp. 4, 8.

46. G. T. Curtis, "Can Hawaii Be Constitutionally Annexed to the U.S.?" *North American Review,* Vol. CLVI (March, 1893), p. 284.

47. March 2, 1893.

48. *St. Paul Dispatch* in *Literary Digest,* March 18, 1893, *op. cit.,* p. 55.

would not be sustenance, but indigestion—born of unfamiliarity with the product and anxiety in its consumption. Debate on the Hawaiian question was to continue, but it was apparent at this juncture that the American people were not yet ready to begin the imperial feast and that the "first fruit" would be left to wither.

CHAPTER 4

Stalemate

While the matter of Hawaiian annexation, both in the islands where Blount was unobtrusively but assiduously gathering information for his monumental report and in Congress, was temporarily quiescent, the focus of the imperialist-anti-imperialist debate had shifted to the nation's intellectual journals. Here it was largely to remain, except for a brief interval at the time of Blount's submission of his report in July, until mid-autumn.

Mahan's notable article provided the most significant offensive thrust for the imperialists. It was quickly parried, however, by E. L. Godkin, the outspoken editor of *The Nation.* In a series of incisive editorials Godkin noted and criticized the logical relationship among the demands of Mahan and his confrères for Hawaiian annexation, a larger Navy, and a wholesale shift in our foreign policy toward imperialism. He pointed out that Mahan's stress upon the military importance of Hawaii was intimately connected with the desire of the Captain and his comrades "to get if they can, the largest and most powerful Navy ever seen." [1] He observed in a subsequent editorial that Mahan's "exposition and illustration of the role which the American Navy is to play in the future of the country is highly serviceable to the expansionists and annexationists. . . ." [2] Godkin and his fellow anti-imperialists believed, however, that the large offensive Navy

---

1. "Naval Politics," *The Nation,* Vol. LVI (March 9, 1893), p. 173.

2. "Armed Evangelists," *The Nation,* Vol. LVI (March 16, 1893), p. 191.

which Mahan advocated, instead of being a national asset, would be a source of international friction and a threat to our institutions.

Godkin, whose anti-imperialism was tinged with the Irishman's almost inherent anglophobia, denounced the desire of Mahan and other American imperialists to emulate English foreign policy. "He asks us," Godkin remarked with obvious disparagement, "to follow England's example by such annexations of foreign territory and populations as seem likely to promote certain undefined things which he calls national 'influence' and national 'greatness' by securing naval predominance on the Pacific." [3] Countering the imperialists' "closed frontier" argument, the editor of *The Nation* implied that it was ridiculous to contend that "because our population has reached in scanty numbers the shores of the Pacific . . . that we are bound, on any theory of national greatness, to seek further expansion by annexing the islands of the sea and the mongrel nations of the tropics." [4]

Godkin emphasized a fundamental matter which was of grave and lasting concern to the anti-imperialists when he noted that Mahan failed to consider "what effect this policy of general annexation, and general readiness to subjugate would have on our domestic institutions." [5] Finally, he raised a related issue, which the anti-imperialists were to reiterate for over a decade until their position was widely adopted during the Progressive era, when he pointed out that many domestic "social and political problems of the gravest order remain to be solved before we can consider ourselves fit at all for the role of armed evangelists." [6]

The powerful pens of Mahan and Godkin provided only part of the material for the great debate in the month of March. Lorrin Thurston, who was one of the prime movers behind the Hawaiian revolution and who currently headed the Provisional Government's annexation delegation, contributed a good deal of propaganda on "the advantages of annexation" to the nation's

---

3. "Naval Politics," *loc. cit.*
4. "Armed Evangelists," *loc. cit.*
5. "Naval Politics," *loc. cit.*
6. "Armed Evangelists," *loc. cit.*

newspapers and magazines.[7] He was supported by Americans like James O'Meara employing familiar imperialist shibboleths. "Manifest Destiny," O'Meara asserted, "impels the people of the Hawaiian Islands. . . . They simply anticipate the inevitable." [8]

The anti-imperialists, however, questioned whether the Hawaiian populace desired annexation. Graham Gribble, writing in the March issue of *Engineering Magazine,* suggested that this aspect of the debate could be easily resolved by simply holding a plebescite and allowing the Hawaiian people to vote on the matter. Frederick R. Clow, in his article in the *Journal of Political Economy,* contended that desire for the "sugar bounty" was the sole reason anyone in Hawaii favored annexation.[9]

The March issue of the *Californian Magazine* carried a very influential anti-annexationist article by George W. Merrill, former U.S. Minister to Hawaii. Writing from first-hand experience that few of the participants in the debate could bring to the subject, Merrill insisted that the political, social, and racial conditions in the islands were so completely undesirable from the American standpoint that the United States would be acting in an extremely foolish and paradoxical manner if it voluntarily were to burden itself with them. Merrill felt that the United States already possessed every influence in the islands which was desirable and that a closer tie would only bring unnecessary problems. In reply to the argument that if we did not take the islands quickly some other power would, Merrill commented that the annexationists had always attempted to employ this as a ruse, but that it was nothing more than that; "the danger of interference in the affairs of Hawaii by any European power is so extremely remote that any need to annex them in order to save the islands from the greed of other powers is entirely eliminated." [10]

---

7. For example, "The Sandwich Islands: the Advantage of Annexation," *North American Review,* Vol. CLVI (March, 1893).

8. John O'Meara, "Hawaiian Annexation," *Californian Magazine,* included in *Literary Digest,* Vol. VI, No. 22 (April 1, 1893), p. 593.

9. In *loc. cit.*

10. *Literary Digest,* Vol. VI (March 11, 1893), p. 511.

This phantom threat of intervention by another power, especially Great Britain, was one that the anti-imperialists felt constrained to refute repeatedly simply because the annexationists raised it repeatedly. Thus the *Buffalo Express* stated emphatically that "this cry about forestalling England is a mere bugaboo." [11] James Schouler, in his "Review of the Hawaiian Controversy," viewed the matter in historical perspective and insisted that "no fear of British or other foreign interference to seize these islands if we do not need trouble us. That fear has been the usual goad for driving our people, if possible, into filibustering and oppression toward the weaker nations of this hemisphere ever since the days of San Jacinto." [12]

The anti-imperialists' contention that British interest in annexation was merely a bête noire created by the imperialists would seem to be corroborated by a perusal of surveys of British opinion on the matter, e.g. the rather extensive sampling of opinion in the British press in *The New York Times* of January 30, 1893. Similarly, a later survey conducted by *The Nation* in London in April reported: "The unanimity with which all the leading English journals of every shade of political opinion have refused to treat the Hawaiian question, from the outbreak of the trouble down to the present time, as a matter of special British concern is very striking." It reported that the English in general displayed a disposition of either indifference or else outright objection to British interference in Hawaiian affairs. [13]

Another issue that was to be an important facet of the debate over imperialism in the years to come which first received extensive attention in the spring of 1893 was the matter of the relation of foreign acquisitions to the U.S. Constitution. The anti-imperialists claimed that such acquisitions were not provided for by the Constitution or its recognized usage, and, hence, were unconstitutional.

---

11. Cited in *New York Times,* February 17, 1893.

12. James Schouler, "A Review of the Hawaiian Controversy," *Forum,* Vol. XVI (February, 1894), p. 671.

13. "Hawaii and British Interests," report from London (April 25, 1893), in *The Nation,* Vol. LVI (May 18, 1893), p. 362.

The constitutional and related aspects of the Hawaiian question were raised by several noted legal scholars, including George T. Curtis [14] and Judge Thomas M. Cooley. Cooley, who was considered the nation's leading authority on the Constitution, was eminently qualified to speak on this subject. In addition to his reputation as a juridical scholar, Cooley was highly respected as a former justice (1864-1885) of the Michigan Supreme Court, Chairman (1887–1891) of the Interstate Commerce Commission, and professor of law and American history at the University of Michigan. It is therefore not surprising that his commentary on Hawaii should be widely read, frequently reprinted, and often commented upon. An intriguing indication of the great and even lasting influence of Cooley's article is that during the Hawaiian debates five years later, in 1898, Senator William Frye, a zealous imperialist, had a reply written by Judge John Caton printed as a government document.[15]

Judge Cooley presented a lengthy, abstruse legal argument which boils down to his flat statement that the Constitution "was not made and shaped for the establishment of any colonial systems. Our government is not suited to that purpose." Judge Cooley, acting here rather as counsel for the anti-imperialist plaintiffs, widened his case against Hawaiian annexation beyond the constitutional issue. He averred that the evidence did not indicate that the Provisional Government was supported by a majority of the people, and observed that "this distant country" was being offered to the United States "by what is at most a pro tempore government," which had no right to bargain away the nation's sovereignty.

The Judge considered the racial question. "The proposed treaty," he remarked, "is one that will justify our annexing other countries regardless of the differences of race and the discordant elements that might be brought into the Union by the

---

14. See Curtis' "Can Hawaii Be Constitutionally Annexed?" *op. cit.*

15. See *Senate Document 214,* 55th Congress, 2nd Session—"Argument Favoring Annexation of Hawaii," by J. D. Caton (Washington, 1898). Caton was former Chief Justice of Illinois.

act." Like many anti-imperialists, including such staunch friends of the colored races as Moorfield Storey, Herbert Welsh, and Charles Francis Adams, Jr., Cooley recognized the fact that the United States already had a plethora of unresolved racial problems, which would only be increased by colonialism.

Cooley took up the imperialists' argument that we would need Hawaii in time of war. He questioned whether the islands "situated as they are, two thousand miles away," would not constitute an element of weakness rather than strength "in case of a war with . . . any great naval power, unless we proceed at once to create a Navy as great as that which could . . . be hurled by our antagonist against them." This latter possibility—the creation of a large modern military establishment—was precisely what the imperialists wanted. Cooley and his fellow anti-imperialists, however, were completely opposed to such a move on the part of the United States. Speaking of contemporary Europe, he made a statement which is very interesting in light of our present world situation:

> Immense armies and navies are created as the necessary preparation for war, and maintained at enormous expense and at all times, in order that they may be ready for immediate use in case of hostilities springing up with some foreign nation. Their very existence is a menace to the peace of the world; the more powerful are the armies and navies of leading nations, the greater the liability of destructive conflicts.

The Judge was quite wary of the belligerent international competition that Mahan, Roosevelt, Lodge and other imperialists felt would be such a stimulating and beneficial influence upon the United States. Like all anti-imperialists, he condemned the idea that we should compete with England, France, and Germany in establishing colonies and said that the proposition should be rejected as alien to our institutions.[16]

Judge Cooley's influential essay was the epitome of anti-imperialist thought as it developed in the turbulent first six months

---

16. Thomas M. Cooley, "Grave Obstacles to Hawaiian Annexation," *Forum,* Vol. XV (June, 1893), pp. 392-396.

of 1893. While the points that it raised were being debated by the nation's intelligentsia, James Blount was concluding his sweeping investigation of affairs in Hawaii. The former Congressman had succeeded Stevens as U.S. Minister on May 17; the latter, realizing that his position was untenable, had resigned. Blount accepted the additional job reluctantly as a duty, and informed the State Department that he could only consider the position as an ad interim one to be held until a suitable successor could be found. Blount had no desire at his age to begin a new career in the diplomatic corps. He wanted merely to terminate his investigation with thoroughness and dispatch and to write the concluding section of his monumental report. He completed it on July 17 and sent it immediately to Washington.

The report deals with a host of subsidiary matters, but delves quite deeply into two principal questions which especially troubled President Cleveland and many other Americans. These issues were the role played by Stevens and the American Marines in the coup d'état and the attitude of the islands' people toward American annexation. Blount gave conclusive, and apparently incontrovertible, answers to both questions.

He provided a strong, detailed indictment of the actions of the American Minister in the revolution and stated that the information which he had gathered demonstrated that the "undoubted sentiment of the [Hawaiian] people is for the Queen, against the Provisional Government, and against annexation." [17] Blount's report was not made public until autumn, but when it did appear, it severely denigrated the annexationist movement and elated the anti-imperialists.

The anti-imperialists were also heartened by the continuing production and widespread acclaim of anti-imperialist literature that flowed from the prolific pen of Carl Schurz. Schurz, who was to remain the leading anti-imperialist publicist for over a decade, was serving at this time as the chief editorial writer of *Harper's Weekly*; and he used this position to advantage in the

---

17. *United States Foreign Relations, 1894,* Appendix II, pp. 594, 598.

anti-imperialist cause. It was, however, an article which he published in October in *Harper's Monthly* which seems to have had the greatest influence upon important public figures, as well as upon a large segment of the general population.

On October 6 Walter Gresham wrote to Schurz praising this essay. The Secretary of State said: "I think it will do a great deal of good. . . . It is the best article of the kind that I have seen, and I sincerely hope to see something else from your pen upon the same subject." The noted contemporary historian, James Ford Rhodes, also said that he felt that Schurz's latest anti-imperialist effort would "have a large influence and do a great deal of good." [18]

Schurz's work, titled simply. "Manifest Destiny," advanced his belief that this pseudo-philosophy was responsible for much of the agitation in favor of American imperialism, as well as for some of the difficulty of the anti-imperialists in combating it. He observed that all endeavors to annex foreign territory to the United States were invariably accompanied by raucous statements about "Manifest Destiny" in an attempt to make the opposition seem to be a foolish battle against fate.

Schurz expressed displeasure that President Harrison's attempt to annex Hawaii had "called forth the cry of 'Manifest Destiny' once more." Comparing the type of expansion now envisaged with that in which the United States had engaged previously, Schurz, keeping a wary eye on the theories of Mahan, pointed out that "the new Manifest Destiny precept means, in point of principle, not merely the incorporation in the United States of territory contiguous to our borders, but rather the acquisition of such territory, far and near, as may be useful in enlarging our commercial advantages, and in securing to our Navy facilities for the operations of a great naval power."

The anti-imperialists felt strongly that it was not only a question of Hawaii today, Cuba tomorrow, but also of a general and very dangerous tendency, which must be eliminated now, lest it, like some malignant growth, clutch at the very vitals of the

---

18. Schurz Papers.

American system. Schurz hurled the imperialists' favorite euphemism back at them and in Cassandra-like tones issued a grave prophecy of possible impending disaster: If the American people "yield to the allurements of the tropics and embark upon a career of indiscriminate aggrandizement, then Manifest Destiny points with certainty to a total abandonment of their conservative traditions of policy, to a rapid deterioration in the character of the people and their political institutions, and to a future of turbulence, demoralization, and final decay." [19] The anti-imperialist cause would find no more forthright or eloquent paladin than this brilliant German emigré, and perhaps no more sobering and concise statement of what the anti-imperialists felt would be the unhappy fate of the nation if it heeded the siren-song of imperial destiny.

Cleveland and Gresham agreed thoroughly with Schurz, and said as much, but this did not solve the immediate and specific problem of what to do about Hawaii. The President and Secretary of State felt that since an agent of the American government had conspired in the revolution and American troops were instrumental in its success the United States, like it or not, was at least temporarily quite involved in the Hawaiian problem.

By the middle of October, Cleveland and Gresham had come to the conclusion that since representatives of the United States had improperly interfered and contributed in large measure to the downfall of the Hawaiian Queen, we had an ethical obligation to see that she was restored to the throne. Their decision may also have been partly prompted by that most lofty of Victorian motivations—the desire to aid a fair maiden in distress, at least this is what the Secretary of State's wife suggests in her biography of her husband. [20] The fact that the "damsel" in question was the formidable and even rather truculent Liliuokolani does tarnish the ideal chivalrous image of "Sir Walter" a bit.

---

19. "Manifest Destiny," *Harper's New Monthly Magazine,* Vol. LXXXVII (October, 1893), pp. 737-739, 746.

20. Matilda Gresham, *The Life of Walter Quintin Gresham, 1832-1895,* 2 vols. (Chicago, 1919).

There is little doubt, however, that Gresham's view of the situation was highly idealistic, if not so romantic.

The Secretary of State viewed the matter in terms of morality rather than expediency, and asked rhetorically whether the "great wrong done to a feeble but independent State by an abuse of the authority of the United States [should not] be undone by restoring the legitimate government?" [21] To implement the policy of restoration Gresham sent instructions on October 18 to Albert Willis, who had replaced Blount as American Minister. The Secretary told Willis to convey to Liliuokalani the President's regret at the reprehensible conduct of Stevens and the unauthorized use of American troops and to inform her that the President expected her to grant complete amnesty to those responsible for the revolution if she were reinstated.

Willis subsequently met with the former Queen and related the designated message, including the key part concerning amnesty. To this the still haughty erstwhile monarch replied disdainfully that she thought that all "such persons should be beheaded and their property confiscated by the government." [22] This, of course, somewhat complicated the American administration's plans for restoration.

When word of the administration's Hawaiian policy reached the press it created quite a stir. It was, on the whole, not favorably received. The Republican newspapers, as was to be expected, castigated both the restoration policy and its authors. The Democratic and independent journals tended to question the wisdom of the move. There were a few publications which praised it. The *New York Herald* and *New York Evening Post* endorsed it, and *The Nation* commented that "President Cleveland's decision in the Hawaiian case is the only just one possible. He has simply undone the wrong which Minister Stevens, acting without authority, committed. . . ." [23]

---

21. Cited by *The Nation,* Vol. LVII (November 16, 1893), p. 389.

22. *House Executive Document 70,* 53rd Congress, 2nd Session, p. 2.

23. *The Nation,* November 16, 1893, *loc. cit.*

Whatever wrong had been done, the role of the United States acting to restore an absolute monarch, particularly one so intransigent and unpredictable as Liliuokalani, and especially when force might well have to be used against the American community in Hawaii to effect this end, did not appeal to many Americans. Even the majority of anti-imperialists, while highly critical of the actions of Stevens and the Provisional Government, were rather loath to see the United States intervene to put Liliuokalani back on the throne. Thus Theodore Woolsey said: "One wrong cannot be cured by another. Our duty is simple. It consists in keeping our hands off." [24] They seemed to feel that the wisest course was simply to leave Hawaii alone to work out its own salvation.

Cleveland believed, however, that this would merely result in an ineffectual stalemate. His sense of honor still indicated to him that the Queen should be restored, if this could be done by persuasion rather than force. In his annual message to Congress (December 4, 1893), he said that a perusal of Blount's findings had led him to conclude that the only honorable course of action was to redress the result of Stevens' unauthorized acts and to restore "as far as practicable the status existing at the time of our forcible intervention." [25] The key word here obviously is "practicable," and the proposed solution simply was not. The President tacitly admitted as much in his special message to Congress (December 18, 1893) on the Hawaiian problem.

He reviewed the entire situation, criticizing the role of the U.S. Minister, the precipitance with which the treaty of annexation was drawn up, the unseemly haste with which ratification was sought, and the validity of the whole policy of annexation. He noted the abortive efforts made to reconcile the Queen and the members of the Provisional Government and virtually conceded that he and Gresham were at a loss to work out a more effective solution than the present status quo. He thereupon referred the entire matter to the "extended powers and wide discretion

24. Theodore S. Woolsey, "The Law and the Policy for Hawaii," *Yale Review,* Vol. II (February, 1894), p. 351.

25. Richardson, *op. cit.,* Vol. IX, p. 441.

of the Congress, [offering cooperation] in any legislative plan which may be devised for the solution of the problem before us which is consistent with American honor, integrity, and morality." [26]

Cleveland's special message was well received by the anti-imperialist camp. "No one who cares for the honor of American diplomacy and statesmanship," said E. L. Godkin's editorial in *The Nation*, "can read the President's Hawaiian message without a touch of honest pride. His statement of the reasons why we cannot annex Hawaii is the finest expression of real Americanism which this country has heard. It is the old gospel preached first by the founders of the republic." [27] A prominent descendant of the "founders," Charles Francis Adams, Jr., was one of a number of men who were to assume an increasingly important role in the anti-imperialist cause in the coming years who wrote to Cleveland at this time, praising his courage and "defiance of jingoism." [28]

Opinion in Congress was far more divided on the question, and was to remain so during the ensuing six months, when it was a subject of frequent debate. The division was largely partisan, with the Republicans combining criticism of the administration's stand with support for annexation.

It is interesting that George Hoar, who was to lead the anti-imperialist forces in the Senate in the battle over the ratification of the Treaty of Paris six years later, was one of the principal thorns in the side of the anti-imperialist Cleveland administration. In the same vein, it is intriguing that Senator Henry M. Teller of Colorado, who in 1898 was to offer the nationally self-abnegating amendment which was instrumental in preventing American annexation of Cuba, revealed himself in 1894 as a disciple of Seward and one of the most outspoken advocates of

---

26. *House Executive Document 47*, 53rd Congress, 2nd Session, p. XVI.

27. "The Hawaiian Message," *The Nation*, Vol. LVII (December 21, 1893), p. 460.

28. Grover Cleveland Papers, Library of Congress, Washington, D. C.

American imperialism.[29] But then perhaps Hoar and Teller would have agreed with Senator Hoar's fellow citizen of Concord, Ralph Waldo Emerson, that "a foolish consistency is the hobgoblin of little minds."

One of those whose crossing of party lines was most notable at this time was Senator John T. Morgan (Democrat) of Alabama. He insisted that Cleveland's message be referred to the Committee on Foreign Relations, of which he was Chairman, with instructions that the committee be empowered to conduct a full-scale investigation of the Hawaiian matter. The proposal was adopted on December 20, 1893, in spite of the cogent observation by its opponents that Commissioner Blount had recently submitted a thorough report of the results of an investigation of the same subject.

While the Morgan Committee pursued its self-appointed task, the debate over Hawaiian annexation and the broader issue of imperialism, per se, continued in the press. One of the most notable items was an article, entitled "A Plea for Annexation," penned with what the anti-imperialists felt to be unmitigated gall by the individual who was the very center of the controversy, former Minister John L. Stevens.

The anti-imperialists certainly accepted Stevens' opening statement that "a grave and serious question is now before the American people, the wrong solution of which will deeply affect the moral standing of the United States before the world," [30] but they had an antithetical idea of what constituted the "wrong solution." The remainder of the article, which contained a specious

---

29. For example, Teller said in the Senate on January 29, 1894: "I am in favor of the annexation of the [Hawaiian] islands. I am in favor of the annexation of Cuba; I am in favor of the annexation of that great country lying north of us. I expect in a few years to see the American flag flying from the extreme north to the line of our sister Republics to the south. I expect to see it floating over the isles of the sea—not only these [i.e. the Hawaiian islands], but in the Great Gulf and in West India [sic] seas." *Congressional Record,* 53rd Congress, 2nd Session, p. 1579.

30. John L. Stevens, "A Plea for Annexation," *North American Review,* Vol. CLVII, No. 445 (December, 1893), p. 736.

account of the genesis of the revolution and amounted to little more than an elaborate *apologia pro vita sua,* met with complete derision. Typical of the anti-imperialist reaction to the article was that of E. L. Godkin, who denounced the "harangue of Mr. Stevens which is filled with personal assaults and irrelevancies, but carefully avoids the crucial and cumulative evidence against him." [31]

While Stevens' article elicited quite a bit of commentary, most of it was adverse, and the anti-imperialists certainly had the edge in the number of significant essays on the Hawaiian situation published in the nation's journals during this period (December 1893—February, 1894). Eugene Chamberlain attacked Stevens in an incisive article, which utilized a dossier of damning factual information and substantiated testimony. He emphasized the basic anti-imperialist position that the annexation of Hawaii was extremely "repugnant to the traditions and temper of the American people, and clearly involves adherence to the theory of insular colonial expansion by conquest." [32]

Frederick R. Coudert agreed with Chamberlain and praised the Cleveland administration for "laboring to assert the wise and wholesome principles which it has been our policy as a government to observe from the beginning." [33] William M. Springer also surveyed the Hawaiian situation and came to the conclusion that annexation was, at least, of "doubtful expediency" and advised against it. [34] James Schouler in his lengthy "Review of the Hawaiian Controversy" stressed the political, social, and racial problems which he believed were inherent in annexation. [35] Professor Theodore S. Woolsey, in his article on "The Law and the

31. "Steven's Defense," *The Nation,* Vol. LVII (Dec. 7, 1893), p. 422.

32. Eugene T. Chamberlain, "The Invasion of Hawaii," *North American Review,* Vol. CLVII (Dec., 1893), pp. 731-732.

33. Frederick R. Coudert, "The Hawaiian Question," *North American Review,* Vol. CLVIII (Jan., 1894), pp. 57-58.

34. William M. Springer, "The Hawaiian Situation: Our Present Duty," *ibid.,* pp. 745-752.

35. James Schouler, "Review of the Hawaiian Controversy," *The Forum,* Vol. XVI (Feb., 1894), pp. 670-689.

Policy for Hawaii," stated quite simply and directly the fundamental anti-imperialist theorem that "annexation of territory beyond the sea" was contrary to traditional American policies and
principles.[36]

The Hawaiian problem was also being debated in both houses
of Congress. Public attention naturally focused more on the Senate, which would have to approve any possible treaty of annexation. There the anti-imperialist cause was sustained principally
by Senators Gray, Vilas, George, Mills, Pettigrew, Turpie, Gor-
don, and Vest. Some of the Senators confined their remarks to
facets of the question of Hawaiian annexation, while others, like
Vest, stated categorically that "we want no colonies." He asserted
that he was unalterably opposed to those men who "proposed
now that instead of having a compact, continental republic, as
our fathers intended, we are to have a great, expansive territory-
acquiring Government, extending even to the islands of the ocean
and the uttermost parts of the earth." [37]

A highlight of the proceedings in the Senate was the submission on February 26, 1894, of the report of the Senate Committee on Foreign Relations. The report had been written by the
Committee's chairman, the strongly imperialistic John T. Morgan
of Alabama. There was considerable disagreement among the
members of the Committee itself over the validity of various
conclusions of the report, and Morgan was the only one who
accepted it in toto.

Morgan was clearly prejudiced in favor of annexation. He
set out to substantiate certain prejudgments and conducted the
inquiry accordingly. His principal aim was to present a document
which would at least balance (its 809 pages do so almost literally), if not refute, the findings and conclusions of Blount's investigation. Even Morgan admitted that Blount had been as-
siduous in his investigation, had carried out his instructions with
"impartial care," and had submitted a "sincere and instructive"
report. He contended, however, that the situation in Hawaii had

---

36. Woolsey, *Yale Review,* Feb., 1894, *op. cit.,* p. 354.
37. *Congressional Record,* 53rd Congress, 2nd Session, p. 190,
191.

made it exceedingly difficult for Blount to obtain the "real" facts, and therefore his conclusions were invalid. In short, Morgan claimed that Blount was wrong and that annexation was right.[38]

The nation's anti-imperialists were incensed by Morgan's report. The anti-imperialist press fulminated against it. The *Philadelphia Record* referred to the report as "a mere incoherent yawp of jingoism.." [39] *The Nation* greeted Morgan's efforts with sarcasm and derision:

> The report of the Senate Committee in relation to the Hawaiian Islands is a document full of mysteries, but the key to most of them is to be found in the well-known jingoism of the chairman, Senator Morgan. . . . His main intent was to make his report a powerful argument for a big navy, and the Nicaragua Canal, and coaling stations thick as blackberries and general bumptiousness and insolence in foreign relations.[40]

The anti-imperialists did not, however, simply criticize the presentations of the opposition and offer no suggestions of their own. In the middle of January Senator Turpie of Indiana, who was a member of the Senate Committte on Foreign Relations, had introduced the following resolution:

> Resolved, that from the facts and papers laid before us by the Executive and other sources, it is unwise, inexpedient, and not in accordance with the character and dignity of the United States to consider further at this time either the treaty or project of annexation of the Hawaiian territory to this country; that the provisional government therein having been duly recognized, the highest international interests require that it shall pursue its own line of polity. Foreign intervention in the political affairs of these islands will be regarded as an act unfriendly to the Government of the United States.[41]

The anti-imperialists greeted Turpie's efforts with immediate approval. *The Nation* stated that "the passage of Mr. Turpie's res-

---

38. See *Senate Report No. 227,* 53rd Congress, 2nd Session (Washington, 1894), especially pp. 1-36.

39. *Literary Digest,* Vol. VIII (March 8, 1894), p. 455.

40. *The Nation,* Vol. LVIII (April 19, 1894), p. 284.

41. *Congressional Record,* 53rd Congress, 2nd Session, p. 1220.

olution at this time is the very best disposition that can be made of the Hawaiian question." [42] The resolution was actively debated, but an attempt made on March 20 to fix a date for a vote upon it was obstructed, and it did not receive further formal consideration.

However, after the debate had dragged on intermittently for two months more, Turpie on May 31 submitted a revised version of his resolution that read as follows:

> Resolved, that of right it belongs wholly to the people of the Hawaiian Islands to establish and maintain their own form of government and domestic polity; that the United States ought in nowise to interfere therewith, and that any intervention in the political affairs of these islands by any other government will be regarded as an act unfriendly to the United States. [43]

From the anti-imperialist standpoint this was an even stronger statement.

The members of the Senate, like the general public, by now were quite weary of the whole affair. The request for an immediate vote was granted, and the resolution was adopted by a decisive vote. [44] The House had previously passed a similar resolution by a margin of 177 to 78. [45]

The anti-imperialist position had received a strong vote of confidence. There are a number of reasons for this. The annexation of overseas territory went directly counter to the century-old American policy of avoiding overseas political entanglements. There must be a powerful stimulus to make a nation abandon a policy that it has honored for so long a time. At this point in 1894 no such stimulus existed. The original excitement and en-

---

42. *The Nation,* Vol. LVIII (Jan. 18, 1894), p. 42.

43. *Congressional Record,* 53rd Congress, 2nd Session, p. 5499.

44. *Ibid.,* p. 5500.

45. Introduced by Representative McCreary, it had been passed on Feb. 7, 1894. It reads: "Resolved; that the people of that country [i.e. Hawaii] should have absolute freedom and independence in pursuing their own line of polity, and that foreign intervention in the political affairs of the islands will not be regarded with indifference by the Government of the United States." *Ibid.,* p. 2001.

thusiasm for annexation engendered by the revolution and the original one-sided and incorrect account of it which had been promulgated had subsided. As the American people and their representatives in Congress learned more about the revolution and Stevens' part in it, the whole affair began to seem unsavory. The attempt by the Harrison administration to railroad through a hasty annexation treaty further contributed to this distaste.

The fear that there might be anarchy in the islands if annexation did not take place had not been borne out. The government and life of the Islands seemed to be progressing quite nicely. A second fear—that if the United States did not annex Hawaii immediately some other nation would—also seemed to be increasingly unjustified. Furthermore, both the Turpie and McCreary resolutions contained provisions that put the nation officially on record as opposing any such attempt.

Finally, the political picture had changed in such a way as to work against annexation. The Democrats, who were generally inclined to vote against imperialism, were now in the ascendancy. They controlled both houses of Congress and were led by a very forceful President and cabinet that were decidedly anti-imperialistic.

These factors might have given the anti-imperialists a sense of great victory. Time and events, however, were to prove that the anti-imperialists had simply prevailed in an indecisive skirmish. In spite of all the discussion neither faction had gained anything permanent. In the larger context of the great debate it was merely a stalemate.

CHAPTER 5

Hiatus

With the Hawaiian problem in abeyance as a result of the Mc-Creary and Turpie resolutions, anti-imperialist attention turned to the question of American involvement in Samoa. President Cleveland in his last annual message had given an indication of the administration's position on the matter when he referred to the regrettable deviation from our customary foreign policy "consecrated by a century of observance." [1]

On May 9, Secretary of State Gresham presented his views on the Samoan situation to the President. Like Cleveland and other anti-imperialists, he deplored the Harrison administration's "departure from our traditional and well-established policy of avoiding entangling alliances with foreign powers." Gresham's legal background is evident in his skillful, logical, and precise analysis of the question. "If the departure was justified," he said, "there must be some evidence of detriment suffered before its adoption or of advantage since gained to demonstrate the fact." He maintained that no such evidence could be found and that we had, thus, "without sufficient grounds, imperilled a policy which is not only coeval with our government but to which in great measure may be ascribed the peace, prosperity, and moral influence of the United States." [2]

The anti-imperialist press vigorously applauded Gresham's Samoan report. E. L. Godkin, for example, praised its emphasis

---

1. Richardson, *op. cit.,* Vol. IX, p. 439.
2. *Senate Executive Document No. 93,* 53rd Congress, 2nd Session, p. 10.

upon "old-fashioned American principles" and stated that it "ought to be hung up in every newspaper office in the country and over the bed of every young jingo who thinks foreign meddling a sign of 'good Americanism.' " [3]

President Cleveland also concurred fully with Gresham's Samoan memorandum, and hastened to submit the entire report to Congress for consideration. The time of submission may well have been chosen to coincide with the effort to make final the resolution on non-intervention in Hawaii, the feeling, perhaps, being that the example of Samoa would influence the Congress to prevent the United States from making what the present administration believed to be a similar blunder; i.e. to learn from the history of the Samoan affair to keep out of all insular involvements.

Early in July the Secretary of State offered addenda to his Samoan report to President Cleveland, commenting: "The undersigned finds in these additional papers abundant confirmation of the views heretofore expressed by him touching the unsatisfactory character of the entanglement in which the United States have become involved by reason of their participation in the General Act of Berlin. . . ." [4] To Cleveland's blunt way of thinking, contemplation of the matter led to only one obvious conclusion—the United States should simply get out of what was a bad situation. Therefore, he took up the matter in his next annual message (December 3, 1894) to Congress.

He questioned the character of the present system of governing Samoa and the wisdom of continued United States participation in Samoan political affairs. He criticized our participation in the establishment of the Samoan government against the natives' wishes. In line with the anti-imperialists' fundamental view of American foreign policy, he stated that the action of the

3. "Our Samoan Trouble," *The Nation*, Vol. LVIII (June 28, 1894), p. 480. Also see Godkin's earlier editorials in *The Nation*—"The Samoan Troubles" (May 17, 1894), and " 'Scuttling' out of Samoa" (May 24, 1894), Vol. LVIII, pp. 358, 480.

4. *Senate Executive Document No. 132*, 53rd Congress, 2nd Session, p. 1.

Harrison Administration vis-à-vis Samoa "was in plain defiance of the conservative teachings and warnings of the wise and patriotic men who laid the foundations of our free institutions." In light of these various factors, he requested Congress to consider the possibility of withdrawing from the Samoan situation "on some reasonable terms not prejudicial to any of our existing rights." Congress, nevertheless, took no demonstrative action on the matter during the ensuing year.

Cleveland was not a man who was easily put off; his tenacity, like his physiognomy, suggested a courageous bulldog. Thus he returned to the subject once more in his next annual message. At a time when the imperialists were much given to prating about Manifest Destiny and the national mission, Cleveland was glad to meet them on their own grounds. This illustrates a fact, often overlooked, that the anti-imperialists also believed in the "mission" of the United States. They simply defined the mission differently, even antithetically, from the imperialists. Thus Cleveland again vigorously attacked the Samoan condominium on the grounds that United States' participation was "inconsistent with the mission and traditions of our Government, in violation of the principles we profess, and in all its phases mischievous and vexatious." [5] In spite of the President's emphatic denunciation of the condominium, nothing significant was done toward abrogating it for another five years; and what was done then certainly did not please Cleveland and the other American anti-imperialists.

In 1894, however, with the movement for Hawaiian annexation apparently effectively stymied, and the Cleveland administration urging withdrawal from Samoa, the anti-imperialists had some reason for being optimistic. *The Nation* commented: "The vaunted 'imperial policy' has been checked in its very beginnings, and it will not be heard of, aside from the professional frothings of the incurable jingoes, for years to come." [6] The founding on July 4, 1894 of the Hawaiian Republic, replacing the Provisional Government, was generally hailed by the anti-imperialists as

---

5. Richardson, *op. cit.*, Vol. IX, pp. 531, 532, 635.
6. *The Nation*, Vol. LVIII (Feb., 1899), p. 97.

another encouraging sign. It was their feeling that the more permanent and independent the Hawaiian government was the less likelihood there would be for annexationist agitation.

Domestic stability, prosperity, and contentment were also viewed at the time, and undoubtedly correctly, as being factors which would dampen imperialist ardor, and vice versa. "This mania," observed E. L. Godkin, "for foreign dependencies at great distances from our shores, which breaks so completely with all the best traditions of our Government, seems to increase with the increasing difficulty of our domestic problems."

There was an intimate connection between certain domestic and foreign problems in relation to the matter of trade. "Trade in our time," Godkin insisted, "follows cheapness and durability. All the navies, steamers, and telegraphs in the world will not make people look at your goods unless they are cheaper than other people's—a simple truth which it seems impossible to hammer through a protectionist skull." [7]

Godkin's petulant statement points up a significant dichotomy in economic theory between the typical imperialist, who believed in high protective tariffs and "controlled" markets, and the typical anti-imperialist who believed in very low or, better still, no tariffs, i.e. free trade. It is interesting that this same phenomenon can be observed in Great Britain, where the leading exponents of free trade (e.g. Cobden and Bright) were also leaders of British anti-imperialism. The American free trade anti-imperialist group seems, in fact, to have been rather strongly influenced by the British example.

Some of the more perceptive American imperialists, like Henry Cabot Lodge, commented upon this. While they were glad to attempt to emulate British imperialism and its concomitant economic philosophy, the American imperialists were quick to criticize their ideological opponents for borrowing from

---

7. *Ibid.*, p. 358. The imperialists were even more scathing in their criticism of those who favored free trade. For example see Theodore Roosevelt's denunciation of Edward Atkinson, a leading anti-imperialist, for his free trade views. "True American Ideals," *The Forum*, Vol. XVIII (Feb. 1895), p. 949.

England various "queer and extraneous fantasies." Thus Lodge ridiculed the adherence of American anti-imperialists to "the theory of the Manchester school [which] in its fullest development [states] not merely that free trade was economically correct, but that if universally applied it would prove to be a panacea for all human ills, that it meant universal peace, and that all such things as armies, navies, war, territorial extension or national expansion must be stopped because they were likely to interfere with the complete freedom of trade." [8]

In addition to criticizing imperialism for allegedly impeding progress in trade and international relations, the anti-imperialists censured it for contributing to the "growing disposition to shrink domestic reforms." The anti-imperialists claimed that many political leaders attempted to obscure their indifference to reform by "disputing with European Powers about protectorates and 'coaling stations' in distant seas, and pretending that every little rock in the vast expanse of the Pacific is a 'strategic point.' " [9]

This charge that imperialism was partly a device, like the Roman "bread and circuses," to divert the attention of the masses from pressing domestic problems was to be frequently repeated by the leading anti-imperialists in the years to come. It was natural that they should raise this issue since some of the most important leaders of American anti-imperialism—Godkin, Schurz, Moorfield Storey, Erving Winslow, Edward Atkinson, Herbert Welsh et al.—were simultaneously extremely active in a great variety of reform movements. And when the imperialists justified expansion as a form of altruism that would bring sundry reforms to the backward areas of the world, the anti-imperialists countered by adapting various maxims, such as, "charity begins at home;" "remove the beam from your own eye before worrying about the mote in the eye of your little brown brother," etc.

Attention, nevertheless, was soon again shifted overseas by revolutionary events that began early in 1895. An abortive royalist coup d'état was staged in the Hawaiian Islands early in

---

8. Henry Cabot Lodge, "Our Blundering Foreign Policy," *The Forum,* Vol. XIX (March, 1895), p. 13.

9. *The Nation, loc. cit.*

January of the new year. Although it was an *opéra bouffe* affair, the imperialist clique in the U.S. Senate treated it quite seriously and used it as an opportunity to renew agitation for annexation. Henry Cabot Lodge stated the case for the imperialists in a notable speech in the Senate on January 21. He called for the annexation of the Hawaiian Islands, as well as "all outlying territories necessary to our defense, to the protection of the Isthmian Canal, to the upbuilding of our trade and commerce, and to the maintenance of our military safety everywhere."

The anti-imperialists were just as adamant in their condemnation of overseas expansion as Lodge, Platt, Frye, and others were in support of it. Donelson Caffery of Louisiana, an implacable foe of imperialism, voiced his unalterable opposition "to foreign acquisitions," and George Gray of Delaware criticized Lodge's "scheme of annexation and colonial empire." He stated his anti-imperialist credo forcefully: "I do not believe that the policy, the traditions, or true interests of this country are consistent with annexation. I believe that our policy is a continental one, and that we are not called upon by anything in our past history or by anything in the necessities of our [present] situation to step off this continent in a career of colonial aggrandizement." [10]

On January 24 a resolution calling for annexation of Hawaii was presented. The Senate on January 26, however, by a close vote (24 to 22, with 29 absentions) decided to substitute for this resolution one by George Vest.[11] The Missouri Senator's resolution, in essence, simply reaffirmed the policy of noninterference enunciated in the Turpie resolution, which had been passed the previous spring, albeit by a considerably greater margin. Thus once again the imperialists were thwarted; but it was evident that their strength was growing.

---

10. *Congressional Record,* 53rd Congress, 3rd Session, pp. 1174, 1139, 1172, 1171.

11. *Ibid.,* p. 1411.

It should be kept in mind that the imperialists needed a great many more votes (a two-thirds majority) to secure approval of an actual treaty of annexation.

CHAPTER 6

The Gathering Storm

The debate over Hawaii was not yet ended, but it was soon drowned out by the ominous, premonitory rumblings of a cataclysmic storm which had gathered over Cuba. José Marti, who while in exile in the United States had organized a revolutionary movement to rid Cuba of Spanish oppression, on February 24, 1895, issued a call to arms which initiated the final struggle in a series of wars for Cuban independence extending back over many years of the nineteenth century. Although the insurrectionary leader lost his life that very day during a skirmish with Spanish troops at Dos Rios, the increasingly bitter internecine struggle was to continue for over three years until the United States intervened and ended the conflict and with it Spanish control of the island.

The "pearl of the Antilles" had been coveted by American expansionists for many years. More than half a dozen American presidents, beginning with Thomas Jefferson, had contemplated the annexation of Cuba. John Quincy Adams, James Monroe, James Polk, and Franklin Pierce had been especially interested in acquiring the island. After the Civil War intense interest in Cuban annexation, as in expansion in general, languished.

With the return of expansionist ardor in the late 1880's and early 1890's, Cuba once more became frequently mentioned as a logical target for annexation. One of the earliest influential statements on the subject in the 1890's was an article by Thomas Jordan entitled "Why We Need Cuba," which argued that there

69

were strong geographical, commercial, and military reasons why the island should belong to the United States.[1]

Agitation for this goal was sufficiently great by the autumn of 1893 (two years, it should be noted, before the outbreak of the revolution which eventually precipitated the Spanish-American War and five years before the United States intervened in Cuba) that various anti-imperialists felt constrained to comment upon it. Carl Schurz, for example, ridiculed the imperialists' contention that it was absolutely necessary for the United States to annex Cuba. He warned that if we rationalized this acquisition, it would logically lead to others until "we shall hardly find a stopping place north of the Gulf of Darien; and we shall have an abundance of reasons, one as good as another, for not stopping even there." [2]

By 1895 Schurz's admonition was forgotten and the new Cuban revolution brought a resurgence of annexationist interest in the island. In July of that year the *American Magazine of Civics* conducted an interesting symposium on the subject of Cuban annexation, which it held to be "a fair criterion of American sentiment on the question."

A perusal of the statements of the fourteen prominent men who were interviewed indicates that there was a wide diversity of opinion on the Cuban issue ranging from the ardent imperialism of Ethan Allen, grandson of the Revolutionary War hero, and Colonel Fred D. Grant, son of the Union Army General and President, to the adamant anti-imperialism of ex-Congressman John Warner and former General Martin T. MacMahan. Allen, Congressman William Sulzer,[3] and Grant, who believed "in an

---

1. Thomas Jordan, "Why We Need Cuba," *The Forum*, Vol. XI (July, 1891), pp. 559-67.

2. Carl Schurz, "Manifest Destiny," *Harper's Monthly*, Vol. LXXXVI (Oct., 1893), p. 740.

3. Sulzer frequently called for Cuban annexation in Congress, claiming that the island was a "natural part of our geographical domain . . . and essential to our control of the Gulf of Mexico, our continental supremacy, and our national destiny." *Congressional Record*, 54th Congress, 1st Session, p. 2350.

aggressive foreign policy always on the part of the United States," advocated the immediate acquisition of Cuba by any convenient means. Governors John Evans of South Carolina and William Oates of Alabama represented the moderates who did not discount the benefits of ultimate annexation but who opposed "any interference in the present troubles in Cuba" and did not think that the island should be obtained by "invasion, filibustering or unlawful means." Those who categorically opposed Cuban annexation did so on various grounds. John Byrne based his opposition to annexation on being "a stickler for the Monroe Doctrine," although Ethan Allen contended that the doctrine was outmoded and was "too small a covering to fit us now." Wall Street denizen Henry Clews felt that it would be an unwise policy to acquire additional territory when "we have so much of our own already." Gideon Tucker, who might be described as a reconstructed imperialist, having favored Cuban annexation before the Civil War, claimed that the majority of the people preferred "domestic quiet to the danger of extending territory;" and former Congressman Warner voiced the frequently expressed anti-imperialist view that "until we have a dearth of trouble at home, we need not search for it abroad." [4]

One of the most significant subsidiary matters which the symposium brought up was the question of whether the United States should accord belligerent rights to the insurgents. The imperialists naturally favored this move as an opening wedge for annexation. The anti-imperialists, although sympathetic to the revolution as a movement for freedom and independence, generally opposed either recognition or active intervention for the very reason that the imperialists favored it. The anti-imperialists' greater respect for the niceties of international law undoubtedly also influenced their support of strict neutrality on the part of the United States.

President Cleveland, in the face of considerable criticism

---

4. "Ought We to Annex Cuba: A Symposium," *American Magazine of Civics,* Vol. VII (July, 1895), pp. 37-49.

and urging to the contrary by Lodge, Roosevelt, and company,[5] refused to grant belligerent status to the Cuban revolutionaries. On June 12, 1895, he issued an official proclamation of United States neutrality. Six months later in his annual message to Congress he reviewed the Cuban situation and reiterated the administration's position, which was basically that of the nation's anti-imperialists. He said that neither our traditional sympathy for a people "struggling for larger autonomy and freedom . . . nor our loss and material damage . . .[6] have in the least shaken the determination of the Government to honestly fulfill every international obligation." [7] Cleveland was resolutely to maintain this position of strict neutrality throughout the remainder of his term.

Before considering the Cuban controversy after 1895, we should note an event, the publication of the memoirs of John Sherman, which illustrates a trend which was to be highly significant in the subsequent course of the great debate. Sherman was one of the founders and most important members of the Republican Party. By 1895 he had served in the national government for forty years as Congressman, Secretary of the Treasury, and Senator; he was to serve in the Senate for two more years and to round out his career, although reluctantly, as Secretary of State. Thus when he spoke on a subject, people listened. It is, therefore, important to note that Sherman in his memoirs criticized the American protectorate in Samoa, opposed annexation of Cuba, and spoke out forcefully against the acquisition of any "lands

---

5. See Lodge, "Our Blundering Foreign Policy," *op. cit.;* Cushman K. Davis, "Two Years of Democratic Diplomacy," *North American Review,* Vol. CLX (March, 1895); J. P. Dolliver, "The Work of the Next Congress," *North American Review,* Vol. CLXI (Dec., 1895).

6. The "loss" referred to was incurred by reduction of American trade with the island which was quite substantial, and the "damage" was to American owned property in Cuba, which at the time was conservatively estimated to be worth $30 million—Edward F. Atkins, *Sixty Years in Cuba* (Boston, 1926), p. 209.

7. Richardson, *op. cit.,* Vol. IX, p. 636.

in a far distant sea." [8] It is interesting and quite significant that Sherman chose to conclude his massive autobiography with the following remarks:

> The events of the future are beyond the vision of mankind, but I hope that our people will be content with internal growth, and avoid the complications of foreign acquisitions. Our family of states is already large enough . . . a republic should not hold dependent provinces or possessions. . . . If my life is prolonged, I will do all I can to add to the strength and prosperity of the United States, but nothing to extend its limits or to add new dangers by acquisitions of new territory.[9]

What this meant was that one of the most venerated patriarchs of the Republican Party, a man who was renowned not just as a staunch party man, but rather as a fierce partisan, was parting ideological company with the young Turks like Lodge and Roosevelt who espoused imperialism and who were coming into ascendancy in the party.

It is significant also that Sherman was not alone among the Republican old guard in his views. Senator George Edmunds, who had battled Grover Cleveland on a score of issues, by 1895 was beginning to agree with his opinions on foreign policy and in three years would join him as one of the original vice presidents of the Anti-Imperialist League. George Boutwell, another of the party's founders, Republican Governor of Massachusetts and Secretary of the Treasury under Grant, would become the first president of the Anti-Imperialist League. Thomas B. Reed, noted speaker of the House, was wavering and would break ranks with his party over the Hawaiian issue in 1898, as would still another of the party's oldest veterans—George Hoar—over the Philippine question in 1899. These men and others like them, who were among the most venerated leaders of the Republican Party, because of the issue of imperialism would strenuously oppose the very party which they had helped to

---

8. John Sherman, *Recollections of Forty Years in the House, Senate and Cabinet* (Chicago, 1895), Vol. II, pp. 975, 1040.

9. *Ibid.*, Vol. II, p. 1216.

create. However, it became apparent after 1895 that the older Republican leaders were steadily losing ground to a small but very active and increasingly influential coterie which advocated a much more dynamic foreign policy.

Senator George Gray in a notable article in April of 1895 vigorously attacked this new policy, characterizing it as being excessively "meddlesome and aggressive. It is," he claimed, "envious and suspicious; it is covetous and not very scrupulous; it exemplifies the evil of power without self-control. . . . Its spirit is that of conquest; its first reason, as well as its last, is force. . . . It overthrows by force a Queen in Hawaii in the name of liberty and annexation, and maintains by force a king in Samoa in the name of independence and autonomy. If this be Republican diplomacy, and we are to have more of it, God help the American Republic!" [10]

E. L. Godkin, in an astute essay, "Diplomacy and the Newspaper," written the following month, seconded Gray's criticism of the "new diplomacy" and demonstrated how and why it was furthered by some of his less scrupulous fellow journalists. His penetrating analysis and critique of the nature of both nascent American imperialism and "yellow journalism," appearing in May of 1895, refutes those historians and commentators who have viewed these phenomena as being the distinctive product of only the last two or three years of the century.

Godkin observed that the geographical isolation of the United States had always been considered a great blessing. "But," he said, "a new school of thought on this matter has sprung up, composed largely of naval officers and Republican politicians, who are known by the general name of 'Jingoes' [11] and are

---

10. George Gray, "Two Years of American Diplomacy," *North American Review,* Vol. CLX (April, 1895), pp. 423-424. Gray's article, in addition to castigating the "large policy," was also a reply to the criticism of Cleveland's foreign policy in an article by Senator Cushman K. Davis—"Two Years of Democratic Diplomacy"— which had appeared in the same magazine the previous month.

11. The terms "Jingo" and "Jingoism," often used derisively by the anti-imperialists to refer to their bellicose imperialist opponents,

profoundly dissatisfied with this isolation." He complained that these men wanted to bring the United States "into contact with considerable foreign powers at as many points as possible" and that they wished to acquire many foreign possessions, including Hawaii, Samoa, Cuba, "the West Indies generally," and parts of Central America.

Godkin felt that such aggressive designs could lead only to dangerous international conflicts. He pointed out that this was the very reason why certain newspapers supported the Jingoes. "They rely," he said, "mostly on large sales, and for large sales on sensational news. Now nothing does so much to keep sensational news coming in over considerable periods of time as war. . . . Next to war they welcome the promise of war."[12]

Godkin commented sarcastically upon the histrionic chauvinism displayed by some of the imperialists and their supporters in the sensational press:

The medium through which the newspaper acts most effectively on the enthusiastic temperament is what is known as 'true Americanism,' or 'intense Americanism.'[13] An 'intense American' is constantly on the lookout for somebody who expresses

---

are derived from a London music-hall ballad, which became popular in 1877, when war between Great Britain and Russia over the Turkish situation seemed imminent. The refrain, the first line of which is, of course, antithetical to the actual ebullient belligerence which characterizes the song, is:

> "We don't want to fight
> But by Jingo if we do,
> We've got the ships, we've got the men,
> We've got the money too!"

12. E. L. Godkin, "Diplomacy and the Newspaper," *North American Review,* Vol. CLX (May, 1895), pp. 571, 575.

13. The anti-imperialists were often disturbed by the bombastic chauvinism of the imperialists, whom one of the Vice-Presidents of the Anti-Imperialist League, Bishop Henry C. Potter, was to characterize as "pinchback patriots." Godkin in an earlier editorial contrasted "true patriotism" with "the sham patriotism which has so many times in the past few years tried to palm itself off on the country." He castigated "the fury of our political Jingoes" who have

or implies doubts about the ability of the United States to thrash all other nations; or who fails to acknowledge the right of the United States to occupy such territories, canals, isthmuses or peninsulas, as they may think desirable.[14]

The anti-imperialists believed that the imperialist, when allied with the sensational newspaper editor, who was willing to play upon the patriotic feelings of the public to gain ulterior ends, represented an irresponsible and undesirable combination which could do the nation no good.

This was precisely the case with such newspapers as William Randolph Hearst's *New York Journal* and Joseph Pulitzer's *New York World*. They sought to boost their circulations by publishing lurid, exaggerated, and one-sided accounts of alleged Spanish atrocities. This is not to say that there weren't terrible atrocities—there were some; but they were not quite so extensive, diabolical, and bestial as they were made out to be; nor were they limited to the Spanish side as Hearst et al. would have had their readers believe. Moreover, the rebels initiated much of the widespread suffering of noncombatants, which the "yellow press" attributed solely to Spanish machinations and cruelty, by deliberately adopting a scorched earth policy at the beginning of the revolution. The important matter, however, at the time was not so much what the actual situation in Cuba was, but rather what the American public, influenced by the Jingoes and yellow journals, thought that it was.

The anti-imperialists deplored the methods employed by the yellow journals. In a letter to Senator Donelson Caffery, dated January 5, 1896, President Cleveland strongly criticized the

---

created "a most tiresome and meaningless jargon about 'the flag' and a 'vigorous foreign policy' and making ourselves respected 'in the eyes of the world.' Hence have proceeded the efforts to work up the American people into a towering rage over some far-off island, which nine-tenths of them know nothing and care less about, or to get up a foreign war with some weak power which it would be a disgrace to fight." *The Nation,* Vol. LIX (July 19, 1894), p. 40.

14. Godkin, "Diplomacy and the Newspaper," *op. cit.,* p. 578.

New York World, referring to it as a "maliciously mendacious and sensational newspaper." [15] The yellow press was undaunted by all criticism. It continued to crank out stories, frequently completely unsubstantiated, of Spanish cruelty, and to urge intervention by the United States.

Excitement over the Cuban situation continued to mount. The replacement in early 1896 of the rather conciliatory Spanish Governor General of the island, Martinez de Campos, who had been unable to cope with the aggressive tactics of the rebels, by the sterner General Valeriano Weyler, added fuel to the fire. Weyler, in an attempt to isolate the insurgents from the rest of the population, introduced a policy of "reconcentration," by which the rural people were ordered to come to the Spanish-held towns or be treated as rebels. The Spanish authorities were unable to cope with the *reconcentrados,* widespread hardship and suffering ensued, and many thousands died of malnutrition and disease. The American people were horrified by this spectacle. General Weyler—variously referred to by the yellow journals as the "Butcher," a "mad dog," a "human hyena" and other ingenious and alliterative epithets—became overnight a popular *bête-noire* among American newspaper readers, who enjoyed railing against this real-life villain as much as they had loved hissing Simon Legree.

President Cleveland, however, still held resolutely to his policy of non-recognition of the insurgents. The President's maintenance of this position greatly irritated the nation's imperialists, many of whom hoped to provoke Spain into war over the issue. In April, 1896, noted journalist Mayo W. Hazeltine [16] remarked that it had "come to be felt on both sides of the Atlantic that in this instance a recognition of belligerency would be introductory to a recognition of independence, which

---

15. Allan Nevins (ed.), *Letters of Grover Cleveland: 1850-1908* (Boston, 1933), p. 422.

16. An editor of the *New York Sun,* he also contributed articles on a variety of subjects to a number of magazines including *Harper's Weekly, North American Review,* and *Colliers.*

is a very different thing, and would undoubtedly constitute a causus belli." [17]

This interpretation of the matter undoubtedly made President Cleveland even less likely to alter his position, in spite of a concurrent Congressional resolution to the contrary. This resolution, which had been adopted by the Senate in February, received final approval in the House in April. It stated that it was the opinion of Congress that a state of war definitely existed in Cuba, that the United States should grant belligerent rights to both sides, and that the cordial "offices of the United States should be offered by the President to the Spanish Government for the recognition of the independence of Cuba." [18] The President duly noted the resolution, but viewed it as merely an expression of Congressional opinion and nothing more, and refused to act upon it.

The indefatigable Mayo Hazeltine, in an article written in December, 1896, posed the same question that so many Americans were asking at the time. He inquired, indignantly, why the President had not carried out the Congressional resolution "to recognize the Cuban revolutionists as belligerents." [19] Hazeltine had himself given probably the strongest reason for the President's stand in his previous article when he observed that such a move in the current circumstances would be construed as a *causus belli*. He had also, perhaps inadvertently, revealed why recognition and even intervention was desired as much by the nation's imperialists as it was opposed by the anti-imperialists. He remarked, while speculating whether a war between the United States and Spain was imminent, that "not only would Cuba be lost, but Spain has other insular possessions of which, were she beaten at sea, she might be deprived—Puerto Rico,

17. Mayo W. Hazeltine, "Possible Complications of the Cuban Question," *North American Review,* Vol. CLXII (April, 1896), p. 407.

18. *Congressional Record,* 54th Congress, 1st Session, pp. 3627-3628.

19. Mayo W. Hazeltine, "What Shall Be Done About Cuba," *North American Review,* Vol. CLXIII (Dec., 1896), p. 731.

the Canary Islands, the Philippine Archipelago, and the Balaeric Islands. . . ." [20]

It is interesting to note the incidence of speculation over the likelihood of war between the two powers several years before the occurrence of events, such as the sinking of the *Maine,* which are often spoken of as having caused the war. This speculation was not limited to the United States, where it became rife after 1895. As early as September, 1895, for example, Don Segundo Alverez, former Mayor of Havana, considering the possibility of war between Spain and the United States over Cuba, came to a conclusion with which the American anti-imperialists heartily agreed. He said that "the interest of the United States is not in having war. . . . What is to their benefit is the constant and admirable development of their vast resources, which they are achieving to the admiration of the entire world." [21]

European military men were especially prone to speculation and calculations concerning the causes, conduct, and outcome of a possible conflict between the United States and Spain. They compared the relative strengths of the armies, the size, modernity, and fire-power of the navies. They estimated the reserve capabilities and military acumen of the possible foes. They analyzed probable deployment of forces and did not overlook the likely effects upon international politics and territorial distribution. One of the most interesting examples of this preoccupation is an article entitled "Can the United States Afford to Fight Spain?" The author concluded that it could not. He insisted that a "thorough defeat of the Spanish fleet by the American fleet would be almost impossible" and that "the United States in such a war could do but little damage to Spain." [22]

Public opinion in the United States, to say the least, did not

---

20. Hazeltine, "Possible Complications of the Cuban Question," *op. cit.,* pp. 406, 408.

21. Segundo Alvarez, "The Situation in Cuba," *North American Review,* Vol. CLXI (Sept., 1895), pp. 364-365.

22. The author is simply designated as "a foreign naval officer," "Can the United States Afford to Fight Spain?" *North American Review,* Vol. CLXIV (Feb., 1897), p. 215.

agree with this view. The prevalent belief was that the United States could easily score a stunning victory. President Cleveland, in his annual message of December, 1896, really spoke for all American anti-imperialists. "The correctness of this forecast," he said, "need be neither affirmed nor denied. The United States has, nevertheless, a character to maintain as a nation, which plainly dictates that right and not might should be the rule of its conduct. Further, though the United States is a nation to which peace is not a necessity, it is in truth the most pacific of powers, and desires nothing so much as to live in amity with all the world. Its own ample and diversified domains satisfy all possible longings for territory, preclude all dreams of conquest, and prevent any casting of covetous eyes upon neighboring regions." [23]

The trend of the times, however, was in a different direction. There was an increasingly influential group that did not desire to live in peace but rather dreamed of conquest and imperial glory. "Not in universal harmony," Alfred Thayer Mahan insisted, "nor in fond dreams of unbroken peace rest the best hopes of the world." These bellicose men welcomed the "jarring sounds which betoken that there is no immediate danger of the leading peoples turning their swords into plowshares." They predicted correctly that "in this same pregnant strife the United States will doubtless be led to play a part." [24]

Mahan's fellow naval officer and successor as president of the U.S. Naval War College, Captain H. C. Taylor, preached this same doctrine in February, 1896. His paean of the martial virtues and glories, which was later echoed so often by that more illustrious advocate of the "strenuous life," Theodore Roosevelt, must certainly have shocked the anti-imperialists with their pacifistic proclivities. Captain Taylor said that war might be cruel, but it was also beneficial. "Not only," he stated in words that might have been inspired by Mars himself, "do

---

23. Richardson, *op. cit.,* Vol. IX, pp. 719-720.

24. Alfred Thayer Mahan, "Possibilities of an Anglo-Saxon Reunion," *North American Review,* Vol. CLIX (Nov., 1894), p. 558.

nations that practice too long the arts of peace in forgetfulness of war become enfeebled and the natural prey of neighbors grown strong through combat, but they grow corrupt internally as well and race decadence hastens its steps. The corrupt ease, the luxurious immorality of life, towards which a total absence of war always leads nations, has in it something more degrading for the human race than simple savagery."

The use to which a large, modern American Navy might be put had long worried the anti-imperialists. Their fears were certainly confirmed when Captain Taylor boldly stated that although navies have "found their principal office for generations past in promoting the interests of peace and preserving order on the high seas . . . this cannot always be, and our country, which bids fair to occupy a high place among nations, should no longer be unprepared for those wars which must come." [25]

The anti-imperialists seized every opportunity to combat the belligerent pronouncements of the opposition. Carl Schurz, speaking at the International Arbitration Conference at Washington in April, 1896, denounced "as a wretched fatuity that so-called patriotism which will not remember that we are the envy of the whole world for the priceless privilege of being exempt from the oppressive burden of warlike preparations." [26]

Similarly, Edward Chapman, in a notable article—"The Menace of Pseudo Patriotism"—criticized the chauvinism of the imperialists and their journalistic abettors. Perhaps foreseeing some such incident as the sinking of the *Maine,* he warned that "in an international crisis, when great issues hang in the balance and popular excitement runs high, a democracy contains no more dangerous element than that which would stimulate so-called patriotic passion to gain a vote or sell a newspaper." Chapman and his fellow anti-imperialists were concerned that the jingoes might now cause the nation to forsake the wisdom of its

---

25. H. C. Taylor, "The Study of War," *North American Review,* Vol. CLXII (Feb., 1896), pp. 183, 189.

26. The speech was delivered on April 22, 1896. Schurz Papers.

time-honored policy. "Nothing," he cautioned, "can more surely militate against the fulfillment of our national mission than our adoption of that ideal of military imperialism which is leading the nations of Europe into a labyrinth of increasing complexity and difficulty." [27]

Chapman's admonition was to be less heeded than the continued and increasing saber rattling of Lodge, Mahan, Roosevelt, and other imperialists during the ensuing six months. Carl Schurz, therefore, took up the subject once more in a trenchant editorial, "Armed or Unarmed Peace," in the June 19th issue of *Harper's Weekly.*

He criticized the jingoes and big-Navy men, especially the vigorous new Assistant Secretary of the Navy. Employing his extraordinary forensic skill, Schurz demonstrated the logical fallacy of the position of the imperialists when they attempted to conceal their aggressive designs in specious argument. He pointed out that according to Roosevelt (as had already been argued by naval officers like Luce, Mahan, and Taylor), a lengthy period of peace will tend to make a people "effeminate and unpatriotic," while war will invigorate them and "inspire patriotism." On the other hand, he observed, T. R. also contended that the construction of a formidable battle fleet was a means of preserving peace. "Ergo," Schurz rejoined, "the building of a great war-fleet will effect that which promotes effeminacy and languishing patriotism. Mr. Roosevelt, according to his own theory, will hardly accept this result as satisfactory. His argument in favor of a big war fleet as an instrumentality of peace comes thus to an untimely end."

Schurz succinctly pointed out the nature of the division between the imperialists and anti-imperialists on this issue. "In truth," he said, "those among us who are really in favor of peaceable methods of adjusting international differences are not in favor of building a great war fleet, while almost all the advocates of a great war fleet belong to the jingo class. . . . The

---

27. *North American Review,* Vol. CLXIV (Feb., 1897), pp. 250-252.

reason why the true friends of peace are opposed to the building of a big navy is a very simple one. We do not need such a navy for the maintenance of peace between the United States and foreign nations." [28]

Another very prominent anti-imperialist, Moorfield Storey, who was to serve for more than fifteen years as president of the Anti-Imperialist League, was even courageous enough to beard the opposition in their own stronghold. Speaking at the Naval War College in September, 1897, on "A Civilian's View of the Navy," the outspoken lawyer presented a strong case against a massive, aggressive fleet, which would be quick to lead the United States into an unnecessary war. He disliked the thought of the probable outcome of such a war even more than the war, per se. He must indeed have shocked his hosts when he said candidly: "I can imagine no greater calamity to this country than a successful war, which should lead us to enlarge our boundaries and to assume greater responsibilities." [29]

Schurz, Storey, and the other anti-imperialists were now opposing the prevailing trend of national opinion. Moreover, Grover Cleveland, on whom they could count to uphold the anti-imperialist standard at all costs, was gone from the White House. In place of that stout oak stood William McKinley, who was more like a willow that would bend in the face of the gathering storm.

---

28. Frederic Bancroft (ed.), *op. cit.,* Vol. V, pp. 400-401.

29. Cited by M. A. De Wolfe Howe, *Moorfield Storey: Portrait of an Independent* (Boston, 1932), p. 194.

CHAPTER 7

Cuba Libre

The uncertainties engendered by McKinley's pliable nature were compounded by the disturbing features of the Republican platform of 1896, which called for a "firm and vigorous" foreign policy, control of the Hawaiian Islands, an isthmian canal, strategic naval bases, and some demonstrative action toward Cuba. It is true that foreign policy played a decidedly minor role in this election, being overshadowed by the issues of Free Silver, the tariff, and the unusual and intriguing phenomenon of the mercurial "Great Commoner." More Americans undoubtedly voted against Bryan, whom they feared as a demagogue who like some Pied Piper of the Platte would lead the nation down a silvery path to economic chaos, than voted for McKinley because of the Republican platform's aggressive pronouncements on foreign policy. Nevertheless, these pronouncements had an ominous sound which could not be ignored. This was especially so when the anti-imperialists' ears were assailed by a cacophony of vociferous pronouncements by the domestic imperialists mixed with strident cries of "Cuba Libre" coming from the embattled Caribbean island.

McKinley himself had said very little about foreign policy, and for some time many people were not certain of his position in this area. Whitelaw Reid, editor of the *New York Tribune* and a staunch imperialist, therefore, wrote to the President soon after his election hoping, by appealing to McKinley's known desire for popular praise, to influence him to espouse openly the imperialist cause. "Someday," Reid said, "we will have Cuba, as well as the Sandwich Islands. . . . To get both in your administration would put it beside Jefferson's in the popular mind and ahead of it in history." [1]

Mayo Hazeltine, in an interesting article which appeared soon after McKinley's inauguration, speculated about the new administration's foreign policy. He felt, like many people, that the administration's program would be the antithesis of Cleveland's policy. He predicted that McKinley would favor annexation of Hawaii and recognition of Cuban belligerency. He commented upon the anti-imperialist views of the new Secretary of State, John Sherman,[2] noting with distaste Sherman's opposition to "all annexation." Hazeltine believed that Sherman's views would not hamper expansion, since he was "confident that the words ascribed to him do not express the views of the President." [3]

How Hazeltine could be so sure of McKinley's views on these matters at this point, when the President himself apparently was not, is interesting. There was no question, however, of the basic position of Lodge, Roosevelt, and the other very dedicated imperialists. They were as strongly in favor of insular possessions now as they had been in the past and would be in the future; but the Cuban situation and the public response to

---

1. Cited by Sylvester Kirby Stevens, *The American Frontier in Hawaii* (Harrisburg, 1945), p. 291.

2. Sherman was appointed Secretary of State so that McKinley's political mentor and strong financial backer Mark Hanna could obtain Sherman's seat in the Senate, a position to which he had long aspired. Sherman, whose faculties were failing, preferred to round out his days in the familiar Senate chamber, but accepted the Secretaryship out of his strong loyalty to the party. It was evident, however, as we have noted previously, that Sherman's anti-imperialist views were certainly not acceptable to the younger men in control of the Republican Party. Sherman resigned, probably without regret, after a relatively brief tenure, when the incompatibility of his anti-imperialist views with the trend of opinion in his party and national events rendered his position untenable.

3. Mayo W. Hazeltine, "The Foreign Policy of the New Administration," *North American Review,* Vol. CLXIV (April, 1897), pp. 480, 485.

it seemed to convince the leaders of the American imperialist movement that a change of strategy might be in order.

A definite shift in emphasis can be noted in the pronouncements of the "Duke of Nahant," as the anti-imperialists were to dub Henry Cabot Lodge for his imperial aspirations. Lodge in the spring of 1895, both in his Senate speeches and magazine articles, forthrightly advocated American annexation of Cuba, saying that such a move was an absolute "necessity." This approach had immediately drawn angry criticism from the anti-imperialist camp. *The Nation* denounced this viewpoint, saying that Lodge was like "a highwayman, to whom a traveler's purse is equally a 'necessity,' and is to be had by means as honorable as Lodge seems to have in mind." [4]

It was perhaps this type of reaction to their more candid views that led imperialists like Lodge to soft-pedal their more aggressive tones with euphemistic appeals to duty, destiny, and international altruism. Thus we find Lodge in May of 1896 writing about "our duty to Cuba." Where before he had stressed the interests of the United States, he now said that "the interests of humanity are the controlling reasons which demand the beneficent interposition of the United States." [5]

To question the sincerity of some of the statements of Lodge and other American imperialists, both in relation to intervention in Cuba and to the subsequent acquisitions of territory that followed the Spanish-American War, is not to say that they had no sense of altruism. Their altruism, however, was often merely a sublimation of other motives, growing out of an interesting combination of self-righteousness and self-delusion. Their attitude might be viewed as a precursor, if on a vaster scale, of the philosophy of "what's good for General Motors is good for the country." Many of the imperialists seemed to feel that what was best for the United States was, *ipso facto,* best for the world. The anti-imperialists, on the other

---

4. *The Nation,* Vol. LX, No. 1550 (March 14, 1895), p. 193.

5. Henry Cabot Lodge, "Our Duty to Cuba," *The Forum,* Vol. XXI (May, 1896), p. 287.

hand, simply were not so certain that the United States had a monopoly on the world's wisdom and virtue.

While advocacy of intervention in Cuba was not strictly synonymous with imperialism, those who were most zealous in their support of one most often avidly favored the other and vice versa. The American imperialist leaders welcomed the war, which intervention in Cuba was certain to bring, primarily as a means whereby the United States could both assert itself vigorously on the international scene as a "great power" and obtain the overseas possessions which they felt to be the hall-mark of "greatness." The anti-imperialists, on the other hand, abhorred the means (war) as well as its tangible end (colonies). Moreover, they denied that greatness was in any way inherent in the possession of overseas territories. The greatness of a nation, they contended, lay rather in the excellence of its principles and the degree to which the nation's people adhered to them. And they argued forcefully that to engage in an unnecessary war and the pursuit of foreign conquests was a denial of the nation's true mission, which was to serve as a noble example of peace and enlightened democracy and self-government.

Nevertheless, American intervention in Cuba did not necessarily have to result in imperialism, and there does not seem to have been any widespread awareness of the probable connection between these phenomena in the mind of the public. While the government attempted to remain scrupulously neutral, by the end of 1897 a very large segment of the American people was frankly sympathetic with the Cuban insurgents and began increasingly to feel that the United States should intervene for humanitarian reasons in the internecine struggle.

The anti-imperialists feared that even a war for humanity might degenerate into a war of conquest and that military intervention in the Cuban struggle might lead to American control of this and other Spanish possessions. This fear, however, was not prevalent among the mass of the people whose emotions were being brought to fever pitch by the pro-insurgent propaganda which mounted in volume and sensationalism as time passed.

Newspapers and magazines throughout the country burgeoned with articles expressing righteous indignation at the situation in Cuba. The demand was reiterated that the United States should intervene in the interests of humanity, if for no other reason. Now while it is true that Hearst's *New York Journal* and Pulitzer's *New York World* resorted to the most sensational type of reporting of the Cuban situation apparently from crassly commercial motives, a great many other periodicals, although not in such a sensational manner, echoed the intensely chauvinistic and militant sentiments displayed by the yellow journals. However, it seems that even the yellow journals were reflecting as well as fomenting the interventionist sentiment of the public.

The anti-imperialists, although censuring the imperialists for inducing the popular demand for the war, agreed that McKinley's decision was responsive to public opinion. Thus David Starr Jordan, President of Stanford University and a leading anti-imperialist, commented: "McKinley was evidently reluctant to yield [to the demand for war], but his weakness [6] as well as his strength lay in 'holding an ear to the ground'—in other words, leading wherever the people seemed willing to push him." [7]

It was the force of events combined with public emotion that pushed McKinley toward the war. Mayo Hazeltine, in the early days of McKinley's administration, had sagaciously prophesied that "there may arise at any moment—out of the situation in Cuba—a crisis which will compel the United States to depart from the [official] attitude of indifference which they have maintained for the last two years." [8]

---

6. Paul Holbo has recently challenged in an interesting article the prevailing opinion of the majority of historians, who have tended to agree with Jordan's contemporary estimate. See "Presidential Leadership in Foreign Affairs: William McKinley and the Turpie-Foraker Amendment," *American Historical Review,* Vol. LXXII (July, 1967), pp. 1321-1335.

7. David Starr Jordan, *The Days of a Man* (New York, 1922), Vol. I, p. 614.

8. Hazeltine, "The Foreign Policy of the New Administration," *op. cit.,* p. 479.

Actually two crises arose—both in February, 1889. The first incident grew out of the interception and publication (in the *New York Journal* of February 9, 1898) of an indiscreet letter by the Spanish Minister at Washington, Enrique Dupuy de Lôme. In this controversial missive de Lôme referred to President McKinley as "weak and a bidder for the admiration of the crowd." Although this was certainly uncomplimentary, it was a view that was shared by quite a few Americans, including the majority of the anti-imperialists; and even Theodore Roosevelt is reputed to have said that McKinley had "no more backbone than a chocolate eclair." De Lôme's commentary, while offensive, was not intrinsically that important; but placed in juxtaposition to the startling occurrence of the following week—the sinking of the *Maine*—it seemed to an already aroused American public to be further evidence of sinister machinations by Spain.

The U.S. battleship *Maine* blew up in the harbor of Havana and sank with the loss of 260 American lives on February 15, 1898. To this day, the responsibility for the explosion and its exact cause remain a mystery. Anti-imperialist leader Edward Atkinson, an authority on such matters, stoutly maintained at the time that the explosion was caused by spontaneous combustion and, hence, could hardly be even a minor *causus belli*.[9]

Atkinson's opinion that the sinking was simply an unfortunate accident was not shared by the American public, which clamored for revenge. Joseph Wisan has remarked that peace "was made impossible by the high emotional pitch to which the public was raised following the destruction of the *Maine*."[10] Nevertheless, the anti-imperialists did what they could to stem the bellicose tide.

---

9. Atkinson also later implied in a letter to H. H. Thompson (August 1, 1898) that the whole thing would have been obviated if the anti-imperialists' advice had been heeded: "If we had not built the new navy, there would have been no *Maine* to be blown up in the harbor of Havana. . . ."

Atkinson Papers, Massachusetts Historical Society.

10. *The Cuban Crisis as Reflected in the New York Press,* (N.Y., 1934), p. 458.

Many of the most prominent anti-imperialist leaders—David Starr Jordan, E. L. Godkin, Andrew Carnegie, Carl Schurz, Samuel Gompers, Edward Atkinson, and Moorfield Storey—believed very strongly in the peaceful settlement of all international controversies and devoted themselves to the causes of international arbitration and peace. They naturally opposed the chauvinism which would lead the United States into war, even if the nation had been directly provoked, and they denied such provocation. Atkinson suggested that the nation's churches should forward a huge petition to Congress protesting against a possible war; but Julius Pratt has demonstrated that this was the wrong place to look for support.[11]

Carl Schurz, in a thoughtful editorial in *Harper's Weekly* of March 19, 1898, suggested that the American people should not be stampeded into an unnecessary war by a false sense of national honor. He criticized the belligerent attitude of the Roosevelt-Mahan circle, saying that "swaggering and boasting of prowess are not a part of true honor." "This Republic," he stated, "is very strong. Spain is, in comparison, very weak. Our manifest superiority is so great that there would be little glory in our triumph." [12] The imperialists did not agree. They felt that Spain should be "taught a lesson," and claimed that the United States "needed a war."

The anti-imperialists believed that the President was reluctant to undertake hostilities, and they did what they could to support him in this inclination. Schurz praised "the self-contained dignity with which so far President McKinley and his Ministers have conducted our foreign affairs amid the excitements of the day." [13] Edward Atkinson wrote to various members of Congress urging them to uphold the President in a pacific policy and to stymie the war-spirit "by long and earnest debate in Congress until

---

11. Pratt contends in *Expansionists of 1898* (Baltimore, 1936) that a majority of the nation's clergy, especially the Protestants, strongly supported the war.

12. Bancroft (ed.), *op. cit.*, Vol. V, pp. 453-54.

13. *Ibid.*, p. 456.

it shall become first an object of derision and finally of contempt." [14]

The anti-imperialists were joined in their anti-war protests by the nation's major financial interests, who feared that a war at this time might easily disrupt the recovery which had gained momentum since the depression which followed the panic of 1893. Theodore Roosevelt, always opposed to the anti-imperialists, now roundly denounced the financial group, saying that the United States would have the war "in spite of the timidity of the commercial interests;" [15] and as it turned out, Roosevelt had his way.

In spite of communiques from the American Minister in Madrid that augured well for a peaceful settlement,[16] the United States moved inexorably toward war in the early days of April. On April 8, 1898, three days before the President was to send his war message to Congress, Moorfield Storey, in addressing the Massachusetts Reform Club, stated the essence of the anti-imperialist position. He outlined the immediate evils he saw as a result of U.S. intervention in Cuba, and then spoke of even farther-reaching consequences:

> If all these imaginings are in vain, and our success is a rapid and bloodless one as the most sanguine can hope, such a victory is more dangerous than defeat. In the intoxication of such a success, we would reach out for fresh territory, and to our present difficulties would be added an agitation for the annexation of new regions which, unfit to govern themselves, would govern us. We would be fairly lauched upon a policy of military aggressions, of territorial expansion, of standing armies and

---

14. Harold Francis Williamson, *Edward Atkinson: The Biography of an American Liberal* (Boston, 1934), p. 224.

15. Henry F. Pringle, *Theodore Roosevelt* (New York, 1931), p. 179.

16. For example, Woodford cabled on March 31, 1898: "I believe the ministry are ready to go as far and as fast as they can and still save the dynasty here in Spain. They know that Cuba is lost. Public opinion has moved steadily towards peace."—*Foreign Relation, 1898* (Washington, D.C., 1901), p. 684.

growing navies, which is inconsistent with the continuance of our institutions. God grant that such calamities are not in store for us.[17]

On the same day that Storey was delivering his jeremiad in Boston, Carl Schurz wrote to President McKinley, saying wishfully that he hoped that "the war fever stirred up by the 'yellow journals' is on the point of receding." He pleaded with McKinley to avoid war. "If availing yourself at the last moment of the last chance, you succeed in saving the Republic from so terrible and hopeless an estrangement, the American people will never cease to be grateful to you." [18]

The President, more astutely, read public opinion the other way. He had come to feel that it was best to acquiesce and give the people the war they were demanding. He, therefore, went before Congress on April 11, and in the name of "humanity, civilization, and American interests," requested authority to intervene with military forces in Cuba.

Debate on the matter began almost immediately, and several stormy sessions followed. Interestingly enough, it was the statement of a man known for his strong imperialist sentiments which largely led to the capitulation of the anti-imperialist opposition to the war in Congress. Senator Henry M. Teller took a very active part in the spirited debate over Cuba. He surprised a great many people by saying that he wanted the Senate to declare that "we do not intend in any way to derive benefit from the intervention . . . that whatever we may do as to some other islands, as to this island, the great bone of contention, we do intend to take it." Teller said, furthermore, that he would offer an amendment to the joint resolution that would "make it clear to the world that . . . when we go out to make battle for the liberty and freedom of Cuban patriots, that we are not doing it for the purpose of aggrandizement for ourselves or the increasing of our territorial holdings."

---

17. Howe, *op. cit.,* pp. 194-195.
18. Letter to McKinley, April 8, 1898, Schurz Papers.

The anti-imperialists in Congress undoubtedly felt that if there had to be a war this was certainly the altruistic spirit in which it should be approached. There was that ominous phrase about "whatever we may do as to some other islands," but the anti-imperialists probably felt that the nation could not with honor go back on the overall self-abnegating spirit of the resolution; in any case, such a resolution coming from the likes of Teller was certainly a step in the right direction. They, therefore, supported the measure with enthusiasm.

The majority of the anti-imperialist leaders—men like Storey, Cleveland, Jordan, Schurz, and Gamaliel Bradford—still held out against the war in any form. Schurz at a meeting of the New York Chamber of Commerce on April 7 drew up a set of resolutions stating that war with Spain would be a calamity and a crime. Similarly, a group of anti-imperialist leaders who were later all officers of either the New York or New England Anti-Imperialist Leagues—including Charles Francis Adams, William Dean Howells, John S. Crosby, Bolton Hall, Ernest H. Crosby, and Henry C. Potter—assailed the war in speeches before the New York Central Labor Union. Finally, on April 16, in a last anguished editorial in *Harper's Weekly* Schurz demanded: "Can true patriotism possibly be eager to rush our country into war while there is a chance for honorable peace?" [19] But this voice of reason was lost amid the overwhelming clamor for war and "Cuba Libre."

On April 19 the die was cast. Congress passed a four-part joint resolution which amounted to a declaration of war. It declared that: 1) Cuba was to be free; 2) Spain should immediately withdraw from the island; 3) the President should utilize the nations' armed forces to effect these ultimata, and 4) (the so-called Teller Amendment) "the United States hereby disclaims any disposition or intention to exercise sovereignty, jurisdiction, or control over said island except for the pacification thereof, and asserts its determination, when that is accomplished,

---

19. Bancroft (ed.), *op. cit.*, Vol. V, p. 464.

to leave the government and control of the island to its people." [20]

President McKinley signed the official declaration of war on April 24, and the emotionally aroused people of the United States went forth, in a crusading spirit, to battle "for human lives and the liberty of human beings, for 'Cuba Libre.' " [21]

---

20. *Congressional Record,* 55th Congress, 2nd Session, p. 3993.
21. *New York Sun,* March 25, 1898.

CHAPTER 8

Bitter Harvest

Just one week after the formal declaration of the war supposedly initiated solely to liberate Cuba, Commodore George Dewey steamed into Manila Bay and annihilated the Spanish fleet there. Dewey's swift and complete victory on May 1, 1898, focused the nation's attention upon the Pacific. One of the most significant byproducts of this phenomenal action was an immediate quickening of interest in the annexation of the Hawaiian Islands.

The question of annexing Hawaii had been hanging fire for almost a year when Dewey's gunnery practice off Cavite brought it once more to public attention. Soon after his inauguration, President McKinley had moved to carry out that part of the Republican party platform which called for American control of Hawaii. A treaty of annexation was drawn up in June 1897, by Assistant Secretary of State William R. Day and former Secretary of State John W. Foster. The current head of the State Department, John Sherman, was known to oppose annexation and was, therefore, effectively bypassed. Sherman, however, was induced to sign the handiwork of Day and Foster on June 16, 1897. The treaty, which was very similar to the abortive pact of 1893, accompanied by a message from McKinley, was submitted to the Senate the same day.[1]

---

1. See *Senate Report No. 681,* 55th Congress, 2nd Session, for the text of the treaty and accompanying papers.

News of the treaty brought an official protest from the Japanese government. This protest, however, was intended primarily for its effect upon Japanese public opinion, and Japan made it clear that she had no territorial designs on Hawaii.[2] Despite this disclaimer and the subsequent withdrawal altogether of the Japanese protest on December 22, 1897, the imperialists made very effective use of the "Japanese menace" as a propaganda device in the campaign for annexation.

Another factor that might have influenced the Japanese protest is that John Sherman had shortly before the treaty was drawn up apparently informed the Japanese ambassador that annexation was not under consideration. The ambassador might well have viewed the subsequent appearance of the treaty as American duplicity, but this was not the case. There are several explanations. First, Sherman, himself, was opposed to annexation and undoubtedly said so at the time. Second, the negotiations for the treaty were not conducted by Sherman. Third, Sherman's seventy-odd years were weighing heavily upon him, and he was known to be quite forgetful at times.

Such an explanation will not suffice in the case of McKinley's statements on the matter to Carl Schurz. Schurz met with McKinley in New York soon after his inauguration. He questioned the wisdom of appointing Sewall of Maine, a friend of John L. Stevens and James G. Blaine, as Minister to Hawaii. The President said that if Sewall were appointed, as he subsequently was, it would be with the definite understanding that he was not to emulate Stevens and take part in any schemes for annexation. McKinley assured Schurz that annexation was not within his purview, saying "you may be sure that there will be no jingo nonsense under my administration." Later, at a dinner at the White House on July 1, 1897, Schurz reminded the President of this and questioned why, in light of his previous assurances to the contrary, he had gone ahead with a treaty of annexation. McKinley seemed embarrassed and replied rather

---

2. F. Hilary Conroy, *The Japanese Frontier in Hawaii, 1868-1898* (Berkeley, 1953), pp. 137-138.

evasively that he had merely sent the treaty to the Senate so that he could test public opinion on the issue.[3]

There was no doubt at any time just where President McKinley's predecessor, Grover Cleveland, stood on the issue. Just three days after the treaty had been submitted to the Senate, Cleveland wrote to his former Secretary of State, Richard Olney. "Did you," he inquired disgustedly, "ever see such a preposterous thing as the Hawaiian business? The newspapers I read are most strongly opposed to it, and there ought to be soberness and decency enough in the Senate to save us from launching upon the dangerous policy which is foreshadowed by the pending treaty." [4]

The Senate was not to disappoint the former chief executive's anti-imperialist sentiments on this occasion. Although the Committee on Foreign Relations reported favorably upon the treaty on July 14, 1897, the existence of a group of determined anti-imperialists in the Senate made it clear that the necessary two-thirds majority could not be obtained at that time, and so no further action was taken upon the matter before the end of that particular session of Congress.

The debate over annexation then shifted from the halls of Congress to the periodicals. From the legislative forum Senator Stephen White of California carried his opposition to the pages of the *The Forum* magazine. To the dismay of some of his California constituents, who by 1898 owned a good proportion of the Hawaiian sugar industry, he strongly criticized the proposed annexation of Hawaii. He pointed out the paradoxical position of the President and Secretary of State, citing McKinley's warning in his inaugural address against the "temptation of territorial aggression," and remarking that the participation of Sherman, whose views were decidedly anti-imperialistic, "in the present scheme has not failed to excite surprise." White examined the imperialist position in detail and endeavored to

---

3. Claude Moore Fuess, *Carl Schurz: Reformer* (New York, 1932), pp. 349-50.

4. Richard Olney Papers, Library of Congress, Washington, D.C.

demonstrate that "none of the arguments made in advocacy of the outlined program is sound, that Hawaiian annexation is detrimental to the interests of the United States, and that its accomplishment . . . must be alike impolitic and dishonorable." [5]

The imperialists countered White's incisive essay in the next issue of the same journal. John Proctor insisted, in an article significantly titled "Hawaii and the Changing Front of the World," that "our interests, as well as our national honor, now demand the annexation of the Hawaiian group." He scorned the anti-imperialists for their opposition to Hawaiian annexation in a manner typical of the American imperialists, saying that "every acquisition of territory since the formation of our government has been opposed by men who seem to have had little appreciation of the manifest destiny of our race." [6]

Daniel Agnew, former justice of the Pennsylvania Supreme Court, had a far different conception of the nation's destiny should it ratify the Hawaiian treaty. Agnew was one of the original members of the Republican party and had vigorously supported the G.O.P. over the years, but like many others broke with the party over the issue of imperialism. He and his fellow anti-imperialists seemed to feel that the treaty would be a covenant with Hell which would release all of the seven deadly sins. "Let it be confirmed," he warned, "and a precedent will be established having no limit to danger. Folly may seize San Domingo, Avarice covet Cuba, and Greed grasp the islands of the Caribbean Sea. The Union, stretched and distended, will fall to pieces of its own weight and weakness, a prey to discord and foul ambition." [7]

The same issue of *The Forum* in which Judge Agnew's anti-

---

5. Stephen White, "The Proposed Annexation of Hawaii," *The Forum,* Vol. XXIII (Aug., 1897), pp. 730, 723.

6. *The Forum,* Vol. XXIV (Sept., 1897), pp. 41, 45.
Albert Shaw had earlier written in a similar vein, saying that "we need a broad and masculine quality of leadership at Washington, which will disregard the timid plaints of those critics who are forever opposed to anything that involves a decisive attitude on the part of the government." *Review of Reviews,* Vol. XV (May, 1897), p. 528.

7. Daniel Agnew, "The Unconstitutionality of the Hawaiian Treaty," *The Forum,* Vol. XXIV (Dec., 1897), pp. 469-70.

imperialist jeremiad appeared also carried a very influential article by James Bryce. His classic work *The American Commonwealth,* published in 1888, had established Bryce as the foremost foreign authority on the United States, and his opinion on annexation carried great weight.

The sage, friendly foreign commentator remarked that he was writing "from an American point of view," which is intriguing because his views and those of the leading American anti-imperialists are virtually identical. He emphasized the tremendous significance of the proposal that the United States should acquire possessions in the Caribbean and the Pacific. He insisted that annexation of Hawaii and Cuba, instead of strengthening the nation as the imperialists claimed, would actually prove to be a source of weakness. Bryce believed that there were a multitude of virtually insurmountable obstacles in the way of American administration of tropical colonies. "The fact is," he said, stating the case as bluntly as Carl Schurz or Moorfield Storey, "that American institutions are quite unsuited to the government of dependencies."

One of the most interesting aspects of Bryce's critique of incipient American imperialism concerned the American mission, about which the exponents of the new Manifest Destiny talked at such length. His views on this subject could have been adopted without emendation as the basic creed of the American anti-imperialists. He said America needed no new imperial mission. "The United States has already a great and splendid mission in building between the oceans a free and prosperous nation." One of the finest facets of this mission had been to give the European nations "an example of abstention from the quarrels, wars and conquests" that form such a large part of their history. The United States had fortunately been free from the burden of armaments and the problems of colonial rivalries which afflicted Europe. Like the American anti-imperialists, he believed that entering this arena would be "un-American policy, and a complete departure from the maxims—approved by long experience—of the illustrious founders of the Republic." [8]

8. James Bryce, "The Policy of Annexation for America," *The Forum,* Vol. XXIV (Dec., 1897), pp. 385-95.

While Bryce's cogent criticism of nascent American imperialism was influencing the intelligentsia, another stratum of American society—the organized labor movement—was also questioning the wisdom of annexation. Many trade journals, including the *Iron Molder's Journal,* the *Coast Seaman's Journal,* and the *American Federationist,* came out strongly against imperialism in the fall of 1897.[9] The nation's foremost labor unions —the American Federation of Labor and the Knights of Labor —vigorously attacked Hawaiian annexation.

The more articulate spokesmen of the labor movement denounced imperialism. James W. Jamieson criticized the "vainglory of territorial extension," and Samuel Gompers feared that annexation of Hawaii would be merely the first step on the path of imperialism, which would lead to "the decadence of our Republic and the degeneration of our people." [10] While men like Jamieson and Gompers were opposed to imperialism both philosophically and practically, the majority of the labor movement opposed imperialism on the expedient basis that annexation might bring increased competition for jobs and lower wage rates.

Formidable demonstration of anti-imperialist sentiment in the United States in late 1897 and early 1898 disturbed the American imperialists. President McKinley, in his annual message to Congress in December, 1897, again urged that Hawaii be annexed. Mahan,[11] Lodge, and Roosevelt worked assiduously

---

9. John C. Appel, *The Relationship of American Labor to United States Imperialism: 1895-1905* (unpublished doctoral dissertation—University of Wisconsin, 1950), pp. 92-103.

10. James W. Jamieson, "Hawaiian Annexation from a Labor Standpoint," *Iron Molder's Journal* (Sept., 1897); Samuel Gompers, "Should Hawaii Be Annexed," *American Federationist* (Nov., 1897), cited by Appel, *ibid.,* p. 103.

11. Mahan's principal contribution to the cause, other than his letters of encouragement and counsel to other laborers in the imperialist vineyard like Theodore Roosevelt, was in the form of two articles—"A Twentieth Century Outlook" and "Strategic Features of the Caribbean Sea and the Gulf of Mexico"—published in *Harper's Monthly Magazine* in September and October respectively.

to build up sentiment in favor of annexation. When the Senate failed to take favorable action upon the treaty, Roosevelt was especially disappointed. He wrote to W. L. Clowes on January 14, 1898, that he was "a good deal disheartened at the queer lack of imperial instinct that our people show." [12]

If a future President was displeased, a former President was elated. Grover Cleveland wrote to Richard Olney that "all the influence of this administration appears unable thus far to bring to a successful issue the Hawaiian monstrosity." [13] Professor Hermann Von Holst, who was to become very active in the movement, serving as an officer of several anti-imperialist organizations, echoed Cleveland's sentiments in a speech before the Commercial Club of Chicago on January 29, 1898. He warned that the annexation of Hawaii would tempt the nation to seize other areas overseas and "to pass behind us the warning counsels of Washington and his farewell address and enter upon a new era as to our international policy." [14]

Annexation of Hawaii was being debated by a variety of local groups throughout the nation. Halfway across the country, just the day before Von Holst's speech to the Commercial Club, Harry Bingham took the opposite side of the question in his address before the Bar Association at Woodville, New Hampshire.[15] Bingham's primary method of presenting his case—attempting to counter the critiques of those who opposed annexation—when placed in juxtaposition with the current feelings of more prominent imperialists like Lodge and Roosevelt indicates that the imperialists were on the defensive at this time.

Bingham cited many anti-imperialist objections to annexation, but had difficulty in effectively refuting them. Instead, like many imperialists, he resorted to an attempt to denigrate the anti-imperialists by comparing them to the Tories in the Amer-

---

12. Cited by William Adam Russ, Jr., *The Hawaiian Republic, 1894-1898* (Selinsgrove, Pa., 1961), p. 219.

13. Cited by W. Stull Holt, *op. cit.,* p. 164.

14. *Pittsburgh Dispatch,* January 30, 1898.

15. Bingham was an attorney and president of this local bar association.

ican Revolution and claiming that they were simply opposed to "the growth and prosperity of the country." [16] The truth, as Grover Cleveland observed in a statement released to the Associated Press, was that the anti-imperialists felt that the true mission of the nation was to "build up and make a greater country of what we have, instead of annexing islands." [17]

When the Senate reconvened in January, 1898, debate on the treaty of annexation was renewed in executive session. The current occupant of the White House, unlike his predecessor, had no intention of removing the treaty. In fact, President McKinley had now become an enthusiastic annexationist, claiming in words that echoed the mid-century expansionists that "we need Hawaii just as much and a good deal more than we did California. It is Manifest Destiny." [18]

Such a destiny was considerably less manifest to a sufficient number of Senators of anti-imperialist persuasion. It became apparent by March that the two-thirds majority required to pass the treaty could not be mustered. Therefore, after spending almost three months of the session attempting in vain to round up the requisite number of votes for the treaty, those favoring annexation decided to resort to the less demanding joint resolution, which requires only a simple majority. Senator John T. Morgan offered such a resolution, and on March 16, Cushman K. Davis, Chairman of the Senate Committee on Foreign Relations, issued a favorable report upon it to the Senate.[19]

The joint resolution meant, of course, that the House would also be called formally into the debate. The question had already been raised informally during the session by individual Congressmen who were especialy interested in the matter. The most notable example of this was a long critique of annexation

---

16. Harry Bingham, *The Annexation of Hawaii: A Right and a Duty* (Concord, 1898), pp. 10-22.

17. *Cleveland Letters, op. cit.,* pp. 491-92.

18. O. S. Olcott, *Life of McKinley* (Boston, 1916), Vol. I, p. 379.

19. *Congressional Record,* 55th Congress, 2nd Session, p. 2853.

by Henry U. Johnson of Indiana, one of the most steadfast and outspoken anti-imperialists in the House, who was soon to become one of the original officers of the Anti-Imperialist League.

Johnson criticized the Senate for considering the matter in the closed executive session and called for open and public discussion of the treaty. He presented a variety of objections to annexation. He contended that the United States did not need any more land; that overextension would weaken the nation; that the Hawaiian Islands were vulnerable to attack and would require undesirable increases in military forces and expenditures for their defense; that annexation would establish a bad precedent; and that the United States had enough problems without foolishly going out of its way to seek others.[20]

The introduction of the joint resolution did satisfy Johnson's complaint about Hawaiian annexation being officially considered only by the Senate and within the closed executive session. However, the joint resolution was a tactical device which could not have pleased the gentleman from Indiana and his anti-imperialist colleagues. They were undoubtedly disturbed when a resolution similar to the one introduced in the Senate in March was offered by Francis G. Newlands in the House on May 4—just three days after Dewey's stirring victory, and certainly influenced by this event.

Johnson attempted in vain to counter Newlands' move by introducing a resolution to neutralize the islands, a measure which the anti-imperialists were later often to propose for the Philippines, and with a similar lack of success. A majority of the Committee on Foreign Affairs approved Newlands' resolution, and the Committee's Chairman, Robert R. Hitt of Illinois, so reported to the House on May 17.[21] Hugh A. Dinsmore of Arkansas submitted a minority report opposing annexation, and the final Congressional debate over Hawaii began.

The anti-imperialist cause in the House initially received very important tactical support from the powerful Speaker of the

---

20. *Ibid.*, pp. 2031-2034.
21. *Ibid.*, p. 4989.

House, Thomas B. Reed.[22] Reed, like so many of the Republican party's elder statesmen, was strongly opposed to imperialism; [23] and he was in an excellent strategic position to make his opposition felt. Acting in his capacity as Chairman of the Rules Committee, he was able to prevent consideration of the resolution. He held firm for three weeks, in spite of great pressure from the McKinley Administration and the majority of his Republican colleagues. Finally realizing that his Fabian tactics could not be maintained indefinitely, he acquiesced and the resolution was allowed to come before the House for official consideration on June 10.

In the interim the anti-imperialists both inside and outside of Congress were marshalling their forces. Carl Schurz took his indignant opposition directly to President McKinley. He wrote to the President on May 9 insisting that the annexation of Hawaii "would amount to a needless and reprehensible conquest." [24] On June 1 he wrote again urging the President to avoid all annexation schemes, but his earnest advice fell upon deaf ears. McKinley by now was irrevocably committed to the policy of annexation. Lodge wrote to Roosevelt, who was serving as the dashing lieutenant colonel of the Rough Riders, and assured him on this score, saying that the "President has been very firm about it and means to annex the islands." [25]

The debate which ensued in the House (June 10–15) and Senate (June 20–July 6) on the joint resolution for annexation of Hawaii was intense and bitter. The anti-imperialists criticized

---

22. E. L. Godkin interestingly had predicted several years earlier that Speaker Reed would be a bulwark against annexation. He had written on November 22, 1894: "When the furious Boutell tries to annex by resolution in the next Congress he will find Speaker Reed as stubborn and noisy with the gavel as ever Speaker Crisp was." *The Nation,* Vol. LIX, No. 1534, p. 374.

23. See the excellent sketch of Reed in Robert Beisner, *Twelve Against Empire* (N.Y., 1968), pp. 203-211.

24. Schurz Papers.

25. Letter of June 15, 1898, H.C. Lodge (ed.), *Selections from the Correspondence of Theodore Roosevelt and Henry Cabot Lodge* (New York, 1925), Vol. I, p. 311.

annexation from every conceivable angle. They employed both logic and ridicule in their refutation of the expansionists' arguments.

They scoffed at the idea that propinquity was a valid basis for annexation. Congressman Kitchin of North Carolina put it most vividly: "Start in London, cross the English Channel, cross the Austrian Empire, cross Turkey, and stand in the palace of the Sultan and you have not traveled as far as from San Francisco to Honolulu . . . and yet gentlemen speak of their proximity as a reason for annexation!" [26] In the Senate William Roach of North Dakota scored a related point when he said sarcastically that "if we need to annex Hawaii to protect our Pacific coast, it is absolutely necessary that we annex the British Isles and Europe to protect our Atlantic coast." [27]

The anti-imperialists offered various critiques of the claim that Hawaii was a military necessity, a subject which naturally was stressed since the Spanish-American War was in progress. Congressmen John C. Bell and Hugh A. Dinsmore were prominent among those who argued that Hawaii would be more of a liability than an asset militarily since it would be a difficult outpost to defend.[28] Champ Clark displayed his trenchant wit: "We are told," he said, "that we need these islands as a strategic base in military operations. All the admirals, rear admirals, commodores, generals, colonels, majors, and captains say so. How does it happen then that we have gotten along splendidly for 109 years without these volcanic rocks?" He stole some of the annexationists' thunder when he stated that if Dewey's "great victory [which the imperialists were always mentioning in connection with Hawaiian annexation] proves anything at all about these islands, it is that we have no earthly use for them, for he could not have done better if we had owned all the islands in all the seas." [29]

The anti-imperialists claimed that annexation of the islands

---

26. *Congressional Record,* 55th Congress, 2nd Session, p. 5934.
27. *Ibid.,* p. 6360.
28. *Ibid.,* pp. 5834, 5779.
29. *Ibid.,* p. 5789.

would pervert the lofty motives with which the war had begun. Senator McEnery read a moving letter to his colleagues from Herbert Myrick, the editor of several agricultural journals who was to become one of the original officers of the Anti-Imperialist League, in which he lamented that Hawaiian annexation "would degenerate the holiest war ever waged into a campaign of conquest." Hugh Dinsmore was one of many who expressed the same view in the House. "Think of it!" he exclaimed. "This war was inaugurated for humanity's sake, with a distinct disavowal of motives of conquest!" [30]

Extending their argument beyond the war, per se, the anti-imperialists objected to Hawaiian annexation on the ground that it would require a larger permanent military establishment "along European lines." Senator Bate of Tennessee and Congressman Fitzgerald of Massachusetts emphasized in their respective chambers that a large standing Army and Navy were opposed to American tradition and would lead to undesirably large military expenditures and greatly increased taxes.[31] Henry Johnson said it would be foolish for Congress to pay much attention to the pleas of military men for annexation since they were largely motivated by self-interest. "Bred to arms, is it at all surprising that they should desire that which will give them opportunities for employment and distinction?" [32]

The anti-imperialists often reiterated during the Congressional debates their fear that annexation would be, in the words of Senator William Bate, "the commencement of indefinite extension of our territory." [33] In the House, Champ Clark, Henry Johnson, and Hugh Dinsmore were particularly eloquent on this subject and cogently predicted that if we took Hawaii, Spain's colonies would be next on the list.[34]

The anti-imperialists felt that the very reason for our entry

---

30. *Ibid.*, pp. 6270, 5777.
31. *Ibid.*, pp. 5968, 6528.
32. *Ibid.*, p. 5996.
33. *Ibid.*, p. 6525.
34. *Ibid.*, p. 5777.

into the war and our experience in it should have taught the United States something about the deleterious effects of colonialism. Congressman Bland of Missouri pointed out that "colonies and the support of them have brought Spain to ruin and bankruptcy so that she is hardly a respectable enemy in a conflict with a nation that has pursued the opposite policy and eschewed colonization. Let us not," he urged his colleagues and country, "depart from our policy. This is a departure and a dangerous departure." [35] Congressmen Fitzgerald, Dinsmore, and Clark, and Senators Morrill, Bland and McEnery all stressed this point. They insisted that our traditional policy was a wise one proven by long usage to be beneficial and claimed that annexation would immediately lead the United States into dangerous foreign entanglements which it had always wisely avoided.

One element of American foreign policy which the anti-imperialists felt would be particularly jeopardized was the Monroe Doctrine. In the House Congressman Bell of Colorado said that the acquisition of Hawaii would operate "ipso facto as a renunciation of our further intention to maintain the Monroe Doctrine and would proclaim that we had joined the horde of European greed in attempting to absorb as many of the weaker powers on earth as possible." In the Senate Justin Morrill of Vermont, one of many Republican patriarchs who opposed imperialism, indicated the hypocrisy of denouncing European colonial enterprises in the Western Hemisphere while embarking "in a thus be damned enterprise ourselves." [36]

The anti-imperialists in Congress contended that the acquisition of Hawaii would constitute a renunciation not only of our traditional foreign policy but also of the basic principles of American government.[37] Champ Clark was only one of a large group including Congressmen Bell, Dinsmore, and Fitzgerald, and Senators Pettigrew, Morrill, and Baker, who claimed that "this annexation violates the principle that governments derive

---

35. *Ibid.*, pp. 5841-5842.
36. *Ibid.*, pp. 5832, 6143.
37. *Ibid.*, pp. 5777, 6145.

their just powers from the consent of the governed." [38] The anti-imperialists always maintained that impartial investigations had shown that a majority of the Hawaiian people were not represented by the Provisional Government and were opposed to annexation.

Their solicitude about the rights of the Hawaiian people was not merely altruism, for some members of Congress felt that the Hawaiians were unfit for U.S. citizenship. Senator Clay of Georgia and Representative Dinsmore both made the point that the value and permanence of American institutions depended upon enlightened citizens and expressed the belief that the Hawaiians would not be such. In addition to questioning whether the native islanders possessed the requisite intelligence for American citizenship, some asserted that they were physically objectionable, because of the incidence of leprosy in the islands. Senator Morrill decried the prevalence of this disease in the area of annexation; and Congressman Johnson went so far as to read into the *Congressional Record* an entire article, "Shall We Annex Leprosy?" which had appeared in the March issue of *Cosmopolitan*.[39]

While the principal leaders of the anti-imperialist movement in the United States—the officers of the Anti-Imperialist League —were among the staunchest friends of colored races in the United States, a noticeable element in the Congressional objections to admitting the Hawaiians to U.S. citizenship was racial. This was founded partly upon prejudice, partly upon popular common sense (the United States, it was said by many, already had too many unsolved racial problems) and in part upon adherence to U.S. laws which excluded Orientals.

The Oriental question came under particular scrutiny in the House. Representative Fitzgerald, (President John Fitzgerald Kennedy's grandfather) inquired indignantly: "Are we to have a Mongolian State in this Union?" Representatives Johnson, Richardson, and Dinsmore all dwelled on this theme, asking

---

38. *Ibid.*, p. 5793.
39. *Ibid.*, pp. 6351, 5777, 6144, 6001-6002.

increduously: "Are you to take into full citizenship those whom your laws exclude from coming into this country?" Champ Clark, who could always be counted upon to enliven Congressional proceedings with his picturesque speech, asked: "How can we endure our shame when a Chinese Senator from Hawaii, with his pigtail hanging down his back, and with his pagan joss in hand, shall rise from his curule chair and in pigeon English proceed to chop logic with George Frisbie Hoar or Henry Cabot Lodge? O tempora! O mores!" [40]

The racial issue was to a certain extent related to the anti-imperialists' objection that the annexation of Hawaii would be detrimental to American labor. Senator Allen of Nebraska exclaimed: "I am not prepared to put the American father and son, in the field or shop, in deadly competition with Chinese, who live on a bowl of rice and a rat a day." Congressman Clark insisted that the American people did not want "Chinese and Japanese slave labor brought into our country to compete with our free white labor," and pointed out that "organized labor is against this scheme." [41]

This was certainly labor's position. The previous national convention of the American Federation of Labor had officially and vigorously denounced annexation. On June 11 Samuel Gompers wrote to Speaker Reed explaining the A. F. of L. stand. He pointed out the federation had worked for years to obtain laws excluding Orientals and that Hawaiian annexation would "obliterate that beneficent legislation and threaten an inundation of Mongolians to overwhelm the free laborers of our country." [42]

Herbert Myrick, acting as spokesman for "nearly one million" farmers, wrote to J. W. Wadsworth, Chairman of the House Committee on Agriculture, claiming that colonial expansion would also be disastrous for the nation's agricultural inter-

---

40. *Ibid.*, pp. 5967, 5888, 5778, 5790.
41. *Ibid.*, pp. 6705, 6707, 5789, 5793.
42. *Ibid.*, p. 6270; see also Samuel Gompers, *Seventy Years of Life and Labor* (New York, 1925), Vol. II, p. 325.

ests. He predicted that the "coolie labor of these tropical colonies . . . manipulated by world-wide trusts, would close up every beet-sugar proposition and cane-sugar mill in the United States," and sound the "death knell in the United States," of the tobacco, cotton, rice, and fiber industries.[43]

Representatives of the sugar-producing states, especially Congressman Broussard and Senators Caffery and McEnery—all of Louisiana—gave particularly strong support to Myrick's claim of the detrimental effect of annexation upon the domestic sugar industry. Some other opponents did not seem to be sure whether annexation was more a plot of the sugar oligarchy in the islands or the sugar trust in the United States, so they often attacked both sides simultaneously. Thus Champ Clark asserted that the annexation of Hawaii was largely a vicious scheme of "the sugar kings," without making it clear precisely to whom he was referring.

While the emphasis in the debate naturally was upon Hawaiian annexation as a phenomenon in the nation's foreign affairs, the anti-imperialists were greatly disturbed by what they felt would be the undesirable reverberations upon the domestic scene. Senator Bate predicted ominously that imperialism would condemn the United States to a situation in which the entire body politic would suffer an infection beginning in its extremities. "This process," he said, "will by degrees wear away the muscular power of our great republic and dwindle it to a shadow and death." Others were less dramatic, but did assert their belief that the imperialists would divert attention from pressing domestic problems by conjuring up foreign schemes.[44]

The anti-imperialists in Congress objected strongly to annexation on constitutional grounds. Senators Bate of Tennessee and Roach of North Dakota were prominent among many members of both Houses who insisted that the Constitution did not give the federal government any power to "establish or maintain colonies." The latter, like so many of his colleagues, also pro-

---

43. *Congressional Record, loc. cit.*
44. *Ibid.,* pp. 6528, 5968, 6270.

tested against the means (i.e., the joint resolution) by which it was proposed to annex the islands and cited an editorial in the *Philadelphia Record* which complained that "Hawaii will make its entry into the Union by an avoidance of natural, popular and Constitutional means." [45] Senators Allen, Caffery, Turley and Bacon all spoke vigorously against the propriety of the joint resolution, claiming that it represented a usurpation of the Senate's prerogatives. They insisted that if annexation were brought about in this way it would be unconstitutional. Even members of the House, especially Bell and Dinsmore, criticized the resolution for being an encroachment upon the functions of the Senate, the latter saying that he did not believe there was "any constitutional authority by the method proposed to us now to take them." [46]

The question of whether "to take them" was, however, viewed differently by a great many members of Congress. On the penultimate day of the debate in the House, Congressman Gibson stated forcefully: "Manifest Destiny says 'Take them in.' The American people say 'Take them in.' Obedient to the voice of the people, I shall cast my vote to take them in; and tomorrow this House of Representatives will by a good round majority say 'Take them in.'" [47] Gibson's prediction was an accurate one; the following day (June 15, 1898), the joint resolution was approved by the House by a vote of 209 to 91. [48]

Although there were some defections from party ranks, the votes in favor were predominantly Republican and those opposed predominantly Democratic. Analyzed on a geographical basis, the principal areas of opposition were the West (29% negative votes) and especially the South (76%). Leaving aside for the moment more lofty motives, there are several practical factors which help to explain this alignment. First is the fact that the South was a Democratic stronghold and annexation was proposed by a Republican administration. Second was the racial

45. *Ibid.*, pp. 6359, 6363.
46. *Ibid.*, pp. 6145, 5975, 5776.
47. *Ibid.*, appendix, p. 549.
48. *Congressional Record, op. cit.*, p. 6019.

issue; the Southern Representatives objected strongly to the polyglot nature of the Hawaiian population. (The "yellow peril" aspect of Hawaiian annexation also probably influenced votes in the Pacific Coast states.) Third was the economic issue: Hawaiian products, principally sugar, competed with those of the South.

The passage of the joint resolution brought reactions of dismay and displeasure from anti-imperialists throughout the United States. The *Boston Evening Transcript, Springfield Republican,* and *New York Evening Post* on June 16 all expressed disappointment, deprecated the measure, and predicted dire consequences. John Sherman, who had resigned in disgust from the State Department late in April,[49] and Speaker Reed, who had further demonstrated his opposition by refusing to preside in the House on the day the vote was taken,[50] also swelled the chorus of anti-imperialist complaint in mid-June.

Many anti-imperialists at this time (i.e., between the passage of the resolution by the House and the vote upon it in the Senate) seized opportunities, especially at commencement ceremonies, to denounce annexation of Hawaii as being but a harbinger of further imperialist ventures which the war was sure to bring if the tide of public sentiment did not soon change. Tennant Lommax,[51] speaking at the University of Alabama on June 20, pointed out that the imperialists, in addition to clamoring for Hawaiian annexation, also "demand that we shall hold the Philippines as a conquered province, convert the island of Puerto Rico to our own use . . . permanently occupy Cuba." His commentary on these specific objects of American imperialist ambition at this juncture is especially interesting when one considers

---

49. He was replaced on April 28, 1898 by Assistant Secretary of State William R. Day.

50. Representative Dalzell of Pennsylvania occupied the Speaker's chair during the vote on the joint resolution in the House.

51. Lommax, a scion of an old and distinguished Southern family, was a graduate of the University of Alabama (M.A. 1878, LL.B. 1879), a prominent lawyer, active in Democratic politics in the South, and renowned as an orator.

TROUBLES WHICH MAY FOLLOW AN IMPERIAL POLICY
Cartoon by Charles Nelan in the *New York Herald,* 1898.

that it was made before a single U.S. soldier had set foot in Cuba, well over a month before General Miles' invasion of Puerto Rico, and almost two months before the American assault upon Manila. Lommax observed that if the United States took even one of the Spanish islands it would "give the lie" to our claim to have entered upon the war for the sake of humanity and would mean the loss of our moral leadership—something which was far more valuable than "conquered islands" and "subjugated provinces."

Reflecting upon the range of the plans of the American imperialists, Lommax exclaimed that "Rome in the days of her mightiest Republican power never conceived at one fell swoop a bolder scheme of territorial aggrandizement, nor one fraught with more danger to the life of the Republic." There was for the intellectuals of his day, educated as they were in classical studies, a further tacit prediction. This was that the United States, in passing from the status of republic to empire as Rome did, would also, like Rome, eventually become corrupt and unwieldy, and, in Gibbon's phrase, "decline and fall." And yet, Lommax bitterly complained, referring to a matter creating increasing personal enmity between individual members of the imperialist and anti-imperialist camps, "he who, as a lover of his country, jealous of her liberty and mindful of the lessons of history, dares oppose these schemes of Colonial power, is in danger of being denounced as a traitor, and held up as an object of public contumely and scorn."

The anti-imperialists felt that imperialism was not only bad foreign policy, but also bad domestic policy. They deplored its probable effects upon the American economy, fiscal structure, national institutions and principles. They sincerely feared that tyranny abroad might logically lead to tyranny at home, and that if we denied liberty and democracy and popular self-determination to others, we would eventually lose these rights ourselves. Thus Lommax protested against "this so-called Imperial Colonial policy as the entering wedge of the most dangerous and insidious assault ever made upon the liberties of the American people." [52]

Former President Cleveland also used a commencement address to warn the nation at this time against incipient American imperialism. Speaking the following day at Lawrenceville School in New Jersey, Cleveland condemned wars of aggression and conquest, foreign acquisitions, and the entire panoply of American imperialist ideology. Employing some of the same terms and shibboleths employed by the ardent American imperialists and apostles of a latter-day Manifest Destiny, he denied the validity of their arguments. He insisted that foreign conquest and an-

---

52. Tennant Lommax, *An Imperial Colonial Policy: Opposition to It the Supreme Duty of Patriotism* (Commencement address, U. of Ala., June 20, 1898).

nexation were "dangerous perversions of our national mission," and urged the American people to firmly resist the "schemes of imperialism." [53]

In spite of such condemnation of imperialism, the joint resolution, which had been introduced in the Senate for debate on June 20, moved inexorably toward passage. The anti-imperialists in the Senate continued to harangue the opposition, almost to the point of mounting a filibuster. Somewhat paradoxically, the final blow to the anti-imperialist cause was struck by the very man, George Frisbie Hoar, who within six months was to lead the opposition to the annexation of the Philippines in the Senate.

Hoar did not, as one might suppose, recant in the interim between the summer of 1898 and the winter of 1899. He was no annexationist apostate, for the seeds of his sincere anti-imperialism are readily apparent in his curious and memorable speech of July 5. His reasoning, while completely honest, was too tortuous, his distinctions too subtle, abstruse, and personal for his colleagues who stood on both sides of the Hawaiian issue, which he so awkwardly straddled. The imperialists were glad to have his vote, although they could not countenance the process by which he arrived at it. The anti-imperialists, on the other hand, while certainly applauding his astute commentary on imperialism, felt that his categorization of the Hawaiian question was faulty because it was too fine. In short, Hoar was forced to adopt a heterodox position on the Hawaiian issue because he was a man, unfortunately for his own peace of mind, whose keen intellect frustratingly discerned shadings of gray on a vital question, in a body the majority of whose members did not understand nor honor such intellectual halftones, but preferred clearly defined images that were either entirely black or white.

Hoar sought to make a distinction between two types of expansion. The first, of which he felt Hawaii was representative, "is the invitation to willing and capable people to share with us our freedom, our self-government, our equality, our education, and the transcendent sweets of civil and religious liberty." The

---

53. *New York Evening Post,* June 22, 1898.

second "is the dominion over subject peoples, and the rule over vassal states. It is forbidden to us by our Constitution, by our political principles, by every lesson of our own history and all history." Possibly even some anti-imperialists might have granted that, perhaps, the case of Hawaii was unique, but still they feared, with Senator Donelson Caffery, that "this Hawaiian scheme is but the entering wedge that cleaves a way open for empire." Hoar's uncompromising New England conscience was troubled by this possibility. He admitted, undoubtedly referring to the men who would comprise the leadership of the New England Anti-Imperialist League, that "some very good friends of mine, with whom I have been accustomed to agree all my life, look with an unconquerable apprehension upon this matter." He also conceded that he was disturbed by "the nature and character of the arguments by which a great many friends of annexation have sought to support it."

If his Concord and Boston friends were right in contending that the advocates of Hawaiian annexation were committing the United States irrevocably to a policy of imperialism, then this was an insidious development that must be opposed. "If it be true," he said, "that the passage of these resolves is to commit the United States to such a policy [i.e. imperialism] as we have heard advocated on this floor, and has been advocated in many parts of the country in the press, then the people of the United States are confronted at this moment with the most serious danger they have encountered in all their history." "If," he continued, "this be the first step in the acquisition of dominion over barbarous archipelagoes in distant seas; if we are to enter into competition with the great powers of Europe in the plundering of China, in the division of Africa. . . . If we ourselves are to be governed in party by peoples to whom the Declaration of Independence is a stranger, or, worse still, if we are to govern subject and vassal states, trampling as we do it on our own great character which recognizes alike the liberty and dignity of individual manhood, then let us resist this thing in the beginning, and let us resist it to the death."

Hoar, however, felt that the annexation of Hawaii was an

isolated incident, that it did not represent imperialism, and would not lead to it. He asserted: "I do not agree with those gentlemen who think we should wrest the Philippine Islands from Spain and take charge of them ourselves. I do not think we should acquire Cuba, as the result of the existing war, to be annexed to the United States." Hoar assumed ingenuously and fallaciously that there were a great many people who felt as he did—who saw an inherent dichotomy between the annexation of Hawaii and all other possible cases of overseas expansion. He also presumed that the imperialists were but a vociferous minority. Thus, in a statement which he was soon to regret, he said that he was "satisfied, after hearing and weighing all arguments and much meditating on this thing, that the fear of imperialism is needless alarm." [54] Hoar, therefore, threw his support and considerable influence behind the joint resolution which was to be voted upon the following day. Other anti-imperialists did not care for what they felt to be the janus-faced quality of Hoar's stand. Senator Allen of Nebraska, speaking on the day on which the vote was taken, said he took it for granted that no one who voted for the joint resolution would ever be allowed to say that he was not in favor of imperialism, "for it will be well understood" that Hawaiian annexation is only "the first act in the drama of colonization" which will go on until we have annexed the Philippines, Cuba, Puerto Rico, and "every little dimple that may force its head above the water." [55]

In spite of all the vigorous efforts of the opponents of Hawaiian annexation down to the final hour, the joint resolution was approved on July 6 by the considerable majority of 42 to 21,

---

54. *Congressional Record,* 55th Congress, 2nd Session, pp. 6661-65.

Hoar also remarks in his autobiography that he was influenced in his decision by President McKinley who convinced him both that there was a real Japanese threat to the Hawaiian Islands and that he was opposed to imperialism, per se. "President McKinley . . . expressed his earnest and emphatic dissent from the opinions imputed to several leading Republicans." George F. Hoar, *Autobiography of Seventy Years* (New York, 1903), Vol. II, p. 308.

55. *Congressional Record,* op. cit., p. 6702.

with 26 abstentions.[56] Politically, as well as geographically, the Senate vote lined up just about the same way as the vote in the House, and for the same reasons.

In view of the fact that the imperialists heretofore had been unable to obtain anything approaching a two-thirds majority for a treaty of Hawaiian annexation, and thus had been constrained to resort to the more controversial method of the joint resolution, one may well wonder why the vote in favor of annexation was, at this juncture, a solid two-thirds majority in the Senate and over two-thirds in the House. The key to the explanation can be found in the remarks of Representative Dinsmore, who noted that men in Congress "by the score" had changed their minds on annexation because "the war fever has gotten into their blood." [57] The war fever had indeed gotten into the nation's blood, and it provided the requisite catalyst for the long-debated annexation of the Hawaiian islands.

As we have noted, the question had been vigorously debated for five years. The major and minor points on both sides had been skillfully presented many times by able and articulate spokesmen. The new and deciding element interjected in 1898 was the war. It was, however, not the logic of the imperialists' military arguments which was decisive, for the anti-imperialists countered this successfully; rather it was the spirit of the times —the "war fever"—which tipped the scales in favor of annexation.

President McKinley, acting with unwonted celerity for a man usually so phlegmatic, signed the joint resolution providing for the annexation of Hawaii on July 7. Stevens' "ripe pear," Mahan's "first fruit," had at last been harvested. The following day,

---

56. *Ibid.*, p. 6712. The Senators who cast negative votes were: Allen, Bacon, Bate, Berry, Caffery, Chilton, Clay, Daniel, Faulkner, Jones (Nev.), Lindsay, McEnery, Mallory, Mitchell, Morrill, Pasco, Pettigrew, Roach, Turley, Turpie, and White. Of those who were "paired," the following indicated that they would have voted "nay": Vest, Cockrell, Jones (Ark.), Martin, Gray, Spooner, Thurston, and Tillman.

57. *Congressional Record, op. cit.*, p. 5781.

Grover Cleveland wrote to Richard Olney, remarking disgustedly: "Hawaii is ours. As I look back upon the first steps in this miserable business and as I contemplate the means used to complete the outrage, I am ashamed of the whole affair." [58] It was for Cleveland and anti-imperialists throughout the United States a bitter harvest.

58. Olney Papers.

CHAPTER 9

The Opposition Organizes

Hawaii was but the first of a number of insular possessions acquired by the United States during the imperial years of 1898 and 1899. The others, with the exception of American Samoa, were obtained as a direct result of the Spanish-American War. Many astute anti-imperialists had foreseen that American imperialism, in gestation for so long, would be born and baptized, with Mars serving as godfather, amidst the flaming ruins of the Spanish Empire. Quite a few of these men, like Carl Schurz, Edward Atkinson, Gamaliel Bradford, Charles Francis Adams, Moorfield Storey, and David Starr Jordan, therefore, had labored assiduously to avert the war. Having lost this phase of the struggle, they then turned their attention to alerting the American people to the probable imperialistic outcome of the conflict which was in progress, and to urging them to beware of the risks and evils inherent in the adoption of this policy.

Dewey's startling May Day victory at Manila Bay, half-way around the world from Cuba, while it elated the nation at large, only served to confirm the fears of the anti-imperialists. On the following evening, David Starr Jordan, president of Stanford University, was scheduled to speak on an educational topic at Metropolitan Hall in San Francisco. Instead he chose to discuss "the risks which might follow our success," taking as the title of his address Kipling's phrase "Lest We Forget." [1] Jordan was con-

---

1. The phrase comes from Kipling's poem "Recessional," which was published the year before. The anti-imperialists were quite fond of parts of this poem. Charles Francis Adams terminates his widely

cerned that in their elation over a swift and easy victory in the war the American people might lose sight of the nation's basic principles. They might forget that our government was based on the concept that all just powers are derived from the consent of the governed and hold Cuba and the Philippines as vassal states.

Jordan told his audience that it was too late to ask how we got into the war. "The crisis comes," he said, "when the war is over." He touched upon the source of much of the imperialist ardor of such men as Theodore Roosevelt, John Hay, Henry Cabot Lodge, and Albert Beveridge, when he questioned anxiously: "What will be the reflex effect of great victories, suddenly realized strength, the patronizing applause, the ill-concealed envy of great nations, the conquest of strange territories, the raising of our flag beyond the seas?" [2] The anti-imperialists feared that it might act as a siren song which would lure the nation to doom. Therefore, they attempted to convince their countrymen that this appeal of imperialism was meretricious. Like Old Testament prophets, or like the New England divines from whom many of the anti-imperialist leaders were directly descended, they railed against "the temptation to substitute for our fundamental law of political equality and our fundamental rule of political justice the dream of empire, the greed of gain, the lust of the flesh, the lust of the eyes, and the pride of life." [3]

Jordan reminded his immediate audience and the nation at large that the war in which the country was engaged was supposed to be a war of mercy, not of conquest. "If we retire with clean hands," he said, "it will be because our hands are empty. To keep Cuba [as many imperialists, in spite of the Teller resolu-

---

disseminated essay *Imperialism and the Tracks of our Forefathers* (Boston, 1899) by citing the final four stanzas of "Recessional," saying of the verses: "I have heard none in the days that now are which strike a deeper chord" (p. 29).

2. David Starr Jordan, *Days of a Man, op. cit.,* Vol. I, p. 516, Appendix, p. 695.

3. George F. Hoar, *Congressional Record,* 55th Congress, 2nd Session, p. 6645.

tion, advocated] or the Philippines would be to follow the example of conquering nations." [4]

Across the nation in New York, Carl Schurz nodded his assent and prepared to write a letter of advice to President McKinley on this matter, as he had been advising American Presidents for three decades on important issues. In his letter of May 9 he pleaded with McKinley that the war be kept from degenerating into one of "greedy ambition, conquest, and self-aggrandizement." Several weeks later he again wrote to the President, warning that "if we turn this war, which was heralded to the world as a war of humanity, in any sense into a war of conquest, we shall forever forfeit the confidence of mankind." He urged McKinley, if he had the best interests of the nation at heart, to put an immediate end to "the imperialist noise." [5]

McKinley did nothing to terminate the "imperialist noise," but an organizational effort got under way in the spring of 1898 which was to attempt to muffle the noise completely. For more than half a decade the individual sensibilities and personal principles of many prominent men throughout the nation had been offended by the thought of the United States adopting the policy of imperialism. These men had individually, acting upon their own initiative, spoken out forthrightly against imperialism. They had done what they could personally to counteract the drift of the nation toward acquiescence in this policy, which they believed was antithetical to the traditions, principles, and best interests of the United States. A concerted effort was now made in June, 1898, to set up the first organization that would attempt to unite the myriad individuals who opposed imperialism and thus make their opposition more effective.

The first impetus for such an organization was a letter written by Gamaliel Bradford, a retired Boston banker and indefatigable publicist for many causes.[6] The letter was published on June

---

4. Jordan, *op. cit.*, p. 697.

5. Letters of May 9 and June 1, 1898, Schurz Papers.

6. He wrote literally thousands of letters on public issues, a great many of which can be found in scrapbooks at the Massachusetts Historical Society, of which Bradford was an active member for many years.

2, 1898, in the *Boston Evening Transcript,* a newspaper which was consistently sympathetic to anti-imperialism. Like many of the leaders of the American anti-imperialist movement, Bradford was opposed to the Spanish-American War. He mentioned in his letter that a few months earlier he had tried "to get up a Faneuil Hall meeting to protest against the war," but was denied the use of this historic building for fear of the possible repercussions of such a conclave. Now he was issuing a "cry for help" in obtaining the use of Faneuil Hall to hold a meeting in opposition to the colonial empire which he and many others feared would be the result of the war. "If any other men will join with me," he said, "to secure the hall, I, for one, will stand up and have my say against the insane and wicked ambition which is driving the country to moral ruin." [7]

Thus it was that a notable meeting was held at Faneuil Hall on June 15, 1898 (ironically the date on which the joint resolution for Hawaiian annexation was approved by the House of Representatives) "to protest against the adoption of an imperial policy by the United States." Bradford, naturally, served as chairman of the meeting. In spite of the fact that the active phase of the war had only recently begun, Bradford insisted that the terms of peace should immediately be accorded close attention "because a faction is hard at work to commit the country to action from which it cannot afterwards recede." Although the war was undoubtedly undertaken primarily in the interests of humanity, Bradford believed that the cause had been manipulated by people with other motives. He felt that self-serving private interests, unscrupulous politicians, and "imaginations thirsting after military and naval glory had a large share. And the same forces are urging us to the establishment of a military empire in Asia with all which that involves." [8]

---

7. *Boston Evening Transcript,* June 2, 1898.
Erving Winslow recalled this important letter thirteen years later in his eulogy of Bradford upon the latter's demise.—*Report of the Thirteenth Annual Meeting of the Anti-Imperialist League* (Boston, 1912), pp. 3-4.

8. *Anti-Imperialist Speeches at Faneuil Hall,* Boston, June 15, 1898 (Boston, 1898), pp. 2, 6.

In addition to Bradford, the Reverend Charles Ames, George E. McNeil, and Moorfield Storey also addressed the assembly at some length, while those honored by presence on the platform included many men who were to be active in Anti-Imperialist League affairs for years to come. Among them were: Erving Winslow (Secretary of the Anti-Imperialist League throughout its existence), Francis A. Osborne (first Treasurer of the League and one of its important financial backers), Albert S. Parsons (for many years a member of the League's Executive Committee —the group that ran the League on a day-to-day basis), David Greene Haskins, Jr. (Treasurer of the League for over twenty years), Edward Atkinson (who authored the controversial *The Anti-Imperialist* and in whose office the League was formally founded), Francis E. Abbot, and William Endicott.

The keynote speech of the meeting was given by Moorfield Storey, who was to serve for many years as president of the Anti-Imperialist League. Storey emphasized, as had Bradford earlier, that they had not come together "to oppose the war or to throw any obstacles in the way of its speedy and successful determination," but rather to insist that "an attempt to win for the Cubans the right to govern themselves shall not be made an excuse for extending our sway over alien peoples without their consent." Storey and his fellow anti-imperialists insisted, and would continue steadfastly to insist, that "to seize any colony of Spain and hold it as our own, without the free consent of its people is a violation of the principles upon which this government rests."

Storey pointed out that any imperialistic venture would be a dangerous break with our prudent and time-honored traditional foreign policy. It would mean that the United States must "become a military power burdened with a standing army and an enormous navy, threatened with complications thousands of miles away, and exposed to constant apprehension." As the anti-imperialists were increasingly wont to do, Storey remarked upon the probable reverberations on the domestic scene. "Our domestic difficulties," he insisted, "will be neglected, for our attention will be divided. Our taxation must increase, our currency become more disordered, and worst of all, the corruption which threatens us cannot fail to spread." Storey concluded his address with a lengthy allusion to the fate of Rome, of which the anti-imperialists were so fond: "When Rome began her career of conquest, the Roman Republic began to decay. . . . Let us once govern any considerable body of men without their consent, and it is a question of time how soon this republic shares the fate of Rome."[9]

The meeting unanimously adopted several long resolutions designed to express and make public the feelings and tenets of those assembled. In addition to strongly condemning the annexation of any territory as a result of the war, they insisted, much like groups opposed to the war in Vietnam, that "our first duty is to cure the evils in our own country." They specifically mentioned protecting "the rights of . . . the colored race at the South and the Indians at the West" and improving the condition of life in the cities, labor relations, "our disordered currency, unjust system of taxation, the debasing influence of money at elections, /and/ the use of offices as spoils."[10]

This body of opinion is noteworthy in several respects. Basically it demonstrates three of the anti-imperialists' related fundamental arguments, i.e. that the nation had enough pressing problems at home without seeking others; that foreign ventures would divert attention, energy, and funds from the solution of these grave domestic problems; and that the nation should prove that it was thoroughly competent in the management of its own affairs before seeking to administer those of other countries. It also illustrates the broad interest in reform of the men who comprised the nucleus of the anti-imperialist movement, and it foreshadows in an intriguing way many of the specific reforms which were to receive much wider attention from the general populace during the Progressive Era. Finally, it indicated that anti-imperialism itself had become essentially a reform movement.

A significant result of the meeting at Faneuil Hall was the

---

9. *Ibid.*, pp. 19-25.
10. *Ibid.*, pp. 2-3.

formation of a committee of correspondence which was to make contact with persons and organizations throughout the country in an effort to weld a strong, nationwide anti-imperialist phalanx. In utilizing this device they emulated their revolutionary forebears. In opposing nascent American imperialism, they acted as their ancestors had in combating British imperialism a century earlier.

The men selected for the Anti-Imperialist Committee of Correspondence—Gamaliel Bradford, David Greene Haskins, Jr., Albert S. Parsons, and Erving Winslow—all remained active in the cause of anti-imperialism for the rest of their lives.

During the summer and early autumn of 1898 the Anti-Imperialist Committee of Correspondence, although limited in size and funds, worked effectively to promote the anti-imperialist cause. Committeemen systematically contacted prominent individuals in the various states and requested names of influential men in each congressional district who were opposed to imperialism and might help the movement. They then got in touch with these men, sending them anti-imperialist literature and urging them to set up local groups to aid in the campaign against imperialism.

The Committee also approached various religious, commercial, labor, and social organizations and attempted to enlist them in the crusade. Members of the Committee wrote to newspaper and magazine editors and had anti-imperialist propaganda published wherever possible. Locally, they worked closely with the anti-imperialist committee of the Massachusetts Reform Club, the majority of whose members were strongly opposed to imperialism.

The movement's institutional stature was enhanced immeasurably by the formal founding [11] on November 19, 1898, of the Anti-Imperialist League. The League was the prototype of all other anti-imperialist organizations throughout the nation and provided the principal institutional spearhead of anti-imperialism

---

11. At a meeting of the Anti-Imperialist Committee of Correspondence.

throughout the years that it remained a vital force in American life.

The Committee of Correspondence drew up a constitution for the new organization. Like the Constitution of the United States, the League's constitution contained seven articles that outlined the organization's formal structure and procedures.

The League's activities were to be conducted by three principal officers with the aid of a small executive committee. The men named to these key posts were: George S. Boutwell, president; Erving Winslow, secretary; and Francis A. Osborn, treasurer. The original members of the Executive Committee were: Winslow Warren, chairman; David Greene Haskins, Jr., Albert S. Parsons, James P. Munroe, William Endicott and James J. Myers. All of these men resided in the vicinity of Boston and were very active in the civic life of Massachusetts.

The League also had a large group of vice presidents who were nationally prominent men. Although the vice presidents were honorary, they were all devoted to the cause and contributed vitally to the anti-imperialist movement. The original eighteen vice presidents were: Charles Francis Adams, Jr., Edward Atkinson, Samuel Bowles, John C. Bullitt, John G. Carlisle, Andrew Carnegie, James C. Carter, Grover Cleveland, Patrick A. Collins, Theodore L. Cuyler, George F. Edmunds, Samuel Gompers, Reverdy Johnson, Herbert Myrick, Hazen S. Pingree, Henry C. Potter, Carl Schurz, and John Sherman.[12] Sometime during the late

---

12. The list was later changed slightly and enlarged, but several documents attest to the fact that this was the group which served for the first six months: *Report of the Executive Committee of the Anti-Imperialist League,* Feb. 10, 1899; The Anti-Imperialist League "Appeal" of April 13, 1899; Erving Winslow's article "The Anti-Imperialist League," *The Independent,* Vol. LI, part II (May 18, 1899), pp. 1347 ff.; the initial issue of Edward Atkinson's *The Anti-Imperialist* (Brookline, 1899). This should clear up the misconceptions on this score in F. H. Harrington's article, "The Anti-Imperialist Movement in the United States, 1898-1900," *Mississippi Valley Historical Review,* Vol. XXII (Sept., 1935), pp. 211-230; and Maria Lanzar's "The Anti-Imperialist League," *Philippine Social Science Review,* Vol. III (Aug., 1930), pp. 7-41.

spring or summer of 1899, the number of vice presidents was increased to forty, and this is the group of men whose signatures are listed on the back of the few Anti-Imperialist League membership certificates still extant.[13] Reverdy Johnson was dropped from the list and the following group of men added:

Felix Adler, Leonard Woolsey Bacon, Gamaliel Bradford, Donelson Caffery, W. Bourke Cockran, William H. Fleming, Patrick Ford, Austen G. Fox, Thomas Wentworth Higginson, Henry U. Johnson, David Starr Jordan, William Larrabee, Charlton T. Lewis, George G. Mercer, Patrick O'Farrell, Emil Preetorius, Henry Wade Rogers, Edwin Burritt Smith, William Graham Sumner, Benjamin R. Tillman, John J. Valentine, Hermann Von Holst, and Herbert Welsh.

Between September and November 25, 1899 (the date of the League's first annual meeting), Charles Henry Parkhurst, I. J. McGinty, and Moorfield Storey became members of this loyal legion. Since the League's officers receive detailed attention in the following chapter, it need only be said here that they all did yeoman service for the cause in these months when the anti-imperialist opposition was organizing on an institutional basis and attempting to mount a strong protest movement against imperialism.

The Executive Committee of the League declared that the center of the movement should be Washington, D.C. This location was doubtless intended to indicate the movement's national scope and to serve as a strategic base for influencing governmental personnel. However, although the League's secretary did maintain an office in Washington for about a year, most of the work was carried on, even at this time, from Boston. After the formation of the Washington Anti-Imperialist League in the fall of 1899, that body handled the movement's work in the nation's capital, and the original League definitely made Boston its headquarters for the remaining two decades of its existence.

---

13. Copies may be found at Widener Library, Harvard University, and in the Croffut Papers, Library of Congress.

The first official act of the Anti-Imperialist League was the promulgation, on its founding day, of an "Address to the People of the United States." Included in it were the following assertions: First, "a true republic of free men" derives its just powers from the consent of the governed, and if this principle is abandoned, the republic exists only in name. Second, the U.S. Constitution contains no provisions for holding vassals and "recognizes no distinction between classes of citizens." Third, the anti-imperialists are in sympathy with "the heroic struggles for liberty of the people in the Spanish islands, and therefore . . . protest against depriving them of their rights by an exchange of masters." Fourth, "expansion by natural growth in thinly-settled contiguous territory, acquired by purchase for the expressed purpose of ultimate statehood, cannot be confounded with, or made analogous to, foreign territory conquered by war and wrested by force from a weak enemy." Fifth, the "new Imperialism" seeks "to set up the law of might and to place commercial gain and false philanthropy above the sound principles upon which the Republic was based." Sixth, the war with Spain was to be fought "solely for humanity and freedom," not for conquest. Seventh, imperialism "must result in foreign complications which will imperil and delay the settlement of pressing financial, labor, and administrative questions at home." The address finally stated that an Anti-Imperialist League had been formed by those "impressed with the importance of these views . . . in order to give evidence of the opposition to a foreign expansion policy by a vast body of our people. . . ." [14]

This is a highly significant document for several reasons: It was the first official statement of the position and philosophy of the Anti-Imperialist League. It succinctly expresses the League's raison d'être and what it opposed. The League was to maintain these same tenets throughout its entire existence.

The whole tenor of the document is reminiscent of the Dec-

---

14. "Address to the People of the United States" (broadside) (Boston, Nov. 19, 1898).

laration of Independence. The anti-imperialists were saying to their countrymen that all Americans should hold these truths to be self-evident; and if they did, the nation could not logically adopt a policy of imperialism. The very first assertion indicated that if the United States espoused imperialism, it would cease to be a democratic republic. The anti-imperialists always insisted that a republic and an empire were antithetical entities and that the United States could not be both at the same time. They also wanted it clearly understood that overseas expansion definitely constituted imperialism and should not be confused with earlier continental expansion.

The anti-imperialists, of course, invoked the second classical American governmental document—the Constitution. They contended that imperialism was not only undesirable and unjust, but it was also illegal. The Constitution simply made no provision for subject colonies. Colonies were representative of Old World tyranny. The United States had been born out of a revolt against colonial domination. The inhabitants of the Spanish islands were fighting an anti-colonial struggle. The only possible justification for the war with Spain was the desire to aid those struggling for liberty. The anti-imperialists emphasized here that if we meant what we said and if we truly believed in individual liberty and national self-determination, we could not forsake our anti-colonialist heritage and become the master of any of Spain's former subjects.

The Anti-Imperialist League's next project after issuing this very important address was to "organize the moral forces of the country" for the purpose of presenting a massive protest to the President and Congress against extending U.S. sovereignty to any foreign territory, their contention being that this would be "dangerous to the Republic, wasteful of its resources, in violation of constitutional principles, and fraught with moral and physical evils." [15] The League urged people to make copies of the protest,

---

15. Anti-Imperialist Scrapbook, Widener Library, Harvard University. This device (i.e. the mass petition or protest) was very popular with the Anti-Imperialist League, and they employed it frequently.

obtain as many signatures as possible, and forward them to the Secretary, Erving Winslow, who would then convey them to McKinley and the Congress.

On November 23rd the Executive Committee of the League decided to launch another mass protest, this time using a chain letter, a device which they frequently employed thereafter. This protest was to bear the signatures of as many as possible of the country's "legal voters," the thought of the committee probably being that the electorate—males over twenty-one—might have more influence upon the President and Congress than the earlier more general protest.

The committee indicated that its goal was to obtain ten million signatures and present them to McKinley. The *Boston Evening Transcript* commented that "if the plans work as successfully as they promise in the preliminary steps, a protest will be registered which it will be hard for the President to disregard." The committee selected an initial group of one thousand prominent men who were to begin the chain. "Among them," reported the *Transcript* commenting upon the diversity of the group, "are governors and ex-governors, Republicans, Democrats, gold-bugs, silverites, capitalists, labor reformers, trade unionists and Grangers." [16] Each of the one thousand men was to sign a card bearing a shortened version of the earlier protest, and then persuade ten others to do so, who would in turn contact ten others, and so on. Such schemes always seem better in theory than they prove to be in actual practice. Although the League did elicit a formidable response, it did not obtain anywhere near the desired ten million signatures, which would have constituted almost eighty percent of the people who voted in the previous presidential election.

The Anti-Imperialist League, besides sponsoring these mass protests, was very active in a variety of ways in the autumn of 1898. One of the League's principal activities was the publication and distribution of anti-imperialist literature. A leaflet printed in early December, 1898, advertising the items available shows

---

16. *Boston Evening Transcript,* Nov. 26, 1898.

how soon after the League's founding a considerable body of special anti-imperialist propaganda had been prepared.

This was one of the areas in which the League's vice presidents were most active, as is indicated by the listing in this single early leaflet of materials written by Andrew Carnegie, John Sherman, George F. Edmunds, David Starr Jordan, John G. Carlisle, Leonard Woolsey Bacon, Samuel Gompers, Henry C. Potter, Herbert Welsh, Edward Atkinson, Moorfield Storey, Gamaliel Bradford, Felix Adler, Patrick A. Collins, and the amazingly prolific and ever-faithful Carl Schurz. Another notable attribute of this leaflet is that, like virtually all Anti-Imperialist League publications, it bears the label of the Allied Printing Trades Union Council. This practice was not as prevalent then as now and indicates that the League was interested in the support of the militant unions. This is further borne out by the suggestion made by the chairman of the Executive Committee that "every effort should be made to strengthen the anti-imperialist position of labor and agricultural unions and organizations." [17]

Probably the most notable of the Anti-Imperialist League's early publications was its series of "Broadsides." The first of these rolled off the presses soon after the League was founded. Titled *Arguments Against the Adoption of a So-Called Imperial Policy*, its introduction says that it was compiled so that citizens might learn what "thinking men" from the time of Washington believed was the best policy for the country. There follow quotations from Washington (the Farewell Address), James Monroe (the Monroe Doctrine), Thomas Jefferson, and an interesting selection on "Our Destiny," by Albert Gallatin. There are a few mocking quotations from William McKinley, including the anti-imperialists' favorite, which they cited at every opportunity: "I speak not of forcible annexation, for that cannot be thought of. That, by our code of morality, would be criminal aggression."

---

17. *Report of the Executive Committee of the Anti-Imperialist League,* Feb. 10, 1899.

Finally, there are comments by prominent anti-imperialists from many fields, including Senators Hoar, Edmunds, and Sherman, Andrew Carnegie, the Reverend Edward Everett Hale, T. J. Conaty (the Rector of Catholic University), and Simeon E. Baldwin (president of the American Social Science Association).

In addition to the vigorous propaganda campaign, one of the principal endeavors of this period was to enlist as many people as possible as members of the League. The Executive Committee reported in February, 1899, that "the present membership of the Anti-Imperialist League is considerably over 25,000." [18] The Committee closed its report for the period by urging that strenuous efforts be made to form anti-imperialist organizations throughout the nation. This endeavor was pursued so energetically that Erving Winslow was able to report at the League's first annual meeting in November, 1899, that there were "at least a hundred active centers of anti-imperialist work" throughout the country.[19] The largest and most important organizations were those in New York, Philadelphia, Washington, Cincinnati, Portland (Oregon), Los Angeles, Minneapolis, and Chicago.

In November, 1899, the original League became nominally the New England branch of the American Anti-Imperialist League. This latter organization had been founded in Chicago at a convention the previous month. It was set up to coordinate the activities of the various Leagues which had been established in many parts of the country. Chicago was chosen because of its location "as the most convenient situation for commanding effect and national influence." [20]

Actually, in spite of this formal organizational change, the original Anti-Imperialist League continued to be the most active of the Leagues and remained the institutional leader of the movement. The original League carried the American Anti-Imperialist League, instead of vice versa. Many of its officers served as ex-

---

18. *Ibid.*

19. *Annual Meeting of the* [*New England*] *Anti-Imperialist League,* November 25, 1899, p. 7.

20. *Ibid.,* pp. 7-8.

ecutives of the American Anti-Imperialist League, as they did of some of the local Leagues in other cities. For example, George S. Boutwell was named the first president of the American Anti-Imperialist League; Donelson Caffery, George F. Edmunds, Carl Schurz, and John J. Valentine were four of its six vice presidents; and William H. Fleming, Winslow Warren and Edwin B. Smith were members of its nine-member Executive Committee, Smith being the chairman. Eventually, in November, 1904, the New England League reassumed its title as *the* Anti-Imperialist League, it being at that time the only really viable organization of its kind.

There had been an anti-imperialist league functioning in Chicago even before the creation of the American Anti-Imperialist League. This earlier organization, which like almost all other leagues received its impetus from the original group in Boston, was called the Central Anti-Imperialist League. It was merged with the American Anti-Imperialist League upon the founding of the latter, its officers contributing more to the new national anti-imperialist organization than any other group except the original League. In fact the American Anti-Imperialist League drew almost exclusively upon these two organizations, the officers of the other local leagues (e.g. Minneapolis, Philadelphia, etc.) contributing comparatively little to it.

The leaders of the Central Anti-Imperialist League, like the officers of all the local leagues, were prominent and influential citizens of the community, some of them with national reputations. Occupationally there was a preponderance, as interestingly, there was in each of the principal anti-imperialist leagues, of lawyers among the Central Anti-Imperialist League's officers. Considering the relatively brief tenure of its existence, the Central League was responsible for an impressive number of publications.

The Anti-Imperialist League of New York was also notable as a "publishing league" and produced a multitude of anti-imperialist pamphlets, which is not surprising in view of the fact that its leaders included E. L. Godkin, William Dean Howells, and Carl Schurz. The roster of officers of the New York Anti-

Imperialist League was the most impressive of any league except the original one; and when the original League's members for five years were limited to residents of New England, the officers of the New York League outranked in national stature all others. It is interesting that nine of the twenty-three vice presidents of the New York Anti-Imperialist League were also vice presidents of the original League.[21] The New York League was especially active in sponsoring public anti-imperialist meetings and providing anti-imperialist speakers for all sorts of occasions, and was host to a number of important meetings of officers from anti-imperialist organizations throughout the United States.

The local anti-imperialist league in Philadelphia was known as the American League of Philadelphia. The League's secretary said that this name was chosen instead of anti-imperialist because "it was thought better to assert something positive rather than to take a negative position. It was desired to emphasize the fact that the League stood for American ideas; and that the imperialists and the expansionists were the persons who were attacking them and practically 'hauling down the flag.' "[22] For the same reasons some other local anti-imperialist organizations adopted the title of "Liberty League."

Upon the founding of the American League of Philadelphia, a statement was issued which declared that because the men involved believed that the well-being of the nation depended on strict adherence to its traditional principles and policies, they were forming "an American League for the purpose of sustaining republican institutions against the existing tendency toward imperialism."[23] The American League's aims, which appear on all of the League's documents, were "to maintain the truths set forth in the Declaration of Independence, and to oppose the expansion and establishment of the dominion of the United States,

---

21. Felix Adler, Andrew Carnegie, Bourke Cockran, Theodore Cuyler, Patrick Ford, Samual Gompers, Charlton Lewis, Charles Parkhurst, and Carl Schurz.

22. *New York Evening Post,* November 21, 1898.

23. Brochure entitled "American League," among the William Augustus Croffut Papers, Library of Congress, Washington, D.C.

by conquest or otherwise, over unwilling peoples in any part of the globe." [24]

The American League was quite active in sponsoring various anti-imperialist "mass meetings," at which anti-imperialist speeches were presented, resolutions adopted that were forwarded to Congress, and general enthusiasm and publicity generated for the cause. The League in Philadelphia also served as host for one of the most notable regional anti-imperialist meetings—the "Eastern Conference of Anti-Imperialists," held on Washington's birthday in 1900.

George F. Edmunds was Honorary President of the American League of Philadelphia, but its regular officers were local men of prominence. In contrast to the original League, whose vice presidents could meet only infrequently because they lived so far apart, there is evidence that all of the officers of the various local Leagues, like that of Philadelphia, attended meetings with some regularity and took an active part in the organization. Also, there were usually a few men—as was the case here with John C. Bullitt, Herbert Welsh, and George G. Mercer—who were affiliated with the original League. These individuals, who were usually the prime movers in the formation of the various local leagues, maintained valuable liaison with the original Anti-Imperialist League.

The formation of the Washington Anti-Imperialist League illustrates how such organizations were created throughout the nation and demonstrates the vital role of the original league in stimulating the anti-imperialist movement everywhere in the United States. William Augustus Croffut, a former newspaperman, having read material printed by the Anti-Imperialist League, began in the early spring of 1899 to correspond with the League's Secretary, Erving Winslow. Croffut wrote to Winslow during the summer of 1899, expressing the desire to set up a local anti-imperialist league in the nation's capital.

Croffut also sought out Patrick O'Farrell, a vice president

---

24. Herbert Welsh Papers, Pennsylvania Historical Society, Philadelphia.

of the original league and discussed the proposed new organization with him. On August 23, 1899, O'Farrell wrote to Croffut, saying: "Since I saw you I have been speaking with several parties who are very anxious to assist in forming a branch of the Anti-Imperialist League. . . . While we don't vote in Washington, we do a power of thinking, and we can be of great service to our country by the formation and circulation of public opinion." [25] Shortly after this Croffut received a letter from Winslow, remarking that he assumed that Croffut had "communicated with Mr. Samuel Gompers and Captain Patrick O'Farrell, our Vice Presidents, in your league organizing." [26]

A fortnight later, on September 11, 1899, Winslow wrote to Croffut saying: "I am very glad to hear of your preliminary organization. I will enclose you [*sic*] a copy of our Constitution and By-Laws." Two days later, on September 18, 1899, Croffut wrote to Speaker of the House Thomas B. Reed and told him: "There was an assembly of 'insurgents' at my house Saturday night—mostly Republicans—and amid much enthusiasm we organized the Anti-Imperialist League of Washington. . . . We shall hold a mass-meeting soon and tell the people the facts in the case." [27]

The very heavy concentration of Republicans in the Washington Anti-Imperialist League is mentioned by Croffut many times. For example, in a letter to Robert Treat Paine, on October 25, 1899, Croffut writes that 'the Anti-Imperialist League of this city [is] composed chiefly of Republicans." In an earlier missive (September 22, 1899) to Senator George L. Wellington of Maryland, he remarks: "We are mostly Republicans." Again, in a letter of October 29, 1900, to the Chairman of the Democratic Committee of Baltimore, Maryland, Croffut states that "the Anti-Imperialist League of this city [is] composed chiefly of men who have been Republicans all their lives, and have stumped many states for their party, and includes two ex-Senators and others

---

25. William Augustus Croffut Papers, Library of Congress.
26. *Ibid.*
27. *Ibid.*

eminent in public life. . . ." [28] The percentage of Republicans in the Washington Anti-Imperialist League was unusually high. It does, however, provide further evidence of the fallacy of the impression that the adherents to the anti-imperialist cause were virtually all Democrats or independents.

The original officers of the Washington Anti-Imperialist League were president: William Birney; secretary: William A. Croffut; treasurer: Henry O. Hallam; vice presidents: J. W. Fowler, Samuel Gompers, John W. Hayes, John B. Henderson, Charles James, Crammond Kennedy, Franklin H. Mackey, P. T. Moran, Patrick O'Farrell, and Louis Schade. In addition to its decidedly Republican political orientation, this group was remarkably homogeneous occupationally. Nine of the thirteen officers were lawyers, and two of the remaining four were nationally prominent labor leaders.[29]

Organized labor felt that imperialism posed a real threat to the domestic labor market through the possibility of flooding the nation with low-cost workers imported from the colonies. Hence it is easy to see why officers of the leading labor unions took an active role in the anti-imperialist movement. While the number of lawyers among the Washington League's officers was unusually high because of its location in this "lawyers' city," where attorneys are so involved in the formulation and influencing of legislation, there was a substantial percentage of legal talent in all of the anti-imperialist leagues. Throughout the course of the great debate, with its intriguing and vitally important legalistic facets, their professional skill greatly aided the pleading of the anti-imperialist case.

The Washington Anti-Imperialist League because of its location proved very helpful to the other leagues in relaying materials —petitions, mass protests, and other documents and items of anti-imperialist propaganda—to the members of the House and

---

28. *Ibid.*

29. Gompers, of course, was President of the A.F. of L. John Hayes was Secretary of the Knights of Labor. The two occupational mavericks in the group were quondam newspaperman Croffut and P. T. Moran, who owned a wholesale grain and feed company.

Senate. The records of the Washington League contain many letters such as the one of December 7, 1899, from George G. Mercer, president of the American League of Philadelphia, to Croffut, saying: "We . . . are exceedingly obliged for the kind attention you have given our work in Washington." [30]

The way in which one anti-imperialist league stimulated others, beginning, of course, with the initial stimulus of the Boston organization, is demonstrated by a letter written by Charles Roe (again a lawyer) of Rochester to Croffut. Roe wrote on September 26, 1899, less than a fortnight after the Washington League's founding, that he had read of its activity in the *Rochester Union and Advertiser*. He said: "I think an [anti-imperialist] organization should be started in every city and town, literature freely distributed and even public meetings held. I am anxious to see the work started here in Rochester, and any information you may give me about the work in Washington, and any suggestion as to work in Rochester would be appreciated." [31]

Thus it progressed, the formation and activities of one group in one city leading to the formation of another elsewhere, which in turn had an influence on the organization of similar leagues and clubs throughout the nation. Eventually in response to this phenomenon a National Association of Anti-Imperialist Clubs was founded at 13 Astor Place in New York City. This organization had a host of honorary vice presidents drawn from the many local anti-imperialist leagues.[32] At its zenith it claimed a following of over 700,000 people scattered throughout the nation's forty-five states and five territories. One wonders whether Gamaliel Bradford, when he penned his "cry for help," had any idea that the response would be so great.

---

30. Croffut Papers.
31. *Ibid.*
32. Its principal active officers were: Anson P. Stokes, C. C. Hughes, Frederick W. Janssen, George L. Wellington, Edwin B. Smith, Gamaliel Bradford, Theodore M. Banta, Edward M. Shepard, and Herbert P. Bissell.

CHAPTER 10

The Old Guard

In its first year of operation, some fifty-two prominent Americans served as officers of the original Anti-Imperialist League. Since the League was the dominant force in American anti-imperialism, a close examination of its officers sheds much light upon the entire anti-imperialist movement in the United States at the turn of the century.

The leaders of the Anti-Imperialist League were an exceedingly distinguished group of men. It is doubtful whether any other contemporary organization in the United States could boast a more outstanding leadership. If the nation could be said to possess an elite, these gentlemen would surely qualify. While atypical of the general American population, they had much in common with one another.

The number of very well educated men in the group is remarkable. At a time when less than 1 per cent of the nation's population had a college education, thirty-eight out of fifty-two, or over 73 per cent, had college degrees (largely from Harvard and Yale), and twenty-six, or exactly 50 per cent, had graduate training, and in almost all cases graduate degrees. A number of them received their graduate training abroad. William Graham Sumner, for example studied at Geneva, Göttingen, and Oxford; Charles H. Parkhurst did graduate work at Halle and Leipzig; Felix Adler, after graduating from Columbia, studied in Berlin,

---

Material in this chapter is reprinted with permission from *The Historian,* Vol. XXX, No. 3 (May, 1968).

and took his Ph.D. at Heidelberg. [1] Even the imperialists noted the characteristic erudition of their opponents. Theodore Roosevelt complained about the anti-imperialists in a letter to Alfred Thayer Mahan: "The terrible part is to see that it is the men of education who take the lead in trying to make us prove traitors to our race." [2]

From an occupational standpoint these men were also exceptional. The great majority of them were professional people —lawyers, professors, editors, and clergymen. They were not only active in these professional fields, but were leaders in them.

Lawyers predominated—twenty-five out of the fifty-two men having been admitted to the bar. George Edmunds, Edwin B. Smith, Henry W. Rogers, Moorfield Storey, and James C. Carter were among the most outstanding lawyers and legal theorists in the nation.[3] Edmunds, Carter, and Storey were renowned for their brilliant arguments in notable cases, and were engaged, as were many other League officers, in debating the constitutionality of many facets of the imperialist policy.[4] Smith and Rogers were among the country's most respected professors of law, the latter serving as Dean of two of the nation's leading law schools— Michigan (1886–1890) and Yale (1903–1916). Storey and Carter both served as president of the American Bar Association. This wealth of legal acumen was conspicuously absent from the top leadership of the imperialist camp; and there is little doubt that the anti-imperialists had a much greater respect for legal

---

1. Even those who had not attended college were men of great learning such as Grover Cleveland, John Sherman, George Boutwell, George Edmunds, Samuel Gompers, Edward Atkinson, and Andrew Carnegie.

2. Letter of December 11, 1897, Morison (editor), *The Letters of Theodore Roosevelt* (Cambridge, 1951), I, 741.

3. For examples of their writing in opposition to imperialism, see E. B. Smith, *Republic or Empire* (Chicago, 1900), *Shall the United States Have Colonies?* (Boston, no date); Moorfield Storey, *Is It Right?* (Chicago, 1900), *Marked Severities* (Boston, 1902), *What Shall We Do with Our Dependencies?* (Boston, 1903).

4. See especially *Anti-Imperialist Broadside No. 7* (Boston, 1899).

justice and tradition than did the imperialists, who too frequently adhered to the brutal and anti-legalistic concept that might makes right.

Although imperialism received support from various church groups interested in proselytizing through missionary activities in the colonies, the Anti-Imperialist League had some of the nation's most distinguished clergymen among its officers, including Henry C. Potter,[5] Episcopalian Bishop of New York; Leonard W. Bacon, a Congregational clergyman who was well known for his numerous publications; [6] and Charles H. Parkhurst and Theodore L. Cuyler—both nationally famous Presbyterian ministers. In numerous incisive sermons and essays they condemned the immorality of imperialism.

Among the League's officers there were also many editors, who were particularly articulate and demonstrative in their critiques of imperialism. They included Samuel Bowles, editor of the *Springfield Republican*—one of the nation's staunchest anti-imperialist newspapers; Patrick Ford, editor of the *Irish World,* the leading American Irish journal; Herbert Welsh, editor of the controversial *City and State*—another strongly anti-imperialist journal; Herbert Myrick, the foremost editor of agricultural publications in the country; and Emil Preetorius, editor of the *St. Louis Westliche Post,* the nation's leading German language newspaper.

The anti-imperialist movement was especially vigorously supported in colleges and universities, and the list of the Anti-Imperialist League's early officers contains the names of a number of America's leading educators: Hermann E. Von Holst, Chairman of the History Department of the University of Chicago;

---

5. In addition to his devotion to the anti-imperialist cause, Potter, like a great many of the League's officers, had an intense interest in a variety of contemporary problems. See his books: *Sermons of the City* (New York, 1881), *The Drink Problem in Modern Life* (New York, 1905), *The Citizen in His Relation to Society* (New Haven, 1911).

6. For example *A Life Worth Living* (New York, 1879), *A History of Christianity* (New York, 1897).

Felix Adler, one of Columbia University's most renowned professors; William Graham Sumner, Yale's internationally famous professor of economics and sociology; Henry W. Rogers, who was, among other things, president of Northwestern University (1890–1900); and David Starr Jordan, who served as president of Indiana University and for more than forty years as president, chancellor, and chancellor emeritus of Stanford University.[7]

Many of these men were qualified to serve in several professions. For example, Bacon and Jordan, although preferring to follow other careers, both had M.D.'s. Journalist Emil Preetorius held a doctorate in law from the University of Giessen and had even pursued post doctoral legal studies at Heidelberg. Of course, many of these men did serve several professions, especially combining legal practice with teaching, government service, and politics.

Some of them were virtually Renaissance men in their versatile talents. Carl Schurz, the most notable example, was a high-ranking military officer, ambassador, Senator, cabinet member, editor, author, and musician, in addition to being active in a dozen reform movements, a category about which more will be said subsequently. Another such man, although less well known today, was Charlton T. Lewis—who was a clergyman, college professor, editor, lawyer, and publicist for many causes. It was said of him, as it could have been said of so very many of these

---

7. For significant examples of their anti-imperialist views, see Felix Adler, "Parting of the Ways in the Foreign Policy of the United States," *Review of Reviews,* XVIII (November, 1898), 586-588; Hermann Von Holst, *The Annexation of Hawaii* (Chicago, 1898), "Some Lessons We Ought to Learn," *University of Chicago Record,* III (February 10, 1899), 299-304, "Some Expansionist Inconsistencies and False Analogies," *University of Chicago Record,* III (March 10, 1899), 339-345; David Starr Jordan, *Imperial Democracy* (New York, 1899); William Graham Sumner, *The Conquest of the United States by Spain* (Boston, 1899). This last item was originally a Phi Beta Kappa address at Yale, indicating, as does the publication of Von Holst's anti-imperialist views in the *Chicago Record,* that the professors were not reticent about making their opinions known on campus.

men: "In all of his fields of endeavor Lewis was successful, and to most of them he made some permanent contribution." [8]

The family, ethnic, and geographical backgrounds of these men are quite interesting. Of the League's forty-three vice presidents eighteen were born in Massachusetts, six in New York, four in Pennsylvania, three each in Connecticut and Kentucky, two in New Jersey, and one each in Louisiana, Vermont, Georgia, Indiana, South Carolina, Michigan, and Ohio. Thus only thirteen states are represented. When one considers the place of residence of these men in 1898, only three additional states—California, Iowa, and Illinois—are added, making a total of only sixteen states, out of the forty-five states and five territories of the day.

If one looks further into the background of the League's officers, he immediately notes the prevalence of old New England families. The great majority of these men were the descendants of English colonists who had settled in Massachusetts and Connecticut, especially the former, in the early seventeenth century.

Their forebears, furthermore, had frequently been outstanding leaders among the early colonists. For example, Thomas Wentworth Higginson was directly descended on his father's side from Francis Higginson, leader of the first large party of Puritan colonists to sail from England for Massachusetts Bay in 1629, and on his mother's side from John Wentworth, the first royal governor of New Hampshire. Erving Winslow's lineal ancestor, John Winslow, came to America on the ship *Fortune* in 1621 and married Mary Chilton, the first woman to land from the *Mayflower*. Gamaliel Bradford was a direct descendant of Governor William Bradford of Plymouth Colony. William Endicott was an eighth-generation descendant of Governor John Endicott of Salem. Winslow Warren's ancestor, Richard Warren, arrived in Massachusetts in 1623. Moorfield Storey's paternal ancestor settled in Ipswich, Massachusetts, in 1635.

Even many of those who had not remained in New England were descended from the same general stock. William Larrabee,

8. Allen Johnson and Dumas Malone (editors), *Dictionary of American Biography* (New York, 1935), II, 208.

Governor of Iowa, was the descendant of Greenfield Larabee, who settled in New London, Connecticut in 1637. John Sherman of Ohio was descended from Edmund Sherman, who arrived in Massachusetts in 1634, preceding Grover Cleveland's ancestor Moses Cleveland by only a year.

The ancestry of these men indicates several things. First, even in the highly democratic and fluid society of the nineteenth-century United States these men by the very fact of their ancestry inherited considerable status in the community. Second, as historian Allan Nevins has said of Grover Cleveland: "Character is not made overnight. When it appears in transcendant degree it is usually the product of generations of disciplined ancestry, or a stern environment, or both." [9] Their ancestry and family training gave these men a quiet courage and a strong belief in the righteousness of their convictions, which is very evident in their writings and actions during the stormy and protracted debate over imperialism. Third, what was said of Charles Parkhurst might be said of so many of these men: He was "of the distinctly Puritan type." [10] They were high-minded, serious, dedicated individuals. Fourth, they were well aware of their lineage and quite proud of it. So often when composing any autobiographical remarks they took pains to point out, like David Starr Jordan, that their forebears were "all of the old Puritan stock." [11] Similarly, Grover Cleveland observed: "From the time the first immigrant of my name landed in Massachusetts, down to the day of my advent, all the Clevelands from whom I claim descent were born in New England. The fact that I first saw light in the State of New Jersey I have never regarded as working a forfeiture of any right I may have derived from my New England lineage." [12]

---

9. Allan Nevins, *Grover Cleveland: A Study in Courage* (New York, 1934), p. 5.

10. Johnson and Malone, XIV, p. 245.

11. David Starr Jordan, *Days of a Man* (New York, 1922), Vol. I, p. 1.

12. George F. Parker (ed.), *The Writings and Speeches of Grover Cleveland* (New York, 1892), p. 240.

This awareness of the past, sense of tradition, and veneration of their forefathers, including the many who participated actively in the American Revolution, undoubtedly influenced the attitude of these leaders toward imperialism. They believed very strongly in the soundness of traditional foreign policy, and largely subscribed to Theodore Cuyler's favorite maxim that "the true things are not new, and most of the new things are not true."

One of the basic things that bothered them about the adoption of the policy of imperialism was that it represented a change from the policy which the United States had pursued since its inception as a nation. Furthermore, it was their very grandfathers who had fought against the imperial tyranny of Great Britain in the Revolution and who had instituted the policy which the imperialists wanted to change. Changing this policy meant, among other things, the repudiation of the wisdom of their literal forefathers. The adoption of a policy of imperialism, they believed, would mean the denigration of the finest documents of our governmental heritage—the Declaration of Independence, Washington's Farewell Address, the Monroe Doctrine.[13] Thus in combatting imperialism they felt that they were serving as the paladins of the best elements of the American tradition.

Four-fifths of the officers of the Anti-Imperialist League were

---

13. Variations on this important theme are found in a great deal of the anti-imperialist literature. See for example: Anti-Imperialist League, *Arguments Against a So-Called Imperial Policy* (Washington, 1898); Charles Francis Adams, Jr., *Imperialism and the Tracks of Our Forefathers* (Boston, 1899); George S. Boutwell, *Address at Faneuil Hall, February 23, 1900* (Boston, 1900), *Isolation and Imperialism* (Washington, 1898), *Republic or Empire* (Boston, 1898); American Anti-Imperialist League, *Address to the Voters of the United States* (Chicago, 1900); New England Anti-Imperialist League, *To the American People* (Boston, 1901); Andrew Carnegie, "Distant Possessions—The Parting of the Ways," *North American Review,* Vol. CLXVII (August, 1898), pp. 239-248; Erving Winslow, "The Anti-Imperialist Position," *North American Review,* Vol. CLXXI (October, 1900), pp. 460-68.

fifth and sixth generation Americans; the other one-fifth had, themselves, emigrated to the United States. Interestingly, they came from only four areas (of which three were part of Great Britain) out of the dozens of nations whose citizens migrated to the United States during this period. Four came from Ireland, four from Germany, one from England, and one from Scotland. They were certainly an unusually well-educated group of immigrants. Three of the four Germans held doctorates, and Schurz was a doctoral candidate when he left the University of Bonn to take part in the abortive revolutionary movement of 1848–49. Two of the Irishmen—Patrick O'Farrell and Patrick Collins—were law school graduates, the latter from Harvard.

The ready espousal of anti-imperialism by this group was one more example of their total involvement in the affairs and controversies of their adopted land. An earlier indication of this tendency was the fact that every one of these men who was in the United States and of requisite age at the time of the Civil War took some part in it, in each case in behalf of the Union—this latter preference certainly being ideologically in accordance with their later anti-imperialist views. Schurz became a major general in the Union Army and participated in many of the war's most important battles. Patrick Ford served in the Ninth Massachusetts Regiment. Patrick O'Farrell actually came to the United States to enlist in the Union Army; he was wounded five times and rose to the rank of captain, while serving in "Corcoran's Irish Legion" of the New York 69th Regiment. Andrew Carnegie and Emil Preetorius, although non-combatants, made important contributions to the Union cause, the former being instrumental in setting up the transportation system for the Union Army, and the latter helping to keep Missouri from joining the Confederacy.

There is little doubt that the experiences of these men in the Old World conditioned their attitude toward imperialism in the New. The Irishmen definitely equated American anti-imperialism with their very strong and active dislike of British imperialism, of which they felt Ireland was a conspicuous victim. Both Patrick Collins and Patrick Ford were in the thick of the fight for Irish

independence. The other Europeans, too, had personally witnessed the concomitants of an imperial policy—onerous taxation,
autocracy, large standing armies, international jealousy, etc.—in
their former countries, and they were anxious to do everything
they could to see that their adopted nation did not make the
same mistake. Furthermore, what drew such intellectuals as
Schurz, Preetorius, and Von Holst to the United States was the
image of the United States as an idealistic, enlightened, democratic
republic, whose basic creed involved a strong belief in liberty,
equality, and self-government—to all of which imperialism was
antithetical.

It thus seems that what both groups of men among the Anti-
Imperialist League officers—the fifth generation native born and
the first generation immigrants—essentially wanted to do was to
preserve the political ideals and foreign policy precepts which
were the product of the United States of the late eighteenth
century.

Their economic philosophy, or rather that part of their economic philosophy that pertained to foreign trade and international relations, also had its roots in the late eighteenth century
—in the laissez-faire doctrines of Adam Smith. The elaboration
of these free trade concepts by the political economists of the
mid-nineteenth century Manchester School, such as Cobden and
Bright, especially appealed to them. In fact there was a logical
correlation between their free trade views and their anti-imperialism, as there had been for Cobden and Bright, by whom
they were also influenced in both respects. Lodge, Roosevelt, and
other American imperialists noted this connection and condemned it. Lodge criticized the adherence of the American anti-
imperialists to "the theory of the Manchester school," which
maintains that "territorial extension or national expansion must
be stopped because they were likely to interfere with complete
freedom of trade." [14] Roosevelt, in a letter to Mahan lamented
the "fact that we have in America among our educated men a

---

14. Henry Cabot Lodge, "Our Blundering Foreign Policy,"
The Forum, Vol. XIX (March, 1895), p. 13.

kind of belated survivor of the Little England movement among the Englishmen of thirty years back." [15] Lodge's and Roosevelt's observances were correct; and it was not merely coincidence that the leaders in the United States of both free trade and anti-imperialism were the same;[16] for protected colonial markets and free trade were antithetical.

The economic position on the domestic scene of an overwhelming majority of the men who comprised the leadership of American institutional anti-imperialism can be succinctly summed up in two words—"sound money." With only one or two notable exceptions, every officer of the Anti-Imperialist League was an advocate of a strong currency. The writings of Schurz, Sumner, Atkinson, Bowles, Caffery, Carnegie, Cleveland, Cockran, Lewis, O'Farrell, and Edmunds on this subject alone would fill many volumes.

They not only strongly upheld gold as the basis of U.S. currency, but also vigorously attacked silver and its advocates. Their support of gold (or strong currency) and their denigration of silver (or weak currency) furthermore, was of long standing. For example, James McGurrin wrote of Bourke Cockran that "from the day he first entered public life, he had consistently championed the cause of sound money." [17] Andrew Carnegie wrote in June of 1891, expressing the views of virtually all of the men who were to serve as anti-imperialist officers: "Come what may, the stamp of the republic must be made true, the money of the American people kept the highest and surest in value of all money in the world, above all doubt or suspicion, its standard in the future, as in the past, not fluctuating Silver,

---

15. Letter of December 13, 1897, *Roosevelt Letters,* Vol. I, p. 741. Also see Roosevelt's "True American Ideals," *The Forum,* Vol. XVIII (February, 1895), pp. 743-750.

16. For example Edward Atkinson, Samuel Bowles, Gamaliel Bradford, John S. Carlisle, Erving Winslow, Albert S. Parsons, and William Graham Sumner.

17. James McGurrin, *Bourke Cockran* (New York, 1948), p. 148.

but unchanging Gold." [18] In 1893 Edward Atkinson wrote in a similar vein: "Silver dollars are bad money. . . . The proposal to coin silver dollars without limit and to force people to take them by an act of legal tender is an intolerable fraud. The purposes of its advocates can only be justified by commending their sincerity at the expense of their intelligence." [19] In an article two years later Atkinson simultaneously condemned the "Jingoes and Silverites," expressing the hope that "the Jingoes among our politicians will be stamped out of political existence in company with the advocates of the debasement of our unit of value." [20]

The great majority of the Anti-Imperialist League's officers agreed with Atkinson. It thus struck them as an ironical and exceedingly distressing twist of fate that the man who accused those who held their economic views of being about to "crucify mankind upon a cross of Gold" should have been selected by the Democratic Party—the party that strongly opposed imperialism—as its standard bearer in the election of 1900.

As far as political principles were concerned, the officers of the Anti-Imperialist League were in very substantial agreement with one another. However, as far as allegiance to a particular party, or to any party, was concerned, there was a division of opinion. But given the variety of minor parties and factions among the major parties, these men were really not too diverse. Essentially they were divided into four general groups politically, some of which merged almost imperceptibly at times with each other.

First, there were the regular members of the Republican party, of which there was a much larger representation among the League's officers than is usually realized. Included here were men like Boutwell, Edmunds, Carnegie, Jordan, O'Farrell, Sherman, John C. Bullitt, and William Larrabee. They had been

---

18. Andrew Carnegie, "The ABC of Money," *North American Review,* Vol. CLII (June, 1891), p. 750.

19. Edward Atkinson, "How Distrust Stops Trade," *North American Review,* Vol. CLVII (July, 1893), p. 29.

20. Edward Atkinson, "Jingoes and Silverites," *North American Review,* Vol. CLXI (November, 1895), p. 560.

loyal members of the regular Republican party for decades—in almost every case since the party's inception.

The second group was comprised of men who also had been among the earliest members of the Republican party and many of whom nominally still belonged to it. This group, however, believed even more strongly in the primacy of principle over party. These men largely made up the reform element in the Republican party. Most of them had broken with the party first in 1872 and had led the "Liberal Republican" movement. Then they were joined by other political mavericks in the so-called "Mugwump" movement of 1884, whose followers deserted the Republican party and gave their votes to Grover Cleveland, another Anti-Imperialist League officer. This group included Bowles, Bradford, Preetorius, Winslow, Storey, Higginson, and Schurz.

Both of these groups had been first drawn to the Republican party principally by its opposition to slavery. There is a direct connection between this earlier choice and their espousal of anti-imperialism. They equated abolitionism with anti-imperialism and felt that in opposing imperialism they were once again combatting a form of slavery. William Lloyd Garrison—the son of the fiery abolitionist publicist and editor of the *Liberator,* for which publication League officer Patrick Ford also worked—pointed out that "the leaders of the anti-slavery movement . . . little dreamed that only thirty-five years after emancipation the principles of human liberty, which they believed settled for all time, would so soon be openly disputed and denied by the leading party of the land." [21]

The anti-imperialists equated the cause of the Negro in 1860 with that of the Filipino in 1899. Garrison, in another speech, said what was felt by a great many of the anti-imperialists: "To Aguinaldo, fighting in the same cause for which John Brown died, sustained by the same hopes and aspirations, our sympathies are due as were the sympathies of all lovers of liberty

---

21. William Lloyd Garrison, "The Root of Imperialism"—an address before the Henry George Club of Providence, Rhode Island, April 7, 1900.

to John Brown. The contemners of Aguinaldo would have been the denouncers of John Brown in the dark days preceding the glare of the Civil War." [22]

The supporters of Aguinaldo, the Filipino patriot, and Brown literally were identical in the case of men like Boutwell, Higginson et al. Their equating of abolitionism with anti-imperialism is further evidenced in their very frequent citation of Abraham Lincoln's anti-slavery strictures in their attacks upon imperialism. Thus one of the two mottoes of the Eastern Anti-Imperialist Conference, which met in Philadelphia in February of 1900, was the Great Emancipator's statement that "those who deny freedom to others deserve it not for themselves, and, under a just God, cannot long retain it." [23] Similarly, Andrew Carnegie, like so many other prominent anti-imperialists, quoted Lincoln's observation that "when the white man governs himself and also governs another man, that is more than self-government; that is despotism." [24]

The third major segment of the political spectrum represented by the Anti-Imperialist League's officers consisted of the conservative wing of the Democratic party. This group included Cleveland, Endicott, Caffery, Carlisle, Cockran, Lewis, David Greene Haskins, Jr., and Winslow Warren. They were all sound-money men, viewed free silver as economic heresy and its advocates as either fools or charlatans or both, and largely opposed the other demands of that wing of the party which accepted the support of the Populists in 1896. In fact, many of these men refused to support William Jennings Bryan in 1896, and some of them, especially Caffery and Lewis, were very active in the formation of a third party—the National (or Gold) Demo-

---

22. William Lloyd Garrison, "Imperialism," address at the annual meeting of the Progressive Friends, Longwood, Pennsylvania, June 10, 1899. Copies of these two addresses may be found in Widener Library, Harvard University.

23. *New York Evening Post,* "Special Anti-Imperialist Supplement," February 24, 1900, p. 1.

24. Andrew Carnegie, "Americanism versus Imperialism," *North American Review,* Vol. CLXVIII (March, 1899), p. 372.

cratic party—which nominated John M. Palmer of Illinois to run against Bryan and McKinley.

Like Grover Cleveland, most of the Democrats among the League's officers had fought against free silver since their "entrance into national politics." [25] Thus Bryan's candidacy in 1900 put this group in a very frustrating and awkward position. They felt that no matter whether they supported Bryan or McKinley they would be denying strongly held beliefs; the result of this was that a number of these very able men, whom the anti-imperialist forces in 1900 could ill afford to spare, simply decided to sit out the election. Others reluctantly acquiesced and agreed to work for Bryan, but it was evident that they could not give him their wholehearted support. All of this, of course, ultimately redounded to McKinley's benefit by removing completely, or else lessening the ardor of, some of his most articulate and influential opponents.

The fourth political group among the League's officers were the independents. Although there were a few men like Albert Parsons and Edwin Smith who had always styled themselves as that *rara avis,* the true independent, the pure strain of this breed was actually somewhat of an anomaly. For the most part, one encounters under the heading of "independent" rather subtle gradations of party loyalty, or else shifting party loyalty, rather than the actual apolitical attitude which would characterize the literal independent. Furthermore, almost invariably one finds that those officers of the League who were considered independents were actually apostate Republicans. The apostasy of some, like Atkinson and Adams, was so pronounced as almost to amount to a conversion to the opposition. Others, like Bradford, Higginson, and Storey, had, after breaking with the Republican party as "Mugwumps," moved gradually toward an independent position. Still others, like Winslow and Schurz, although having broken with the Republican party on several occasions, still deemed themselves Republicans, and not independents.

The Anti-Imperialist League's officers were not ineffective

---

25. George F. Parker, *Recollections of Grover Cleveland* (New York, 1911), p. 214.

politically because they represented a variety of political backgrounds, nor were they merely victims of the passing of the
"genteel tradition." The crux of the matter is simply that the
American political system is based upon expediency and party
loyalty, not upon abstract political principle. The major American political parties, as Lord Bryce observed during the very
period under consideration, are not parties of principle and do
not reward it. The anti-imperialist leadership was not naively
unaware of this; for over a score of the League's officers had
held public office, and in almost all cases of national significance.[26]

They were men, however, who largely placed principle above
party; therefore, many of them in remaining loyal to their
principles were not disturbed by shifting party allegiance. But
in the election of 1900, they were hampered, not so much by
conflicting political ties, as by conflicting principles and ideologies; that is they approved of Bryan's anti-imperialism, although
many of them doubted his sincerity, but they abhorred other
aspects of his program. Their adherence to a few basic principles,
which were antithetically juxtaposed in the campaign of 1900,
left them with only a dubious choice of evils, and thus greatly
weakened the effectiveness of the anti-imperialist forces in this
crucial election.[27]

The general political outlook of the League's officers, like
their espousal of anti-imperialism itself, was largely an adjunct
of their characteristically idealistic attitude. This is further indicated by their intense interest in and devotion to a great
variety of reform movements. There was, in fact, hardly a sig-

---

26. Cleveland had twice been President of the United States.
Sherman, Carlisle, Endicott, Boutwell, Edmunds, and Schurz had all
been cabinet members. Pingree, Larrabee, Boutwell, Tillman, and
Cleveland had been Governors. Boutwell, Caffery, Carlisle, Schurz,
Tillman, and Sherman had been members of the U.S. Senate. Cockran, Carlisle, Boutwell, Sherman, Collins, Fleming, and Johnson
served in the U.S. House of Representatives.

27. For a complete discussion of the anti-imperialist role in
this election, see my article "Scylla and Charybdis: The Anti-
Imperialist Dilemma in the Election of 1900," *Pacific Historical
Review*, Vol. XXXVI (May, 1967), pp. 143-161, and Chapter XIII.

nificant reform movement in the United States of the late nineteenth century in which some officer, and usually many of them, had not been quite prominent; and some of them like Welsh, Storey, and Winslow, were so intensely involved with such a multiplicity of reform movements as to be deemed "professional reformers."

In discussing other matters we have already mentioned many of these reform movements, such as abolition, tariff reform and free trade, and political reform, e.g. the Liberal Republican movement of 1872 and the Mugwump movement of 1884. However, they were also very active, in addition to those movements considered in detail below, in such diverse areas as prison reform; education; treatment of the blind, deaf, and insane; temperance and prohibition; suffrage; tenement regulation; child labor, etc.

Civil service reform claimed the attention of a great many of the League's officers; and they were among the most prominent members of this movement in the nation. Included in this group were Schurz, Storey, Atkinson, Bowles, Bradford, Edmunds, Sumner, Preetorius, James Munroe and Charles F. Adams. They served in important administrative capacities on the local, state, and national levels of the movement. For example, Parsons was Chairman of the Cambridge Civil Service Reform Association; Munroe was Chairman of the Massachusetts Civil Service Commission; and Schurz was President of the National Civil Service Reform League. Such reforms as were effected were to no small degree due to their untiring efforts.

A somewhat related interest of many of the officers of the Anti-Imperialist League was municipal reform. Bradford, Cleveland, Collins, Carter, Adler, Smith, Parkhurst, John Bullitt, Hazen Pingree, Austen Fox, and Herbert Welsh were all quite active in this area.

Cleveland, Collins, and Pingree worked in a highly practical way in this field while serving respectively as Mayor of Buffalo, Boston, and Detroit, and running sound, honest administrations in the face of considerable opposition from vested interests. Parkhurst was President of the Society for the Prevention of

Crime and his vigorous attacks upon the connection between organized vice and politics led to the famous "Lexow investigation" (1894),[28] on which Fox and Adler also worked. Bullitt and Carter similarly made important contributions to municipal reform. Bullitt was instrumental in the adoption of a new charter for the city of Philadelphia, and the Bullitt Bill (1882) in the Pennsylvania Legislature provided the basis for "better government of cities of the first class." Carter founded and served for nine years as president of the National Municipal League. This interest of these men in municipal reform had a direct relation to their anti-imperialism; for one of their oft-repeated arguments was that the American people should not think of ruling other lands until it could be proven that they could govern their own large cities honestly and efficiently. "What hope is there," Moorfield Storey demanded, "that a people will govern others wisely who cannot govern themselves, who do not care enough for their own interests to make a Tammany Hall in New York, a Quay and a Penrose in Pennsylvania, a Fitzgerald in Boston, or a Cox in Cincinnati impossible?" [29]

Another area of reform in which many of the officers of the League were quite interested, and which also had a direct relationship to their anti-imperialist sentiments, is what we would today call civil rights. Edmunds, Atkinson, Adams, Storey, Higginson, Schurz, Welsh, and George G. Mercer all worked to better the treatment and status of the Negro and the American Indian. Their contributions in this area were many and varied, but perhaps the most notable services were those performed by Schurz when Secretary of the Interior, by Welsh as head of the Indian Rights Association, and by Storey, who became the first president of the National Association for the Advancement of Colored People.

The interest of these men in this area of reform made them especially sensitive to the rights and treatment of colored peoples

---

28. Charles H. Parkhurst, *Our Fight with Tammany* (New York, 1895).

29. *Eleventh Annual Meeting of the Anti-Imperialist League* (Boston, 1910), p. 30.

everywhere, and obviously affected their opposition to imperialism. It was also one of their arguments that the American people, who had shown themselves so delinquent and even cruel in their treatment of colored people in their own country,[30] could not without grossest hypocrisy rationalize their imperialist endeavors on the basis of a desire to altruistically aid their "little brown brothers."

There was a strong ideological connection between anti-imperialism and the international peace movement; it is, therefore, not surprising that many of the Anti-Imperialist League officers [31] were also leaders of the latter movement in the United States. Their belief in peace, and opposition to war and militarism, both on practical and philosophical grounds, was one of long standing with most of these men. Thus Burton J. Hendrick wrote that Andrew Carnegie "was a hater of militarism even as a boy." [32] The Civil War also provided a very strong stimulus in this direction. Bernard Alderson remarked about Carnegie: "The carnage, the bloodshed and the devastation of the land made so deep an impression upon his mind that he has ever since had a horror of war; in season and out of season he has been a strong advocate of peace." [33]

Carnegie is, of course, well known for his great and lasting contributions to the cause of international peace, but the other men mentioned previously all worked very assiduously in this cause, giving their time and energy to many peace organizations, such as the American Peace Society. The vital connection in their minds between militarism and war and imperialism and their opposition to these related phenomena in the peace movement can be seen, for example, in an essay entitled "Annexation

---

30. This was, for example, one of the major points in C. F. Adams' *Imperialism and the Tracks of Our Forefathers* (Boston, 1899). See especially pp. 16-17.

31. Included in this coterie were Atkinson, Carnegie, Mercer, Gompers, Winslow, Storey, Bowles, Schurz, and Jordan.

32. Burton J. Hendrick, *The Life of Andrew Carnegie* (New York, 1932), Vol. I, p. 103.

33. Bernard Alderson, *Andrew Carnegie: The Man and His Work* (New York, 1909), p. 26.

and Conquest," which David Starr Jordan, who headed the American delegation to the Peace Conference at The Hague in 1913, wrote for L'Organization Centrale pour une Paix Durable. He emphasized in this work the principle, which both the anti-imperialists and the peace advocates wished to have accepted categorically, that "no annexation or transfer of territory shall be made by force, as a result of war, or conquest." [34]

It was not only ideologically—in their advocacy of pacifism, free trade, etc.—that the leaders of the Anti-Imperialist League were different from the leaders of American imperialism. There was another salient difference, which, because it is basically such a simple one, might easily be overlooked. It was, however, undoubtedly a contributory factor in determining the stand which these different groups of men assumed. The officers of the Anti-Imperialist League in 1898 were very largely men who were well along in years. The League's president, George Boutwell, was over eighty. Gamaliel Bradford, whose clarion call had resulted in the first formal anti-imperialist meeting, was sixty-seven. Edward Atkinson, in whose office the League was founded, was seventy-one. Carl Schurz, the cause's leading publicist, was sixty-nine. Cleveland, Sherman, Higginson, Potter, Caffery, Carlisle, Carnegie and Adams were all past sixty, as were more than half of the League's officers. Indeed the average age was over sixty, the median sixty, and the mode—that of the last five men named as well as others—was sixty-three. Within a decade many of the League's principal leaders would be dead, and as Moorfield Storey was later to remark, "the young men do not take up the work." In counter-distinction the leading advocates and publicists of imperialism averaged over fifteen years younger and were in their prime. For example, in 1898 Theodore Roosevelt was forty, Albert Beveridge thirty-six, Walter Hines

---

34. Jordan, *Days of a Man,* Vol. II, p. 671.

There are numerous other indications in various items in the Jordan Papers (Stanford University) which evince a strong ideological connection between anti-imperialism and the international peace movement.

Page forty-three, Albert Shaw forty-one, and Henry Cabot Lodge forty-eight.

This difference in age between the groups is significant. Roosevelt, himself, in a letter to Mahan said that he felt that one of the principal reasons for the opposition to imperialism "is due to the men of a bygone age having to deal with the facts of the present." [35] If Roosevelt's petulant remark is taken to mean that the anti-imperialists did not understand the contemporary situation, he was in error; but if it is taken to mean that they did not like the contemporary international situation, were uncomfortable in the present, and preferred the foreign policy of the past, then he undoubtedly was right.

The officers of the Anti-Imperialist League were in general men whose lives, greatest achievements, and greatest influence were largely behind them. This is one of the most important reasons why even those men like Sherman, Boutwell, and Edmunds, who had remained steadfast in their party allegiance until confronted with the spectre of imperialism, were not more effective politically. These old gladiators, while battle-wise, were losing their stamina, and were being crowded out of the arena by younger, more vigorous, and more militant men like Roosevelt and Lodge. As the influence of the elder statesmen, who formed the backbone of the Anti-Imperialist League, declined, that of the Young Turks, like Roosevelt, Lodge, and Beveridge increased. It was, perhaps, only natural that the younger men would be the ones to espouse imperialism. The empire builders have invariably been young; Alexander the Great died at thirty-three; Napoleon became Emperor at thirty-five.

An interesting juxtaposition of the older and younger men and their differing ideologies occurred in the Senate on January 9, 1900. On that occasion Albert Beveridge delivered his maiden speech in the Senate. It was a grandiloquent oration eulogizing American imperialism. It was answered by Senator George Hoar. Hoar, who was not one of the original officers, but who subse-

---

35. *Roosevelt Letters,* Vol. I, p. 741.

quently became an officer of the League, was cast in the typical mold. He was a member of an old and prominent Massachusetts family, his forebears having settled there in 1640; he had graduated from Harvard and Harvard Law School; he had been an abolitionist, was a "sound-money" man, etc.[36] At the time that he rose in the Senate Chamber to comment upon Beveridge's speech, he was seventy-two years old. He said:

> As I heard his eloquent description of wealth and glory and commerce and trade, I listened in vain for those words which the American people have been wont to take upon their lips in every solemn crisis of their history. I heard much calculated to excite the imagination of the youth seeking wealth, or the youth charmed by the dream of empire, but the words Right, Justice, Duty, Freedom, were absent my young friend must permit me to say from that eloquent speech.[37]

It was in fact the contention of the elder statesmen who founded the Anti-Imperialist League that right, justice, and freedom were conspicuously absent from the entire imperialist doctrine, and for this reason, as well as the others we have considered, they steadfastly opposed it and adhered staunchly to the nation's traditional foreign policy.

---

36. George F. Hoar, *Autobiography of Seventy Years*, 2 volumes (New York, 1903).

37. *Congressional Record,* 56th Congress, 1st Session, p. 712.

CHAPTER 11

The Treaty of Paris

The leaders of the anti-imperialist movement were concerned about the possible outcome of the Spanish-American War. The annexation of Hawaii during the summer of 1898 confirmed their fears that the war would lead to imperialism. They felt it would be hypocritical and dishonorable to turn a war begun in the name of humanity into one of conquest and self-aggrandizement, so they did what they could to stem the drift in this direction. Carl Schurz took his objections to acquisition of Spanish territory directly to the President. Writing to McKinley late in July, he reminded him that the government was precluded by its own declaration from annexing any of the Spanish islands and said that if we went back on this solemn pledge it would put "a stain of disgrace on the American name." [1]

The anti-imperialists also felt that it was distressing that the government would in effect be emulating the policies of the adversary which it so vigorously condemned. Although the great majority of the American people in the chauvinistic atmosphere engendered by the war were inclined to view Spain as the very antithesis of the United States, the anti-imperialists pointed out that the American imperialists were employing the same rationalizations that the Spanish had in attempting to justify imperial conquest. Leonard Bacon, Anti-Imperialist League vice president, emphasized this theme in a daring and

---

1. Schurz Papers.

much publicized sermon (delivered on July 10, 1898, while the war was still very much in progress) in which he revealingly compared Spain's heritage of imperialism with the policies advocated by the American imperialists and questioned the wisdom of mingling with the European nations "in their chaffering diplomacies over the balance of power and in the mire and blood of their perpetual wars." [2]

Bacon's sermon represents the prototype of a cogent argument which the anti-imperialists were to reiterate many times in the next several years, and which, with the passage of time, was to prove increasingly disturbing to the American national conscience. This contention—that the United States was, in espousing imperialism, adopting the very system and concomitant policies for which we had so often denounced Spain and other European nations—received probably its most notable statement in William Graham Sumner's incisive essay, "The Conquest of the United States by Spain." [3] As events progressed in the Philippines, and the American Army adopted even such distasteful practices as the "water cure" and reconcentration camps (the latter having been ironically one of the principal items of our censure of the Spanish administration of Cuba, which we ostensibly fought the war to eliminate), the anti-imperialists were able to recall the early admonitions of Bacon, Sumner et al. and say "we told you so."

In July of 1898, however, the nation was enthralled with the idea of military glory and overseas expansion, and the anti-imperialists' earnest words fell upon deaf ears. Thus when Spain late in July sued for peace through the French Ambassador Jules Cambon, the preliminary terms which Cambon received in reply on July 30 included relinquishment of Spanish sovereignty over Cuba, cession of Puerto Rico and an island in the Ladrones to the United States, and the occupation by the United States of "the city, bay, and harbor of Manila pending the

---

2. Leonard Woolsey Bacon, "A Parallel," in *Anti-Imperialist Broadside No. 2* (Washington, D.C., 1898).

3. William Graham Sumner, *The Conquest of the United States by Spain* (Boston, 1899).

conclusion of a treaty of peace which shall determine the control, disposition, and government of the Philippines." [4]

One must recall that at this point American troops had been in Puerto Rico for only a few days and had not yet set foot in the Philippines. Spain, wishing to believe as so many Americans did that the war had been fought over Cuba, demurred over the disposition of the other islands concerned; but she was militarily and economically in no position to carry on the war further. Therefore, when Secretary of State Day presented Ambassador Cambon with a formal protocol almost in the form of an ultimatum, Spain had no real choice but to accept. This she did on August 12, the day before the American attack upon Manila.

The protocol did not settle the central question of the ultimate disposition of the Philippine Islands. There seems to have been a good deal of uncertainty at this time in the mind of the general public as to just what was the best course for the United States to pursue in this regard. There was, however, no uncertainty on the part of the anti-imperialists. For example, in a notable speech on July 29 Senator George Hoar stated emphatically that as long as he represented the Bay State, she would not be the "ruler of vassal states or subject people. She will enter upon no mad career of empire in distant seas." [5]

The Anti-Imperialist Committee of Correspondence, which published and distributed Senator Hoar's speech in pamphlet form, was very active during this trying period. The Committee especially urged that the anti-imperialist position be vigorously presented at the highly important conference on future American foreign policy sponsored by the National Civic Federation on August 19, exactly one week after the signing of the protocol which formally suspended hostilities between the United States and Spain.

Moorfield Storey, Robert T. Paine, Carl Schurz, and Samuel Gompers rose to the challenge. Gompers dwelled on the dele-

---

4. *United States Foreign Relations, 1898, op. cit.,* p. 820.
5. George F. Hoar, "The Opinion of Massachusetts on Imperialism," address before the Massachusetts Club, July 29, 1898.

terious moral consequences of imperialism,[6] while Schurz emphasized the practical side of the issue. Schurz pointed out that the United States had no governmental machinery for controlling colonies. He remarked upon the climatic and racial difficulties the United States would encounter. He reminded his audience that democracy had never flourished in the tropics and that our type of civilization had never been successfully transplanted there on a large scale. Schurz insisted that to annex the areas in question would simply be to garner a myriad of problems, when the United States already had too many that were still unsolved. He warned that if the nation expanded in the Far East it would immediately become involved in the quarrels of the European nations, competing there for colonial prizes, and this would call for "the maintenance of big naval and military armaments, imposing immense burdens upon the people." [7]

Schurz's Saratoga speech can be taken as an epitome of anti-imperialist thought and pronouncements in the late summer of 1898. While his position and that of his fellow officers of the Anti-Imperialist League was clear and unwavering, that of many other prominent Americans at the time was ambiguous and vacillating. A good example of this is the case of John Hay, who at the time (August, 1898) was ambassador to Great Britain and was soon to become Secretary of State.

Hay heartily approved of the war. In fact, he made the most memorable remark of all concerning the brief conflict when he wrote to that "bully" leader of the Rough Riders, Teddy Roosevelt: "It has been a splendid little war; begun with the highest motives, carried on with magnificent intelligence and spirit, favored by that fortune which loves the brave." [8] In light of Hay's subsequently prominent part in the American imperialist surge, it is fascinating to read both his own remarks and those

6. Samuel Gompers, *Seventy Years of Life and Labor: An Autobiography* (New York, 1925), Vol. II, p. 326.

7. Schurz, "Our Future Foreign Policy" in Bancroft (ed.), *op. cit.*, Vol. V, pp. 478-494.

8. William R. Thayer, *The Life and Letters of John Hay* (Boston, 1915), Vol. II, p. 337.

of his good friend Andrew Carnegie at this juncture. Carnegie wrote in his autobiography:

> Philippine annexation was a burning question when I met him [Hay] and Henry White in London on my way to New York. It gratified me to find our views were similar upon that proposed serious departure from our traditional policy of avoiding distant and disconnected possessions and keeping our 'empire' within the continent, especially keeping it out of the vortex of militarism. Hay, White and I clasped hands together in Hay's office in London and agreed upon this.[9]

Further evidence that Hay was either not sincere in his relation with his Skibo host or else had during early September an experience in a secular way analogous to that of Paul on the road to Damascus is found in a letter which Hay wrote to the steel master on August 22: "I have read with keenest interest your article in the *North American*.[10] I am not allowed to say in my present fix how much I agree with you. I am rather thankful it is not given to me to solve that momentous question." Of course, ironically, it was his "strange fate" to perform this role. It is, perhaps, even stranger if one credits Hay with much personal integrity, which Carnegie and others surely did,[11] that he seemed to be so sympathetic to the anti-imperialist position one month and was in the vanguard of the opposition the next. However, many men, chameleon-like, have been known to change their coloring to suit their surroundings.

In the article that Hay so strongly supported, Carnegie stated that "it has never been considered the part of wisdom to thrust one's hand into the hornet's nest, and it does seem as if the United States must lose all claim to ordinary prudence and

---

9. Andrew Carnegie, *Autobiography* (New York, 1920), p. 358.

10. The reference is to Carnegie's article "Distant Possessions —The Parting of the Ways," *North American Review,* Vol. CLXVII (August, 1898), pp. 239-248, in which he castigated the policy of imperialism.

11. Carnegie wrote of Hay that "he inspired men with absolute confidence in his sincerity, and his aspirations were always high."— Carnegie, *Autobiography, loc. cit.*

good sense if she enters this arena and becomes involved in the intrigues and threats of war which make Europe an armed camp." He solemnly admonished his adopted nation that if it espoused the policy of imperialism it would be "making a plunge into an abyss." [12] It was the enigmatic John Hay, who became Secretary of State on September 30, who guided the nation into the "hornet's nest" and the "abyss." It is difficult to assess precisely the significance of Hay's role, but there is no doubt that his approval of Philippine annexation greatly aided the imperialist cause.

Hay was appointed Secretary of State when William R. Day resigned to head the American peace commission, which was scheduled to meet at Paris on October 1. The other members of the delegation were: Senator Cushman K. Davis of Minnesota, chairman of the Senate committee on foreign relations; Senator William P. Frye of Maine, president pro tempore of the Senate; Senator George Gray of Delaware; and Whitelaw Reid, editor of the *New York Tribune*. Since Davis, Frye, and Reid were outspoken imperialists, it was virtually a foregone conclusion that the treaty would be expansionist to some degree.

Both the imperialists and anti-imperialists were quite active in propounding their views in the press in the month preceding the commission's assembly in the City of Light. In the works of the former one finds an interesting potpourri of chauvinism, romanticism, mysticism, Social Darwinism, and historical determinism. The preaching of the doctrine that the people of the United States really had little choice but to bow to inexorable predetermined forces, cosmic tendencies, and primordial urges is especially evident. Thus financial expert Charles A. Conant [13] wrote that "the instinctive tendency of a race or civilization often outruns the wisdom of its leaders. . . . When the current of race

---

12. Carnegie, "Distant Possessions—The Parting of the Ways," *op. cit.*, pp. 245, 240.

13. In 1901 President McKinley selected Conant to reorganize the Philippine monetary system, a service which he later also performed for Cuba, and for years the new Philippine silver pesos were known as "Conants."

or national tendencies runs strongly in a given channel it is apt to override alike the misgivings of its sympathizers and the protests and resistance of those who would obstruct it." [14]

Even more typical of the imperialist mystique of the time was an article by H. H. Powers [15] entitled "The War and Manifest Destiny." Powers claimed that the Spanish-American War was merely "the natural outcome of forces constantly at work in the race." The territorial acquisitions which would come as a result of the war were similarly viewed as the result of a basic natural drive. "We want the earth—not consciously as a formulated program, but instinctively, with a desire that is too deep for consciousness." Strongly influenced by the contemporary penchant for Social Darwinist theory, Powers emphasized that "this universal desire is only the higher psychic phase of a still more fundamental and universal fact, the fact of growth. . . . Into this world struggle the American people is crowded by an inner power of growth that has no equal or precedent." [16]

It is a moot point whether the American imperialists actually completely and sincerely believed in such dicta or whether they simply shrewdly realized that this type of argument, like the arguments based upon missionary and altruistic motives, was difficult to answer; for if one accepted the imperialists' premises, it then seemed as if one were arguing against fate, God, and

---

14. Charles A. Conant, "The Economic Basis of Imperialism," *North American Review,* Vol. CLXVII (Sept., 1898), p. 326.

15. Powers (1859-1936) was a very prolific writer on many subjects, including economics, sociology, art, and travel; but his greatest interest was in foreign relations. See *The Things Men Fight For* (Boston, 1916), *The Great Peace* (New York, 1918), *America and Great Britain* (New York, 1918), *America Among the Nations* (New York, 1921).

16. H. H. Powers, "The War and Manifest Destiny," *Annals of the American Academy of Political and Social Science,* Vol. XII (Sept., 1898), pp. 175-77. Similarly, J. R. Proctor said that one should not underestimate the "inherited racial instincts, restless activities, and aggressive enterprise of our people" from which there must "arise a New Imperialism."—"Isolation or Imperialism," *The Forum,* Vol. XXVI (Sept., 1898), pp. 14, 26.

goodness, or in the more usual and alliterative, contemporary terminology, against destiny, deity, and duty.

Many people, much to the dismay of the anti-imperialists, felt that American imperialism should embrace all of Spain's insular empire. There were those, like Mayo Hazeltine, who argued that the United States should simply ignore the self-abnegating declaration with which the war was begun. "We should," he said, "deal with Cuba precisely as we have dealt with other foreign territory which, from time to time, we have annexed." He maintained that "there is not one American citizen in a thousand who believes that, because we entered upon the war with a philanthropic purpose, we are precluded from exacting some compensation for the outlay which the stiff-necked refusal of Spain to treat her colonists with justice has compelled us to make." [17]

The anti-imperialists felt that it was bad enough, especially in light of the Teller amendment, to advocate the annexation of any of the Spanish islands; but to urge that the nation should not honor the specific pledge made in the case of Cuba was to them unbelievably immoral. They also must have noted with disdain that Hazeltine was, on the other hand, quite willing to support supposed philanthropic purpose where the result would be acquisition of additional territory rather than denial of it. Thus Hazeltine the following month contended in a companion article that "by our victory at Cavite and the subsequent capture of Manila we assumed a moral obligation . . . that can be best discharged by the occupation of all of the Philippines." [18]

Such Machiavellian manipulation of morality thoroughly disgusted anti-imperialists like Carl Schurz. Schurz wrote to President McKinley on September 22, 1898, and told him in reference to the Saratoga meeting that a majority of those attending the conference were against any annexations. Schurz believed, perhaps wishfully, that this was the position of a large majority

17. Mayo W. Hazeltine, "What Is to Be Done with Cuba?" *North American Review,* Vol. CLXVII (Sept., 1898), pp. 318-19.

18. Mayo W. Hazeltine, "What Shall Be Done with the Philippines?" *North American Review,* Vol. CLXVII (Oct., 1898), p. 387.

of the American people. He predicted that popular feeling against imperialism would increase "as the burdens which the imperialistic policy will put upon us become more apparent to the public mind." The accuracy of Schurz's prediction was to be borne out after the turn of the century, but at this time the excitement engendered by the swift victory over Spain and the romantic appeal of imperialism veiled the realities of colonial rule, which the American public would learn only by bitter experience.

Schurz and his anti-imperialist colleagues, however, did their best to warn them. Schurz poured his feelings into a notable article, "Thoughts on American Imperialism," which was published in the September issue of *Century Magazine*. Schurz reiterated the anti-imperialist arguments that imperialism would lead to a huge standing Army and Navy, onerous taxation, increased racial problems and tension, and the abandonment of the Monroe Doctrine. He went into the practical problems of administration and government in some detail. He demonstrated that annexation of the areas in question would offer the nation politically merely a choice of evils. The new areas could be admitted to statehood, but this would have a pernicious effect upon American government and political affairs. The only other, and equally undesirable, alternative would be government without the consent of the governed to which the United States had been opposed since its inception.

Schurz devoted a good deal of attention to attempting to combat what was the most nebulous but most powerful and popularly compelling part of the imperialist doctrine. This was the congeries of mystical phrases, shibboleths, speciously altruistic motivations, pseudo-scientific theorems and doctrines of justification, which were included in the resuscitation of that grand and glorious rationalization of American territorial aggressiveness—Manifest Destiny. He remarked that the American people were once again being told that territorial expansion "is imposed upon this Republic by 'Manifest Destiny.'" He pointed out that this was not the first occasion that this rationalization had been employed. Before the Civil War Manifest

Destiny had been invoked in behalf of " 'extending the area of freedom,' which then really meant the acquisition of more territory for slave states." The American people had resisted this sophistry then, and Schurz hoped that they would once again oppose it when it meant the adoption of a policy of outright imperialism. In making their decision on this momentous issue, he urged them, above all, to avoid being influenced by "high-sounding phrases of indefinite meaning or by seductive catch-words appealing to unreasoning pride and reckless ambition." [19]

Schurz's remarks were directed at just the sort of reasoning and rhetoric that appeared in many of the stirring speeches of Theodore Roosevelt. Roosevelt, in his first important speech in his campaign for the governorship of New York, delivered at Carnegie Hall on October 5, characteristically chose to speak on "The Duties of a Great Nation," the foremost of which he apparently felt to be the adoption of an imperialist policy. His appeal was couched in the sort of phraseology about which Schurz warned the public in his *Century* article. "The guns of our warships," Roosevelt said in an almost classic statement of his philosophy of the strenuous life, which blended so well with the whole fabric of American imperialism, "have awakened us to new duties. We are face to face with our destiny, and we must meet it with a high and resolute courage. For ours is the life of action, of strenuous performance of duty; let us live in the harness striving mightily; let us rather run the risk of wearing out than rusting out." [20]

The implications of such statements caused Schurz, who had been importuned by many influential Republicans—including the nominee himself—to campaign for Roosevelt, to work against him in the gubernatorial campaign. He realized that it was not a matter which simply concerned the state of New York, since election to the governorship might give Roosevelt a step-

---

19. Carl Schurz, "Thoughts on American Imperialism," *The Century Illustrated Monthly Magazine,* Vol. LVI (Sept., 1898), pp. 781-88.

20. *The New York Times,* October 6, 1898.

ping-stone to the presidency. On October 21, 1898, the New *York Evening Post* published an important letter from Schurz stating that he could not support Roosevelt when a vote for him would encourage "a vulgar land-grabbing operation, glossed over by high-sounding cant about destiny and duty and what not. I cannot support him when his hot impulses and extreme notions of militant imperialism might do the country greater and more irreparable harm than anything I can think of."

The debate over whether to annex various parts of the Spanish empire was not, of course, confined to New York. This vitally important issue was being actively debated throughout the entire nation. The men who were to become the officers of the Anti-Imperialist League, upon its founding the following month, were especially active preaching the anti-imperialist gospel in New England. On October 8 George Boutwell, who would become the first president of the Anti-Imperialist League, delivered a very vigorous speech at the Twentieth Century Club in Boston on "Problems Raised by the War." He stressed those of a political, military, administrative and financial nature and warned that if the nation continued to follow the path of militarism and imperialism "evil consequences of the most serious character are . . . inevitable." [21]

Several days after Boutwell's speech, President McKinley began an extensive speaking tour in the mid-west, which was apparently designed to test public opinion on the terms of the peace treaty. Speaking at Ottumwa, Iowa, on October 13, the President said he wanted "the best public sentiment of the country to help determine what the duty of the American nation is." [22] A number of McKinley's contemporaries felt that the

---

21. George S. Boutwell, *Problems Raised by the War* (Washington, 1898), p. 3.

22. *Speeches of William McKinley* (New York, 1900), p. 115. Theodore Roosevelt, speaking the following week at Fort Henry, N.Y., slanted the issue rather differently. "Do you wish," he railed, "to keep or throw away the fruits of what we have won in the war? . . . If you wish to throw them away, then vote against President

cheers which greeted his mention of "doing our duty" by Puerto Rico and the Philippines convinced him that the mass of the American people favored an imperial course.[23] However, even on this tour the President was confronted with anti-imperialist opposition. For example, Samuel Gompers, who shared the speaker's platform with the President at the "Peace Jubilee" in Chicago on October 19, spoke out forcefully against expansion and claimed that "our flag was waving in Hawaii and the Philippines over people subjugated by our superior force." [24]

The anti-imperialist position also continued to appear frequently in the press in October. E. L. Godkin hammered away at imperialism almost every week in editorials in *The Nation*, with those on the 6th ("What To Do with the Philippines") and the 27th ("Destiny and Duty") being particularly notable. Philadelphia lawyer Solomon Solis-Cohen wrote a trenchant article for *The Arena* on "The Spectre of Imperialism." William MacDonald surveyed "The Dangers of Imperialism" in *The Forum*, especially emphasizing the ramifications of the fact that "a policy of imperialism . . . is not in harmony with the historic spirit of American government." [25] Grover Cleveland's former Secretary of the Treasury, John G. Carlisle, took up the fight both in *Harper's Weekly* ("The Policy of Expansion—Cuba and the Philippines") and in *Harper's Monthly* ("Our Future Policy"). Cleveland wrote on October 21 to his former cabinet member and fellow Anti-Imperialist League vice presi-

---

McKinley; vote in favor of his opponents, and give heart . . . to every Spaniard in Spain, to every man in Continental Europe who wishes us ill. Vote that way if you please. . . . But if you choose to vote for America, if you choose to vote for the flag for which we fought this summer . . . then you will vote to sustain the administration of President McKinley."—Pringle, *op. cit.,* p. 206.

23. For example, see Hoar, *Autobiography, op. cit.,* Vol. II, pp. 309-311.

24. Gompers, *Life and Labor, op. cit.,* Vol. II, p. 327.

25. William MacDonald, "The Dangers of Imperialism," *The Forum,* Vol. XXVI (Oct., 1898), p. 185.

dent concerning the latter essay: "I cannot tell you how much I was gratified with your expansion article. I can't for the life of me see how such a thing can be insisted on the face of such a plain exposure of its dangers and the national inconsistency it entails." [26]

Throughout October while the debate was raging in the United States, the members of the American peace commission in Paris had been wrangling with their Spanish counterparts, the State Department, and themselves.[27] There were three basic problems. First, the protocol of August 12 was inadequate and somewhat vague. Second, the instructions from the President, reflecting his own indecision, ranged from imprecise to nebulous. Third, the commissioners, themselves, held varying views and it was difficult for them all to agree on a single presentation of demands.

Day was in favor of taking a part but not all of the Philippines. Davis, Frye, and Reid wanted to take the entire archipelago. Gray, whose position at this point was described by his contemporary James LeRoy as "the typically anti-imperialist attitude," [28] was opposed to acquiring any territory at all in the Philippines. On October 25, 1898, Gray cabled his views to McKinley. "To take the Philippines," he said,

> would be to reverse accepted continental policy of the country, declared and acted upon throughout our history. . . . Policy proposed introduces us into European politics and the entangling alliances against which Washington and all American statesmen have protested. It will make necessary a navy equal to the largest of powers; a greatly increased military establishment; immense sums for fortifications and harbors; multiply occasions

---

26. Cleveland Letters, *op. cit.,* p. 506.

27. For an interesting contemporary account by one of the participants, see H. W. Morgan (ed.), *Making Peace with Spain: The Diary of Whitelaw Reid, September-December, 1898* (Austin, 1965).

28. James A. LeRoy, *The Americans in the Philippines* (Boston, 1914), Vol. I, p. 364.

for dangerous complications with foreign nations and increase burdens of taxation.[29]

McKinley apparently paid little attention to Gray's admonitions; for only three days later he cabled instructions to the commissioners to demand the entire Philippine archipelago. The cable was replete with the usual pious phraseology to the effect that the nation in annexing the remains of the once proud Spanish empire was merely acting "in the interests of humanity," living up to the "moral obligations of our victory," and following the "plain path of duty." [30]

McKinley's own explanation of how he arrived at his decision in regard to the Philippines is classic. "The truth is," he said, "I didn't want the Philippines, and when they came to us, as a gift from the gods, I did not know what to do with them." [31] There is little doubt that McKinley made his decision in response to what he felt to be the trend of public opinion and in response to the urgings of the more aggressive imperialistic wing of the Republican party. He claimed, however, that his decision was a result of divine revelation. Whether he confused the voice of God with that of Theodore Roosevelt or Henry Cabot Lodge one will never know, although it is quite possible that neither of these gentlemen would have denied the similarity. In any case, the explanation of his decision that he gave to a group of visiting clergymen is replete with rationalization and has the familiar ring of the doctrine of Manifest Destiny. He told them that he had prayed for divine guidance and that one night it came to him that "there was nothing left for us to do but to take them all, and to educate the Philipinos, and uplift and civilize and Christianize them,[32] and by God's grace do

---

29. *Senate Document 148,* 56th Congress, 2nd Session (Washington, 1900), p. 31.

30. *Ibid.,* pp. 37-38; also *U.S. Foreign Relations, 1898, op. cit.,* pp. 937-938.

31. Olcott, *op. cit.,* Vol. II, p. 109.

32. McKinley in his unctuous rhetorical flight overlooked the salient facts that parts of the Philippines were highly civilized and that the Catholic Church had been established in the islands in the

the very best we could by them, as our fellowmen for whom Christ also died. And then I went to bed, and to sleep and slept soundly." [33]

The result of McKinley's supposedly divinely inspired official determination in regard to the disposition of the Philippine Islands, however, was to cause many other people to lose their sleep. The members of the neophyte Anti-Imperialist League, which was formed the following month, were especially disturbed and worked strenuously to combat the adoption of imperialism which the treaty involved. We have previously considered the petitions and publications which the League immediately issued in November. The officers were, moreover, very active in correspondence and giving speeches on the matter. George Boutwell, for example, gave an important speech on November 4 on the subject of "Isolation and Imperialism." Although these were not the only alternatives available to the nation as some imperialists claimed, the President of the Anti-Imperialist League was willing to debate the opposition on these grounds, insisting that it was far better to work out our destiny in this continent than to adopt a policy of territorial expansion "such as has already been entered upon by war and which can only be preserved by successive wars." [34]

16th century and by the end of the 19th century numbered a majority of the Filipinos among its communicants. If he had read an interesting article written by his own minister to Siam, John Barrett, he would have been freed from "many a blunder and foolish notion too." Barrett wrote: "It is a mistake to suppose that the Philippines are the home of barbaric, uncivilized tribes. Manila was the seat of colleges, observatories and technical schools before Chicago was founded; roads to all points of the compass had been constructed in Luzon before there was a paved street . . . in New York; and devoted padres had carried the gospel to the heart of the tropical jungle before the Pilgrim Fathers landed at Plymouth Rock,"—"The Cuba of the Far East," *North American Review,* Vol. CLXIV (Feb., 1897), p. 176.

33. Olcott, *op. cit.,* Vol. II, pp. 110-111.

34. George S. Boutwell, *Isolation and Imperialism* (Washington, 1898), p. 3.

Boutwell also carried on an extensive correspondence with Senator Hoar, giving him encouragement, suggestions, and moral support in the battle against the treaty in the Senate, which the latter was preparing to lead. Hoar wrote to Boutwell on November 12 saying that "If the Democrats will stand fast, I think I am sure of enough Republicans to defeat any policy of imperialism. . . . When I left Washington, I had the assurance of a clear majority of the entire Senate that they would resist any acquisition of territory by the war." [35] Two days later Hoar wrote to Senator Hale of Maine, one of the very few of his fellow party members who would ultimately vote with him against the treaty, reporting that he was receiving strong public support for his stand against Philippine annexation. "Certainly," he said, "they cannot get through a treaty which commits us to imperialism." [36]

Senator Hoar simply could not believe that the American people and the U.S. Senate would approve such a treaty, incorporating imperialistic tenets, as was about to be signed. On November 30 he sent an open letter to his constituents via the *Worcester Gazette,* in which he expressed vigorous opposition to the acquisition of the Philippines, and said that he was sure that a great many people felt as he did. He stated: "We have not, so far, any news which is absolutely trustworthy of what they are doing in Paris. But if the report be true, that it is proposed to buy of Spain the 'sovereignty' of the Philippine Islands and to pay $20 million for it, I do not believe that such a treaty will be agreed to and I do not believe that it ought to be agreed to." [37]

---

35. Frederick H. Gillett, *George Frisbie Hoar* (Boston, 1934), pp. 222-23.

36. *Ibid.,* p. 223. Grover Cleveland, however, like many other anti-imperialists, did not share Hoar's optimism. On November 13 he wrote to A. B. Farquhar: "It seems to me that every consideration against this fatal imperialistic folly has been presented to our countrymen, but they do not seem inclined to weigh them."—*Cleveland Letters,* p. 506. See also Goldwin Smith, "The Moral of the Cuban War," *The Forum,* Vol. XXVI (November, 1898), pp. 282-293.

37. Gillett, *op. cit.,* p. 225.

THE WAR DOESN'T SEEM TO BE OVER
The New Arrival—But, you know I am a Peace Treaty.
Cartoon by "Bart" (Charles L. Bartholomew) in *The Minneapolis
Journal,* January 5, 1899.

Carl Schurz agreed so strongly with Hoar that a great proportion of the American people were thoroughly opposed to the
policy of imperialism embodied in the treaty that he wrote to
the Senator on December 1, urging him to introduce a bill
calling for a national plebiscite on the matter. Andrew Carnegie
also favored this idea and on December 27 he wrote to Schurz
saying that "if you could get a plebiscite today [the] Government would be drowned deeper than plummet ever sounded." [38]

38. Bancroft, *op. cit.,* Vol. V, p. 531.

Carnegie was in the thick of the fight over the treaty. On November 20 he had written an open letter entitled "Commercial Expansion Vs. Colonial Expansion," in which he contended that these two phenomena were not linked together as the imperialists claimed, but rather were mutually antagonistic. "Should we undertake to hold the Philippines," he said, "we immediately place the whole republic within the zone of wars and rumors of wars, and the rumor of war, it must be remembered, is in itself destructive to commerce." [39] The cogency of the canny Scotsman's remarks was not lost upon his fellow businessmen, and it is possible that if the desired plebiscite could have been held that a great many of the nation's businessmen, who were always less enthusiastic about imperialism than Roosevelt, Lodge, and Mahan desired, might have voted against incurring the uncertain conditions and the burdens of colonial rule.

The anti-imperialists did not get their plebiscite, so they had to resort to more conventional methods of attempting to influence public opinion. The Anti-Imperialist League increased the volume of its literature, issuing thousands of copies of several different *Broadsides* in the early weeks of December. These contained extracts from various speeches, sermons, and articles written by many of the League's vice presidents and urged the nation's citizens to make their opposition to imperialism known to their representatives in Congress.[40] Whether in response to expressions of public opinion, such as the Anti-Imperialist League endeavored to elicit against annexation, out of strong personal conviction on the matter, or both, Senator George Vest of Missouri on the first day of the new session of Congress (December 1) introduced a resolution to the effect that "under the Constitution of the United States no power is given to the Federal Government to acquire territory to be held

---

39. Andrew Carnegie, "Commercial Expansion Vs. Colonial Expansion: An Open Letter," *Anti-Imperialist Leaflet No. 11* (Washington, n.d., but undoubtedly Dec., 1898).

40. *Anti-Imperialist Broadside Nos. 2, 3, and 4* (Washington, Dec., 1898 and Jan., 1899).

and governed permanently as colonies." [41] Vest's resolution was notable, not only because it was the first of several similar anti-imperialist resolutions (e.g. those of Senators Mason, Bacon, Lindsay, Allen and McEnery), but also because it occasioned most of the recorded debate over the Philippines, the actual debate over the treaty being conducted in the closed executive session.

The treaty of peace, around which all of the heated debate of these months ultimately revolved, was signed in Paris on December 10, 1898. It provided for the relinquishment of Spanish sovereignty over Cuba, and cession to the United States of Guam, Puerto Rico, and the Philippines; and the payment by the United States to Spain of twenty million dollars in connection with the last and most controversial piece of territory.[42] The following day Carman F. Randolph in considering the "Constitutional Aspects of Annexation" for the *Harvard Law Review* wrote: "Assuming that the annexation of the Philippines is embodied in the treaty, it is the most questionable project of domestic concern that a President has ever submitted to the Senate." [43]

Senator Vest reiterated this view the next day in his long speech supporting his own resolution. He based his constitutional argument largely upon Chief Justice Taney's opinion in the famous Dred Scott case. He emphasized the anti-imperialists' fundamental contention that "the colonial system . . . can exist in no free country, because it uproots and eliminates the basis of all republican institutions." [44] The debate continued sporadically in the Senate, and intensively in the nation at large, throughout the rest of December.

William Jennings Bryan, whose role in relation to the treaty was to be an enigmatic one, began in December to attack imperialism, but rather paradoxically not the treaty, wherever he

---

41. *Congressional Record,* 55th Congress, 3rd Session, p. 20.

42. See *Senate Document No. 62,* 55th Congress, 3rd Session (Washington, 1899).

43. Anti-Imperialist Scrapbook, Widener Library.

44. *Congressional Record,* 55th Congress, 3rd Session, pp. 93-96.

found an audience. On December 13 at Savannah, Georgia, he criticized an imperial policy for the United States, saying that the nation must forego a colonial policy or else abandon the concept that governments derive their just powers from the consent of the governed. Ten days later he spoke before the Women's Bimetalic League in Lincoln, Nebraska, on the subject of "The Flag," asking, although he was now on record as favoring the ratification of the treaty, "who will deny to our people the right to haul down the flag in the Philippines if they so desire?" The following week in his speech before the Nebraska Traveling Men's Club Bryan again attacked imperialism. "It has been the boast of our nation that right makes might; shall we abandon the motto of the republic and go back a century to the monarchical motto which asserts might makes right?" [45]

The question of the ratification of the treaty and the larger issue of imperialism, per se, were being discussed everywhere in the final month of the tumultuous year of 1898. Several papers at the annual meeting of the American Historical Association considered various sides of the matter. Professor Henry E. Bourne of Western Reserve, speaking on "Lessons from the Recent History of European Dependencies," observed that the "prospect that the Senate will ratify the action of the President in negotiating the transfer of Puerto Rico and the Philippines has aroused vague apprehensions for the future of our country, and has excited fears that we are not prepared successfully to solve the problem of controlling dependencies in the tropics." [46] Professor Simeon E. Baldwin of Yale delivered a

---

45. Bryan et al, *Republic or Empire, op. cit.,* pp. 13, 16, 17.

46. *Annual Report of the American Historical Association, 1898* (Washington, 1899), p. 303.

William L. Cowles, one of many perceptive foreign commentators who were intrigued by the phenomenon of American imperialism, writing at the same time (December, 1898), emphasized the same point about the United States being unprepared and unequipped for colonial rule.—"American Expansion and the Inheritance of the Race," *Fortnightly Review,* Vol. LXX, pp. 885-887.

paper whose title, typical of this era, reflected Germanic thoroughness—"The Constitutional Questions Incident to the Acquisition and Government by the United States of Island Territories." Striving to maintain proper scholarly objectivity, Professor Baldwin remarked that whether the Senate should ratify the treaty "is a question of political character, with the discussion of which this association has no concern." [47] However, Baldwin's speech demonstrated that the ratification of the treaty would cause many very grave problems.

For Finley Peter Dunne's Mr. Hennessy, as Dunne implied was the case with multitudes of average American citizens, these problems were easily resolved. " 'I know what I'd do if I was Mac [McKinley,]' said Mr. Hennessy. 'I'd hist a flag over th' Ph'lipeens, an' I'd take in th' whole lot iv thim.' 'An' yet,' said Mr. Dooley, ' 'tis not more than two months since ye learned whether they were islands or canned goods.' " The irrepressible Mr. Dooley also sought to set the befuddled Mr. Hennessy straight on the question of our trade with the Philippines, about which the imperialists talked at great length. It was all very simple, Mr. Dooley explained: "We import jute, hemp, cigar wrappers, sugar, an' fairy tales fr'm th' Ph'lipeens, an' export six-inch shells an' th' like." [48] Dunne's devastating Gallic wit, as expressed through the loquacious Mr. Dooley and his foil Hennessy, probably did as much to deflate the American militarists and imperialists as did the erudite treatises of the Boston Brahmins who formed such a force in the affairs of the Anti-Imperialist League.

However, among the nation's intelligentsia the speeches and writings of the latter were quite influential. Probably the most notable example of this at this particular time was Charles Francis Adams' address before the Lexington Historical Society on December 20, which was pointedly entitled "Imperialism and the Tracks of Our Forefathers." In this long scholarly pre-

---

47. *Ibid.,* p. 315.
48. Finley Peter Dunne, "Mr. Dooley on the Philippines," in *Anti-Imperialist Broadside No. 2* (Dec., 1898).

sentation Adams examined the proposed policy of imperialism in the light of the Declaration of Independence, the Constitution, Washington's Farewell Address, and the Monroe Doctrine, remarking with approval that "on these principles of government and foreign policy we have as a people acted for more than seventy years." He analyzed the imperialists' principal arguments and found them to be either specious or inconsistent, and incompatible with our history, traditions, and institutions. He insisted that "it cannot escape our notice that on every one of the fundamental principles discussed—whether ethnic, economic, or political—we abandon the traditional and distinctively American grounds."

Adams' cogent critique of imperialism rang down the curtain on what he said seemed to be "destined to pass into the long record as the Year of Surprises." [49] It was certainly a year that would long stand out as notable. The United States had fought its first foreign war in half a century, had acquired in Hawaii its first major overseas possession, and now by the terms of the Treaty of Paris was to become a full-fledged imperial power.

---

49. Charles Francis Adams, *Imperialism and the Tracks of Our Forefathers, op. cit.,* pp. 13, 20, 9.

CHAPTER 12

Imperialism Ratified

The debate did not even pause with the termination of 1898. In fact, Schurz wrote to Adams on New Year's Day in 1899, sending him a copy of the speech ("The Issue of Imperialism") he was about to give in Chicago. He said that he meant it to be "a sort of vade-mecum for speakers or writers on our side of the question, who will find in it answers . . . to every argument brought forward on the other side." [1] Schurz's speech at the University of Chicago, which with Laughlin, Tolman, Von Holst, and E. B. Smith on the faculty was a hotbed of anti-imperialism, was, as advertised, a virtual compendium of anti-imperialist thought.

In this lengthy oration, delivered the very day that the Treaty of Paris was submitted to the Senate for consideration, Schurz applied all of his great forensic skill to a devastating attack upon imperialism. He forcefully reiterated his many cogent anti-imperialist arguments, which we have considered in his earlier speeches and articles. He emphasized the myriad of political, administrative, racial, religious, military, fiscal, and other problems inherent in colonialism. But above all he insisted that if the United States embarked upon a career of colonial aggrandizement, it would completely forfeit its "moral credit" with the world.

Andrew Carnegie had read an advance copy of the address and was, like many other people, very impressed by it and

---

1. Bancroft, *op. cit.*, Vol. VI, p. 1.

felt that it should be widely disseminated. "Print your speech," he wrote enthusiastically to Schurz, "in pamphlet form and distribute it and I will be your banker. That is the way in which I can aid the good work. You have brains and I have dollars. I can devote some of my dollars to spreading your brains." [2] Carnegie put both his dollars and his brains to work in behalf of anti-imperialism during the crucial month of January. He expressed his strong anti-imperialist views in a thoughtful article entitled "Americanism versus Imperialism." He contended that these two entities were inherently antithetical, saying that he regarded "possessions in the Far East as fraught with nothing but disaster to the Republic." [3]

Senator George Vest, on whose resolution much of the debate in the Senate centered, completely concurred with Carnegie; and he carried his objections to annexation of the Philippines from the floor of the Senate to the pages of the same review utilized as a sounding-board by the steel master. "It is surely time," he said dramatically, "to ask whether the American people are ready to follow these apostles of the New Evangel in revolutionizing our government, and trampling upon the teachings and policies which made us great and prosperous." The irate Senator felt that they certainly should not be; for "nothing but foreign complications, ruinous expenditure, social and political deterioration, and the destruction of free institutions can come from annexation." [4]

While some Senators were making their anti-imperialist views known through the press, others confined themselves to offering opposition to forcible annexation where it would do the most good—in the Senate itself. The Treaty of Paris, after being duly signed by President McKinley, was submitted to the Senate on January 4. It was then immediately referred to the Committee on Foreign Affairs, whose chairman, Cushman K. Davis,

---

2. *Ibid.*, Vol. V, p. 531.

3. Andrew Carnegie, "Americanism versus Imperialism," (Part I), *North American Review,* Vol. CLXVIII (Jan., 1899), p. 1.

4. G. C. Vest, "Objections to Annexing the Philippines," *North American Review,* Vol. CLXVIII (Jan., 1899), pp. 112, 116.

was one of the chief architects of the treaty. While Davis and his committee were going perfunctorily through the motions of examining the treaty, William E. Mason of Illinois startled his Republican colleagues by submitting a resolution condemning forced annexation [5] and by strongly criticizing the immorality of imperialism. Mason questioned the stand of his party on imperialism, and predicted (completely inaccurately as it turned out) that the next Republican national convention would declare in favor of Philippine independence. "God Almighty," he exclaimed, "help the party that seeks to give civilization and Christian liberty hypodermically with 13-inch guns." In the course of the Senate debates Senators Hoar and Caffery emphasized the same general idea, the former lamenting that "some of our worthy clergymen of late [have been] preaching the new commandment to do evil that good may come," and the latter insisting that "Christianity cannot be advanced by force." [6]

Senator Mason was obviously incensed by what he felt to be a hypocritical stance on the part of many of his fellow party members and indignantly demanded: "Will you tell me, please, how grand larceny and 'criminal aggression' become high Christian civilization in the Philippines? Is there," he inquired wryly, "some place in the Pacific Ocean where we change the code of ethics and good morals as we change the calendar and the ship's clocks in crossing?" [7] In spite of the views expressed here, Mason eventually voted for the treaty. This sort of about-face, which can be seen in the case of several Senators, tends to strengthen the contention of some Senators and other contemporary commentators that extreme methods were utilized to induce men to vote for the treaty.

---

5. *Congressional Record,* 55th Congress, 3rd Session, p. 528.
6. *Ibid.,* pp. 530, 500, 438.
The Anti-Imperialist League felt that this facet of the debate was so important that all of *Anti-Imperialist Broadsides No. 5* and *No. 6,* published during January, were devoted to "The Moral and Religious Aspects of the So-Called Imperial Policy—Discussed by Representative Clergymen of Many Denominations."
7. *Congressional Record, op. cit.,* p. 531.

The recorded senatorial debate was ostensibly in reference to the various resolutions, since the discussion of the treaty, per se, was veiled by the covert nature of the executive session. However, as Senator Lodge, the administration's principal and very influential strategist on the treaty, pointed out, the debate on the resolutions was extensive and covered quite well "the broad question of policy involved in the ratification of the treaty." [8] Actually, the recorded debate regarding the basic question of imperialism varied very little from that which we examined in detail in the case of Hawaii in Chapter VIII. The position of most of the participants was largely the same as the previous summer. The most notable exception was Senator Hoar; so it might be well to consider his position.

On January 9 Hoar spoke in support of Vest's resolution. "The question before us," he solemnly stated, voicing the opinion of all the nation's anti-imperialists, "is the greatest ever discussed in this chamber from the beginning of our Government." He delineated the personal difficulty of his position. "I am," he said, "one of those men who believe that little that is great, or good, or permanent for a free people can be accomplished without the instrumentality of party.[9] And I have believed religiously, and from my soul, for half a century in the great doctrines and principles of the Republican Party." It was his feeling that the Republican party was on this issue foolishly casting aside all reason and decency. He said that if he had to part company with his party on this issue, he would do so, being "confident that I am in the company of the framers of the Constitution [and] the signers of the Declaration of Independence." [10]

---

8. *Ibid.*, p. 959.

9. This statement, combined with his distrust of Bryan which was so intensified by what he felt to be Bryan's hypocritical position on the treaty, very largely explains why Hoar, although abhorring imperialism, supported McKinley in 1900.

10. *Congressional Record, op. cit.,* p. 544.

Gamaliel Bradford wrote a letter concerning Hoar's courageous action, which was published in the *Boston Evening Transcript* of

"DONE GONE EXPANDED"

George Washington Dewey—I cannot tell a lie, Granther. I took
them with my little cruiser. We've already got them. The question
is, what are we going to do with them. Don't think you mentioned
that.

Cartoon by Charles L. Bartholomew in the *The Minneapolis Journal*,
January 10, 1899.

Senator Hoar undoubtedly spoke out so forthrightly at this
time because he now felt that he and his fellow anti-imperialists,
although in the right, were losing ground in their battle to defeat
the treaty. One will recall that only two months earlier Hoar
had confidently claimed that a *majority* of the Senate would

Jan. 16, 1899: We should "give every support to Senator Hoar in
the magnificent stand which he has taken, of which the splendor is
only enhanced by the painful sacrifice it has involved in relation
to his party."

oppose the treaty. What had happened in the interim? For one thing the McKinley administration had begun to, and would increasingly, exert considerable pressure in behalf of the treaty. Arthur W. Dunn, a contemporary newspaperman, quoted Senator Gorman's complaint: "It's an outrage the way Hanna and his friends are working this treaty through the Senate. If an honest vote could be taken, I doubt whether there is a bare majority for the treaty; but . . . every interest which can be reached [is] bringing pressure on Senators in the most shameful manner." [11]

It was to be expected that the administration would go all out to obtain passage of its own treaty, but it received unexpected aid from William Jennings Bryan which helped to provide the exceedingly slim margin by which the treaty was ultimately ratified. Bryan had a variety of public explanations for his apparently paradoxical behavior of denouncing imperialism while simultaneously urging his followers to vote for ratification of a treaty which patently involved the United States in an imperial policy. When one contemplates these explanations, he finds that they blithely ignore significant facts and are often rather specious.

His ex post facto presentation of the matter in his memoirs displays the penchant of most autobiographers for rationalization and egotism. He says: "I have never regretted the position taken; on the contrary, I never showed more statesmanship." [12] He insists that if the treaty had not been ratified the Democrats would have borne the responsibility for any "dangers that arose during the continuation of the state of war." It was obvious, however, at the time that Spain was neither capable nor desirous

---

11. Arthur W. Dunn, *From Harrison to Harding* (New York, 1922), Vol. I, p. 282.

12. William Jennings and Mary Baird Bryan, *Memoirs of William Jennings Bryan* (Philadelphia, 1925), p. 121.

Some historians are more inclined to accept Bryan's self-appraisal. See Paolo Coletta, *William Jennings Bryan: Political Evangelist* (Lincoln, 1964), pp. 234-237.

of renewing the fighting and what was really at issue was the content of this particular treaty.

Another one of Bryan's important contemporary arguments was that the treaty really did not cede the Philippines to the United States but merely "severed the Philippine Islands from Spain." [13] This was simply fallacious. As the *Boston Evening Transcript* correctly pointed out at the time, if when the treaty was ratified "that little word 'cedes' remains in it, the Philippines will be as much a part of integral U.S. territory as Alaska, or California, or Massachusetts." [14]

There is no way of knowing precisely whether it was Bryan's tortuous reasoning on the matter that persuaded a number of his followers to change their votes, or whether there were more practical considerations of individual and party benefit involved, although the available evidence points to the latter conclusion. Richard F. Pettigrew, who was a member of the Senate at the time, stated:

> When the Spanish Treaty was pending in the Senate . . . and we believed that we had it defeated beyond a question, Bryan came to Washington . . . and urged a ratification of the treaty. . . . His chief argument was that should the Republicans not give . . . the Philippines their independence . . . such a course would and ought to drive the Republicans from power. . . .[15] Bryan thus made the ratification of the Spanish Treaty an act of political expediency. He was seeking political capital and he was willing to take it where he found it, without paying too much attention to nice questions of principle.[16]

Whether Bryan's enigmatic actions in regard to the treaty

---

13. Bryan *Memoirs*, p. 122.

14. *Boston Evening Transcript,* January 12, 1899.

15. Although Pettigrew was nominally a Republican, he was part of the small, radical "silver" wing of the party. He had by this time become persona non grata with the party regulars, and would not have been loath to see McKinleyism defeated in 1900.

16. R. F. Pettigrew, *Imperial Washington* (Chicago, 1922), pp. 270-271.

were based upon the Machievellian motives that Pettigrew and a number of other contemporary and later commentaries suggest is a moot point; but there is no doubt of the fact that when this dynamic and persuasive leader of the Democratic party joined forces on this issue with the already dominant Republicans that it did great damage to the cause of the treaty's opponents. They were greatly distressed by Bryan's performance and did their utmost to persuade him to change his stand on this vitally important matter. On January 9, the day that Hoar spoke out so eloquently in the Senate against the treaty, Andrew Carnegie cabled Bryan: "Our friends assure me votes enough were secured defeat treaty, but your advice shakes several—the two chief leaders against treaty tell me if you will acquiesce in your friends going with them as fixed, matter settled, reply free." [17]

Carnegie deplored the partisan spirit of Bryan's reply. He wrote in his autobiography: "I thought it unworthy of him to subordinate such an issue, fraught with deplorable consequences, to mere party politics. . . . I could not be cordial to him for years afterwards. He had seemed to me a man who was willing to sacrifice his country and his personal convictions for party advantage." [18] This attitude was shared by quite a few of the most outstanding anti-imperialists, and, coupled with Bryan's continued insistence on the silver issue, was to cost him their valuable support in the election of 1900.

By the middle of January Senator Hoar, like many others, began to realize that the chances of defeating the treaty were being crushed by the pressure being exerted by the administration on one side and Bryan on the other. On January 12 he wrote to Schurz: "It is impossible now to make a confident prediction of the outcome. Until Mr. Bryan spoke I thought we were pretty sure to defeat the treaty. . . . But Bryan has undoubtedly demoralized some of our Northwestern Democrats and one or two

17. W. S. Holt, *op. cit.,* p. 165.
18. Carnegie, *Autobiography, op. cit.,* p. 364.

of the Populists. I still hope to defeat the treaty although I confess to great anxiety and almost despondency." [19]

The coup de grâce to the hopes of the anti-imperialists was administered from abroad. On February 4, two days before the date which had been set for the vote on the treaty, fighting broke out between American and Filipino troops. This apparently caused some Senators who had been wavering to feel that it would now be craven on the part of the United States to withdraw. Senator Thomas M. Patterson of Colorado, in fact, later charged in a speech before the Massachusetts Reform Club that the administration had precipitated the conflict and "deliberately falsified . . . the official dispatches given to the public. . . ." The result was that "Senators who had stood against the treaty, incensed by what they were led to believe was a wanton, deliberate, and unprovoked assault upon the American army by Aguinaldo's forces, changed their purposes and voted for its ratification. The treaty was pulled through by fraud and dishonor." [20]

The administration's purposes were not as malevolent as Senator Patterson claims. The outbreak of hostilities, to the degree that it was the fault of the Americans, was caused more by ignorance and insensitivity (McKinley's provocative "Benevolent Assimilation" proclamation being a case in point), than by evil design. Patterson was correct, however, in implying that the episode was distorted in the American newspapers and the skirmish reported as a deliberate Filipino attack, which

---

19. Gillett, *op. cit.*, p. 225.

A meeting held in New York on Jan. 22, "for the purpose of protesting against the policy of imperialism," passed a resolution expressing "high appreciation and sincere thanks for the conspicuous services rendered to the American people by Senators Hoar, Hale, Mason, and Wellington [all regular Republicans] in preventing the new and dangerous policy of imperialism from being forced through the Senate of the United States without proper and adequate discussion. . . ."—*Boston Evening Transcript,* Jan. 23, 1899.

20. Thomas M. Patterson, *The Fruits of Imperialism* (Boston, 1902), p. 9.

it certainly was not. The Filipinos did not want to fight at this time and quickly asked for a truce, which the Americans refused to grant. The report of the matter may possibly have been an early case of "managed news." The army and the administration at a later date definitely did censor reports to give a favorable impression of affairs in the islands. The important thing here is that the way in which the news was presented to the Senate certainly was detrimental to the cause of the treaty's opponents.

Nevertheless, in spite of any and all machinations in favor of the treaty, the issue remained in doubt until the very end. When the suspense was finally ended and the vote taken on February 6, the margin of ratification proved to be the slimmest possible—one more than the requisite two-thirds majority. The actual vote was 57 to 27,[21] with two other negative and positive votes being paired.

Although a notable commentator on the treaty claims that "Democrats in general, and southern Democrats in particular, favored expansion," [22] the evidence would seem to point to a contrary conclusion. Twenty-four of the twenty-nine Senators in opposition were Democrats. This is a negative ratio of more than two to one of the Democratic votes on the treaty. Of the twenty-two Senators actually casting negative votes, an overwhelming majority—seventeen—were from southern or border states. We previously explored, in analyzing the votes on Hawaiian annexation, the racial and economic considerations which bolstered other motives in the case of many of the southern Senators. It should also be noted that four of the Democratic Senators (two from southern states and two from a border state) who voted for the treaty did so because they were persuaded by personal considerations which had nothing to do with

---

21. An analysis of the vote from a party standpoint shows, although the classification of a few of the Senators is not easy: 42 Republicans, 11 Democrats, 2 Populists and 2 Independents in favor; the negative votes are discussed in the text.

22. Paolo Coletta, "Bryan, McKinley, and the Treaty of Paris," *Pacific Historical Review,* Vol. XXVI (May, 1957), p. 132.

the treaty or anything related to it. Three of these four—Gray, McLaurin, and McEnery—were, as we have noted earlier in the book, very vocal critics of imperialism. In fact, the great majority of the Democratic Senators who voted against the treaty had been for many years and remained consistent foes of imperialism. This opposition, furthermore, was not passive, for many of them spoke and wrote forcefully, certainly conveying a sense of real conviction, against imperialism, and joined anti-imperialist organizations. Caffery from Louisiana and Tillman from South Carolina, for example, although they were not typical of the membership, were among the early officers of the Anti-Imperialist League.

The other five negative votes on the treaty were cast by three Republicans, a Populist, and a Fusionist.[23] The Republicans casting negative votes not only had to oppose, like the Democrats, the titular leader of their party and general public opinion, but also tremendous pressure and blandishments from the regular Republican party machinery, skillfully led by Henry Cabot Lodge—from Hoar's own state of Massachusetts. Their stand showed more than a little courage. Those who stood steadfast in their opposition were lauded by their anti-imperialist supporters outside of Congress. The Secretary of the Anti-Imperialist League, Erving Winslow, called them "the immortal twenty-nine [who] lost all but honor." [24]

Shortly before the treaty was voted upon, Senator McEnery

---

23. The twenty-nine opposition Senators were: Bacon (Ga.), Bate (Tenn.), Berry (Ark.), Caffery (La.), Chilton (Tex.), Cockrell (Mo.), Daniel (Va.), Gorman (Md.), Hale (Me.), Heitfeld (Id.), Hoar (Mass.), Jones (Ark.), Mallory (Fla.), Martin (Va.), Mills (Tex.), Mitchell (Wis.), Mouey (Miss.), Murphy (N.Y.), Pasco (Fla.), Pettigrew (S.D.), Rawlins (Utah), Roach (N.D.), Smith (N.J.), Tillman (S.C.), Turley (Tenn.), Turner (Wash.), and Vest (Mo.). White (Cal.) and Turpie (Ind.) were paired, but would have voted against the treaty.—*Journal of the Executive Proceedings of the Senate,* 55th Congress, 3rd Session, p. 1284.

24. Erving Winslow, "The Anti-Imperialist League," *The Independent,* Vol. LI, Part 2 (May 18, 1899), p. 1350.

of Louisiana had introduced a resolution, the general import of which was simply to leave the issue of the ultimate status of the islands open. The die-hard anti-imperialist faction attempted to put teeth into McEnery's rather nebulous resolution through an amendment offered by Senator August O. Bacon of Georgia, which would have expressly promised eventual independence to the Filipinos. The vote on this crucial amendment ended in a tie, which was broken only by the negative vote of Vice President Hobart. The emasculated McEnery resolution then passed by a vote of 26 to 22.[25]

Henry Cabot Lodge wrote to Theodore Roosevelt, saying that the battle over the treaty was "the closest, hardest fight I have ever known . . . probably we shall not see another in our time where there was so much at stake." [26] The battle over the League of Nations was yet to come.

It was probably natural, given the circumstances which Lodge describes and the closeness of the vote, that there should be many bitter and sorrowful postmortems concerning the vote by those on the losing side. Senator Hoar, who had labored so steadfastly against Philippine annexation, lamented that the treaty would have been defeated "but for Mr. Bryan's personal interposition in its behalf." He regretted that Senator Gray had not maintained his earlier strong opposition to the treaty [27] and that Speaker Reed had not felt it to be "his duty to remain in public life and lead the fight against it." [28]

Some other Senators were less judicious in their consideration of the matter. Senator Gorman intimated that bribery of a sort had been involved, and Senator Pettigrew charged that there was "open purchase of votes to ratify this treaty right on

---

25. *Congressional Record,* 25th Congress, 3rd Session, p. 1846-7.

26. Lodge (ed.), *Lodge-Roosevelt Correspondence, op. cit.,* Vol. I, pp. 391-392.

27. Hoar, Richard Olney, Grover Cleveland et al. also noted that McKinley not long after appointed Gray a Judge of the United States Circuit court. The implication is, of course, that this was either a bribe or a reward.

28. Hoar, *Autobiography, op. cit.,* Vol. II, p. 110.

the floor of the Senate." [29] Arthur Dunn corroborated these general charges and added some specific instances. He stated that Senator McEnery "was promised the appointment of a U.S. Judge of his choice. McLaurin of South Carolina was won over by being allowed to name postmasters in that state. Kenney of Delaware was squeezed by some sort of court proceeding in his state and had to vote for the treaty." [30]

Whether that single vote which was the final margin of passage for the treaty was cast because of administration pressure, bribery, the attack in the Philippines, Bryan's machinations, or simply personal conviction is probably destined to remain forever debatable, and the "moving finger" having writ, not all the ex post facto considerations and recriminations of the anti-imperialists could lure it back to cancel "half a line," or half a vote. The simple fact was that imperialism had, with the advice and consent of the Senate, been ratified.

29. Pettigrew, *Imperial Washington, op. cit.,* p. 206.
30. Dunn, *loc. cit.*

CHAPTER 13

Floodtide

Four days after the approval of the Treaty of Paris by the Senate, the Executive Committee of the Anti-Imperialist League issued a manifesto which stated that the ratification of the treaty would "afford no reason for any change of the purposes of the Anti-Imperialists in regard to the future of the Philippine Islands, nor will it in the least affect the clear duty of the Republic." The manifesto evinced the determination of the League to carry on vigorously with its fight against imperialism. The officers of the League vowed to redouble their efforts in the dissemination of literature, formation of new organizations, promotion of public meetings, and by "every proper means known to a free people . . . oppose the colonial idea." [1]

The Anti-Imperialist League held true to these resolves, and the year 1899 witnessed anti-imperialism in the United States at floodtide. Dozens of anti-imperialist leagues, associations, and clubs were organized; scores of mass meetings were held; hundreds of petitions were drawn up, speeches given and articles written; thousands of pieces of literature were distributed; and myriad Americans enlisted beneath the anti-imperialist banner.

The efforts of Professor Herman E. Von Holst, one of the League's vice presidents, were typical of the work of the anti-imperialist activists during this period. He spoke wherever he could find an audience and contributed many items to various

---

1. "Address Adopted by the Anti-Imperialist League," February 10, 1899.

periodicals. On the same day that the League's Executive Committee issued its resolute manifesto, Von Holst's critique of the disturbing vagueness of the McKinley administration's defense of its imperialist policy was published by the University of Chicago. He pointed out that the President's saying "destiny determines duty" had been widely applauded as indicating the policy which the nation must pursue whether it wanted to or not. The anti-imperialists objected vehemently to this type of Manifest Destiny mystique, and Von Holst dismissed McKinley's slogan as a clever bit of alliteration—"a vague-sounding phrase eminently fit to serve as a dazzling cloak to any vagaries." [2]

William Jennings Bryan, who in the estimation of many of the leaders of the anti-imperialist movement was as prone to vagaries as the opposition, continued to attack imperialism while attempting to justify his stand on the treaty. Speaking at a Democratic banquet at St. Paul, Minnesota, on February 14, he insisted that "the ratification of the treaty, instead of committing the United States to a colonial policy, really clears the way for the recognition of a Philippine republic." Again, speaking at the University of Michigan, he said that he "believed . . . that it was better to ratify the treaty and make the fight for Philippine independence before the American people." [3] The anti-imperialist leaders felt that Bryan's reasoning was specious and his stand on the treaty hypocritical; the majority of them never forgave him for supporting it, and this was to have a profound effect upon their role in the next election.

The anti-imperialists had hoped to thwart the growth of American imperialism directly by defeating the Treaty of Paris. When the treaty, with Bryan's help, was ratified, they then en-

---

2. Hermann E. Von Holst, "Some Lessons We Ought to Learn," *University of Chicago Record,* Vol. III, No. 46 (Feb. 10, 1899), pp. 300-301.

3. Bryan et al, *Republic or Empire, op. cit.,* pp. 28, 31. Former Minnesota Congressman Charles A. Towne, another leading figure in the anti-imperialist movement, also spoke at the University of Michigan several days later on Washington's birthday, informing his audience that if Washington were alive he would "certainly and steadily oppose imperialism."—"Lest We Forget," in *ibid.,* p. 327.

deavored to create a groundswell of public opinion which would persuade the government to give up the islands. Thus Senator Hoar, in replying to a memorial commending his stand in the Senate presented to him early in March by the Anti-Imperialist League, said that since imperialism would influence the entire future of the nation, the "voice of the whole people" should be heard on this great issue.[4]

Throughout the country the voices of thousands of anti-imperialists certainly were heard. During this period American newspapers were deluged with letters and other communications criticizing imperialism. In a typical letter to the *Boston Evening Transcript* Lewis G. Janes denounced the administration's Philippine policy as a great crime and said that it was the "sacred duty of every American citizen to let our public servants in Washington know in the clearest possible language that this crime against liberty and true American principles must stop at once."[5] Half way across the nation from Boston Hermann Von Holst analyzed the reasons for the "crime." He described a great variety of imperialists, one of the most interesting types being the "sham 'conscience' expansionist who, with hot moral indignation, brands as vile calumny the assertion that expansion is the intention of the expansionists."[6] This point is especially interesting, for the great majority of imperialists even after the passage of the Treaty of Paris steadfastly refused to acknowledge that the policy which they advocated was imperialistic. They even frequently eschewed the term "expansionist," a euphemism for "imperialist," preferring instead to talk vaguely of duty, destiny and the White Man's Burden.

Semantics and symbolism were a very important part of the great debate between the imperialists and anti-imperialists at this time. The issue of the flag and what it did and should stand

---

4. Anti-Imperialist Scrapbook, Widener Library, Harvard University.

5. *Boston Evening Transcript,* March 2, 1899.

6. Hermann E. Von Holst, "Some Expansionist Inconsistencies and False Analogies," *University of Chicago Record,* Vol. III, No. 50 (March 10, 1899), p. 341.

for was revived. The imperialists contended that the benighted Filipinos were indeed fortunate to dwell beneath this starry symbol of freedom; but the anti-imperialists claimed that for the Filipinos it in fact represented an alien and oppressive nation which was depriving them of their liberty and simply replacing Spanish tyranny with American tyranny.

That noble lady lifting her lamp beside the golden door was also thrust into the controversy. The Statue of Liberty was created to symbolize the fact that throughout its history the United States had been a marvelous example of a nation thoroughly committed to the ideal of enlightened popular self-government. As such, the United States had been an inspiration for the creation of this type of government throughout the world. The advocacy of imperialism embodied in the Treaty of Paris seemed to have changed all of this. The American people appeared to have forsaken their earlier sentiments and to be intent upon imposing U.S. rule by force over people who were meant to be free. This drastic alteration in attitude seemed to make a mockery of the Statue of Liberty.

Thornton Van Vliet in a mordant essay inquired, in the light of the present circumstances, whether something should not be done with the statue. Should it be dismantled and sent back to its donors with a candid acknowledgment that it no longer suited our condition? Should it be recast into a number of copies to be erected "in our conquered islands to impress the natives with the benevolence of our institutions?" Should a sword be placed in its hand in lieu of the lamp of truth and should it be called "Liberty Conquering the World?" Should the arm of the statue be lowered and its torch extinguished and its head bowed in shame until the nation should change its mind? "We ought," Van Vliet concluded with devastating simplicity, "to do something about this statue. As it now appears it is very inappropriate to the present situation and is an awkward object to have in sight." [7] It was just this type of search-

---

7. Thornton Van Vliet, "Liberty Enlightening the World," *New York Times,* March 13, 1899.

ing examination of the painful contradictions inherent in the adoption of an imperialist policy by the United States, which, when combined with the distasteful realities of colonialism in practice, eventually turned the tide against imperialism.

The leaders of the American labor movement were very active at this juncture in attempting to combat the expansionist policy. For example, John W. Hayes, the General Secretary-Treasurer of the Knights of Labor and one of the officers of the Washington Anti-Imperialist League, issued a pamphlet addressed to the membership of the union in which he vigorously attacked American imperialism and cited with approval various anti-imperialist speeches in Congress, especially those of Congressmen Cockran and Carmack.[8] This support from organized labor and from various members of Congress at this time was particularly helpful to the anti-imperialist cause; for Richard Olney wrote to Grover Cleveland on March 22 that President McKinley was maneuvering "to be in a position to disclaim having any policy of his own and to unload the whole responsibility upon Congress."[9]

In addition to the labor question two other issues were prevalent at this time. The first was the constitutional question. The anti-imperialists contended that imperialism simply was unconstitutional. We have already viewed various aspects of the constitutional debate in our consideration of the protracted controversies, both inside and outside of Congress, over the annexation of Hawaii and the Philippines. Moorfield Storey, renowned for his legal acumen, reviewed many of the salient points in a long letter to the *Boston Evening Transcript*, which was subsequently reprinted as part of *Anti-Imperialist Broadside No. 7.* Storey's "letter" was really a heavily documented essay on constitutional law. It was originally conceived as a reply to Henry Cabot Lodge's speech in the Senate in January defending the constitutionality of imperialism.

---

8. Croffut Papers. Cockran was also an Anti-Imperialist League vice-president.

9. Cleveland Papers.

Storey disagreed sharply with Lodge in regard to the relationship of the Constitution to insular possessions, a question
which was several years later to be officially, if nebulously, resolved in the "Insular Cases." The gist of Storey's long and
involved argument, in which he cited Justices Curtis, Bradley,
Gray, Chief Justice Marshall, the 14th and 15th amendments,
and other sources, was simply that we could not govern the
Philippines as a colony without contravening the Constitution
and established precedent.[10] Senator Hoar, in a more succinct
communication to the *Boston Herald* on March 31 sustained
Storey, and stated simply but emphatically that "governing subject peoples is not a constitutional end and there is, therefore,
no constitutional warrant for that purpose."

The other matter which was especially emphasized at this
time, and which caused the anti-imperialists continuing concern,
was what we would call today a "credibility gap." Soon after
the United States occupied the Philippine Islands, news from
this area began to be censored. Newspapers at home, with the
strong American tradition of freedom of the press, were under-
standably very critical of this practice. One of the earliest critiques of this appeared in the *Boston Evening Transcript* on
January 17, while the Treaty of Paris was still being very actively debated in the Senate. The *Transcript* observed that the
administration had discovered that what was occurring in the
islands was "not favorably affecting the American mind toward
the treaty" and had, therefore, ordered the War Department
to describe the events "in such colors as best suits the purposes
of the administration."

Allowing the people access only to official and carefully constructed news releases from the islands did not sit well with
many Americans. Even after the treaty had been ratified, complaints about censorship continued and actually swelled in
volume. A typical example is the angry letter from John C.
Kimball to the *Transcript*. "It seems to me," he wrote, "that the
action of our Government in keeping up a censorship over the

---

10. *Anti-Imperialist Broadside No. 7* (Boston, 1899).

news sent from Manila is very bad policy. . . . It illustrates how naturally war, even in a free country, carries with it the methods of despotism." [11]

Early in April the *Transcript* took up this controversial subject once more. It noted with approval that Anti-Imperialist League officer Albert S. Parsons "speaks out strongly against censorship as being an evil adjunct of imperialism." Parsons complained in a statement which has an exceedingly modern ring that the country was experiencing a censorship of news from abroad "like that usual in Spain and Russia." He said disgustedly that if the American people submitted to one-man power, to censorship, and to being taxed to obtain sovereignty over men on the other side of the globe, they were, perhaps, better fitted for life in an empire than a republic. He predicted, however, that they "will soon awake, and woe to the party or to the man who has attempted to stop their ears and close their eyes." He went on to mention that an Anti-Imperialist meeting would be held in Tremont Temple, "where that grand old man, covered with honors as a Governor of this state, as a Senator, as Secretary of the Treasury, as a citizen and as a patriot, George S. Boutwell, will eloquently plead for the America of the fathers. Let the first resolution passed there be a demand that censorship be removed, that the American people may have all the facts and then decide what they wish done in the Philippines." [12]

The meeting in question was held the night after Parsons' lengthy critique of censorship was printed in the *Transcript*. It was one of the most important anti-imperialist assemblies of the year. The hall was filled; and the platform was thronged with the regional anti-imperialist leaders, including Thomas Wentworth Higginson, Winslow Warren, Patrick A. Collins, James P. Munroe, Albert S. Parsons, Francis A. Osborn, Pro-

---

11. Kimball's letter was published in expanded form by the Anti-Imperialist League in May under the title *Uncensored Manila News* (Boston, 1899).

12. *Boston Evening Transcript,* April 3, 1899.

fessor Charles E. Fay, Colonel C. R. Codman, Judge Asa French, Rev. George C. Lorimer, Erving Winslow, and Gamaliel Bradford.

The meeting was formally convened in "the name of liberty to protest against the Philippine policy." Albert E. Pillsbury presided. In his opening remarks Pillsbury pointed out that less than a year earlier the nation had declared war against Spain "in the name of liberty and humanity for her barbarous treatment of the Cubans. Today we are doing in the Philippines what we made war upon Spain for doing in Cuba. We are laying waste the country with fire and sword, burning villages and slaughtering the inhabitants, because they will not submit to our rule."

Robert Morse, James Dunbar, Thomas Livermore, and Herbert Parsons all joined the chairman in condemning the policy which had led to the internecine struggle going on in the Philippines. Parsons said he believed that as soon as the American people were made fully aware of the facts they would denounce the war and call for a policy which was more consistent with the "Declaration of Independence, the Constitution, the Farewell Address, and the Gettysburg speech."

The principal speaker of the meeting, George S. Boutwell, pointed out that Congress had not declared war against the Filipinos, so the responsibility for its prosecution rested solely upon the administration. He stated that it would have been much better for all concerned had the United States allowed the Filipinos to set up an independent republic. He said that even those who favored imperialism on a missionary or commercial basis could not be pleased with the present situation.

Boutwell denounced the conflict in the Philippines as an "aggressive, unjustifiable, cruel war." He charged that in engaging in a war with Aguinaldo's forces we were actually betraying our former allies—people who expressed sentiments "worthy of the age of Jefferson and the lips of Lincoln" and who had been led to believe that we had come as liberators not as conquerors.

In behalf of the Anti-Imperialist League, Boutwell submitted a plan calling for the immediate suspension of hostilities in the Philippines and aid to the Filipinos in forming a government of their own, which would then be recognized as an independent and equal state in the community of nations. Boutwell solemnly declared that this would be the League's stand, for "whether it is heeded or derided, it has in it the quality of immortality." [13] Formal resolutions incorporating this plan were unanimously adopted by the meeting, and the League never wavered from this position.

The other major anti-imperialist conference of this period was held in Chicago at the end of April. The notice convoking the meeting was signed by scores of prominent people, including Henry Wade Rogers, Jane Addams, Edwin B. Smith, Hermann Von Holst, James B. Angell, and J. Lawrence Laughlin. The purpose of the meeting was stated as being "to protest against American imperialism and especially against the attempt to subjugate by force the inhabitants of the Philippine Islands."

The "Liberty Meeting" convened in the Central Music Hall in Chicago on April 30. A great percentage of those participating in the program—much like the present-day anti-Vietnam War groups and ideologically rather in accord with them—were academicians, clergymen and social workers. The president of Northwestern University, Henry Wade Rogers, presided. The tenor of the meeting was very similar to the one held earlier in Boston. Rogers, in his opening remarks, pointed out that the anti-imperialists were not opposed to the McKinley administration, per se, but simply to its policy of imperialism. Rogers, a legal scholar, denied that the United States had any legal, constitutional, or moral right to hold the Philippines. The only just solution to the present imbroglio, Rogers suggested, echoing the resolutions of the Boston meeting, was to call a halt to the fighting and help the natives "to establish their own government."

---

13. *Protest Against the Philippine Policy* (Boston, 1899), pp. 3-29.

The Rev. Jenkin Lloyd Jones in his address said that it was distinctly adverse to our traditional principles to oppress those striving for freedom, and that it would be far better to lower the American flag in the Philippines when to do so would "better represent the rights of humanity." Professor J. Lawrence Laughlin of the University of Chicago took up the commercial arguments of the imperialists. He contended that contrary to the imperialists' claims there actually would be very little commercial gain from possession of the Philippines, and what little there might be would be at the expense of the American worker and taxpayer. Edwin B. Smith, Jane Addams, Sigmund Zeisler, and Bishop Spaulding followed Laughlin upon the platform, and all denounced the war and subjugation of the Filipinos as a stain upon the honor of the United States.[14]

At the conclusion of this spirited meeting, a committee headed by Professor William G. Hale presented a long resolution, which was overwhelmingly approved by the assembly. The trenchant criticism of the resolution embodied the essence of the anti-imperialist position at this time and for several years to come. The issues mentioned here were to have an increasingly profound effect upon American public opinion after the turn of the century. The anti-imperialists constantly hammered away at the points made in the resolution: that imperialism is inherently wrong; that it leads inevitably to cruelty, militarism, and despotism; that it represents a form of slavery for the subject peoples; that it is antithetical to the basic tenets of the American creed as expressed in the Declaration of Independence and the Constitution; that McKinley himself had earlier admitted that forcible annexation was despicable; that the United States was adopting the very methods for which it had severely censured Spain and had gone to war over Cuba; and that it was egregiously hypocritical and dishonorable to turn a war that had been announced as a crusade for humanity into a war of conquest and aggrandizement.

---

14. *Chicago Liberty Meeting* (Chicago, 1899), pp. 1, 12, 14, 50.

The meetings in Boston and Chicago did much to stimulate public interest in the anti-imperialist cause. Moorfield Storey later wrote to Edwin B. Smith congratulating him for his instrumental role in convoking the Chicago conference and commenting that "such meetings . . . are powerful forces, and they must continue until the conscience of the people is fully awakened." [15]

The anti-imperialists were quite active in a variety of ways in the spring of 1899 in their attempt to awaken the American people's conscience to the Philippine situation. They increased the circulation of their literature, stepped up their campaign of correspondence to the editors of the major city newspapers, held hundreds of local meetings patterned on those in Boston and Chicago which we have noted, and fought "the colonial idea and the arguments of its friends" through the "active propaganda" of 30,000 members of the Anti-Imperialist League spread throughout the nation.[16]

The propaganda of one of the 30,000 was to prove extraordinarily effective, if in an unexpected way, and was to cause the League, which questioned its wisdom, a certain amount of consternation. Edward Atkinson, one of the group of original founders of the Anti-Imperialist League, decided to send some of the melodramatic anti-imperialist pamphlets which he had composed to the troops stationed in the Philippines. On April 22 he wrote to Washington requesting the government to send him the addresses of five or six hundred officers and men so that he could send them his anti-war pamphlets.

Atkinson's request for this list was not granted, and it was intimated that his materials, in any case, would not be sent to the Philippines through the U.S. Mail. Thereupon, Atkinson mailed copies of three of his pamphlets—"The Cost of a National Crime," "The Hell of War and Its Penalties," and "Crim-

---

15. Storey to Smith, June 27, 1899, Storey Papers, Library of Congress. This letter was subsequently printed as *Anti-Imperialist Leaflet No. 20* (Washington, no date).

16. Erving Winslow, "The Anti-Imperialist League," *The Independent*, Vol. LI (May, 1899), p. 1350.

inal Aggression: By Whom Committed?" [17]—to a number of
men who were prominently connected with affairs in the islands:
Admiral George Dewey, Professor Jacob G. Schurman, Professor Dean Worcester,. Generals Otis, Lawton, and Miller, and
J. F. Bass, correspondent for *Harper's Weekly.*

Atkinson's stated purpose was "to test the right of citizens

WONDER IF HE CAN SEE THE POINT?
Cartoon by Charles L. Bartholomew in *The Minneapolis Journal*,
April 6, 1899.

---

17. These pamphlets pilloried the McKinley Administration for
causing an unnecessary, costly and cruel war. They were replete with
sensational tales of horror, widespread disease, needless destruction
of homes, crops, and livestock, the "water cure," orders to "take
no prisoners," and general brutality. Edward Atkinson, *The Anti-Imperialist* (Brookline, Mass., 1899).

of the United States to the free use of the mail"; [18] but he undoubtedly also felt that no matter how the affair turned out it would publicize the anti-imperialist cause. This it certainly did. Postmaster General Charles E. Smith declared the pamphlets "seditious," had them removed from the mails in San Francisco, and said that they could not be mailed to the Philippines. The matter quickly became a cause célèbre, involving the issues of freedom of speech and the mails in a democracy, as opposed to an imperial state. The Postmaster General's action played right into Atkinson's hands; for the latter was flooded with requests for his controversial pamphlets.

Atkinson then announced in May that he would publish a periodical entitled *The Anti-Imperialist*, in each issue of which his three most controversial articles would be repeated, accompanied by similar propaganda. This curious publication appeared as advertised, and Atkinson continued his strenuous campaign of baiting the McKinley Administration.

This actually provided the most notable anti-imperialist phenomenon of the period, although the other officers of the League continued to busy themselves with less flamboyant writings and speeches throughout the summer. On June 22 Atkinson wrote to journalist Charles Nordhoff, who had earlier been declared persona non grata in Hawaii for similar anti-imperialist activities, saying that he was trying to stir the Administration up again "to provoke another attack." [19] Again, early in September Atkinson wrote to fellow Anti-Imperialist League vice president Herbert Welsh saying that he had written a new pamphlet, which he termed his "strongest bid yet for a limited residence in Fort Warren." [20]

The Secretary of the recently formed Washington Anti-Imperialist League, William A. Croffut, took a cue from At-

---

18. Atkinson, "Prospectus for *The Anti-Imperialist*," leaflet, dated May 12, 1899, in Atkinson Papers, Massachusetts Historical Society.

19. Atkinson Papers.

20. Welsh Papers, Pennsylvania Historical Society. Fort Warren was a Federal penitentiary.

kinson and on September 22 wrote a sarcastic letter to Postmaster General Charles E. Smith, informing him that he was
printing quite a lot of anti-imperialist literature. He taunted
Smith by pointing out that the literature was almost entirely the
work of eminent Republicans such as Senators Mason, Hoar,
Hale, Wellington and Henderson, George Boutwell, Andrew
Carnegie, John Sherman et al. "The demand for this literature
is not yet universal," he said, "and I write to ask if it is practicable for you to issue an order forbidding its circulation in the
mails that go to 'our new possessions?' Such a prohibition would
cause an enormous demand for it, and thus greatly promote
general hostility to the cruel and wicked war against the Filipinos." [21] Smith was undoubtedly very annoyed, but he wisely
refused to give the opposition more ammunition by issuing the
type of decree which he had done in the earlier Atkinson case.

Atkinson continued his agitation during the autumn. In September he began an "anti-imperial chain." He published a leaflet with this title which described his publication *The Anti-
Imperialist* ("which is opposed to tropical expansion and to the
present warfare in the Philippines"), and which solicited sub-
scriptions. There were coupons for people to clip and mail to
others, who were to make additional copies and send them on,
thus building "an anti-imperial chain." Atkinson stated that he
"had been in some measure compelled to conduct this publication by the action of members of the Cabinet in singling him
out by personal defamation." [22] The leaflet also sought information regarding people in various locations throughout the country
who would organize anti-imperialist committees of correspondence, hold meetings, and work for the election of anti-imperialists to Congress.

Some of Atkinson's histrionics did not appeal to some of
the officers of the Anti-Imperialist League and they felt that it
would be wise for the League to disclaim official responsibility
for his actions. In spite of the official disclaimer the League

21. Croffut Papers.
22. *Anti-Imperial Chain,* leaflet (Boston, September, 1899),
Atkinson Papers.

and Atkinson kept up a close relationship. Atkinson wrote that "all facts, addresses, and suggestions which come to him are placed also at the disposal of the Anti-Imperialist League, to which his own work is subsidiary." [23] Also, in mid-October the *New York Evening Post* reported: "Atkinson is in constant receipt of letters from all parts of the country, with money and requests for literature. These are sent to the office of the League, as his literature is largely handled from there." [24]

The month of October was a particularly memorable one for the anti-imperialists, because it was at this time that the American Anti-Imperialist League, which was supposed to become the institutional leader of the movement, was founded. The convention at which the American League was founded was planned at a meeting in Boston on August 15. At this meeting Anti-Imperialist League President George Boutwell reviewed the history of the movement since the founding of the original League. He pointed out that many additional leagues had since been founded throughout the country and observed that "these organizations, as a whole, contain an array of names such as has not been brought together in support of a common cause since the signing of the Declaration of Independence." [25]

A call went out from the Boston meeting for the nation's anti-imperialist leadership to convene at the Central Music Hall in Chicago on October 17-18. The response was a very enthusiastic one in all respects. The *New York Evening Post* commented upon the "determined spirit," fervor and dedication of the delegates. "These meetings," it reported, "recalled vividly the 'old slavery days.' There was the same outburst of pent-up feeling, the same settled determination to sacrifice everything

---

23. *Ibid.*

24. *New York Evening Post,* "Special Anti-Imperialist Supplement," October 18, 1899, p. 2. There was, in general, a great demand for anti-imperialist literature at this time.—See Dana Estes' (who published much of the Anti-Imperialist League's material) comments upon this in a letter (Oct. 7, 1899) to W. A. Croffut. Croffut Papers.

25. Boutwell, "In the Name of Liberty," Boutwell Papers, Massachusetts Historical Society.

to the cause of human rights, to wipe out the stain put on the American escutcheon by this war against a people struggling for liberty, and to sink all party differences in pursuance of this end." [26]

In regard to the political composition of the gathering, the *Post* stated that "at least three-fourths of the active participants were Republicans who had never been Mugwumps, and all except the merest fraction voted for McKinley in 1896. The old-line Mugwumps were relatively few in number, but in the person of Carl Schurz counted for a good deal." [27] The *Post*'s statement, however, is somewhat misleading: for J. Sterling Morton, Secretary of Agriculture under Cleveland, presided over the meeting, and the dozen principal speakers of the two-day meeting included the following prominent Democrats and Independents: former Governor Boies of Iowa, ex-Congressman Charles A. Towne of Minnesota, Congressman Bourke Cockran of New York, Edward Atkinson, Winslow Warren, Louis Ehrich, and Edwin B. Smith. It is true that these men were all economic conservatives and all probably voted for McKinley in 1896 in reaction against Bryan's radicalism. Nevertheless, they were not members of the Republican party. In attempting to demonstrate that the meeting was not anti-Republican (it was actually truly bipartisan), the *Post* distorted the picture the other way.

The *Post*, however, was completely correct when it stated that Schurz's vigorous speech was the high point of the meeting. "A serious trouble of conscience," Schurz said, "disturbs the American heart about this war." He pilloried the Administration for evading the principle underlying the Teller Amendment. He ridiculed the imperialist contention that if we did not keep the Philippines, another power would seize and exploit them. Even if the threat were a real one, the United States could secure an international agreement to accord the Philippines neutral status as was the case with Belgium and Switzerland in Europe.

---

26. *New York Evening Post,* October 21, 1899
27. *Ibid.*

Schurz took up the commercial aspect of the question. He asserted that he was not in sympathy with those "who would sacrifice our national honor and the high ideals of the Republic . . . for a mere matter of dollars and cents." He felt that even if some people would do this, in addition to being immoral, it was impractical. Expressing the usual laissez-faire economic orientation of the anti-imperialists, Schurz ridiculed the "barbarous notion that in order to have a profitable trade with a country we must own it."

Schurz, in a very telling observation concerning the difference between the imperialists and anti-imperialists, pointed out that he had addressed himself to people's reason "without any appeal to prejudice and passion." He inquired whether the anti-imperialists might not ask their opponents to answer the many arguments which he had raised in his long speech in a similar manner, instead of simply assailing them with "wild cries of 'treason' and 'lack of patriotism' and what not?"

The astute old German-American captured much of the nature of American imperialism in his incisive consideration of those who justified imperialism in terms of "destiny, burden, and the flag." Schurz concluded this notable speech by saying that he was confident that the American people were "too wise not to detect the false pride, or the dangerous ambitions, or the selfish schemes which so often hide themselves under the deceptive cry of mock patriotism." [28]

Schurz's speech was very well received. The *New York Evening Post* reported that the audience "constantly interrupted him with shouts of commendation." [29] The following week, William Croffut wrote to Schurz, praising his "great speech in Chicago," and saying: "We have read almost everything that has been published by the Anti-Imperialist League on the burning question, and yours seems to be the most comprehensive and

---

28. Carl Schurz, *The Policy of Imperialism* (Chicago, 1899), pp. 3-26.

29. *New York Evening Post,* "Special Anti-Imperialist Supplement," Oct. 18, 1899, p. 2.

effective statement that has yet been made. In your varied and eventful career you have never done more valuable work than now." [30]

Schurz's speech can be viewed as the high-water mark of the floodtide of active anti-imperialism in the United States. The last of the principal anti-imperialist leagues was founded at the Chicago meeting. Membership in these organizations was reaching its zenith. Enthusiasm for the cause was very high. The war in the Philippines provided a dramatic and immediate example of the problems that the anti-imperialists claimed were inherent in imperialism. The anti-imperialist leadership was at its most vigorous stage. The ranks had not yet begun to be thinned, as they soon would be, by the death of the Anti-Imperialist League's original officers. The anti-imperialist leadership was united in a way that it would never be again. The issue of imperialism now was clearly defined. It would soon be clouded by the numerous exigencies of practical politics in the forthcoming presidential election year.

---

30. Croffut to Schurz, Oct. 25, 1899, Croffut Papers, Library of Congress.

CHAPTER 14

Scylla and Charybdis

The immediate and crucial concern in the mind of virtually every anti-imperialist in the first year of the twentieth century was the relationship of imperialism to the presidential election. The anti-imperialists looked forward to the election as the best opportunity for repudiating the imperialist policy. An interesting combination of personalities, ideologies, and events, however, frustrated this desire.

The leaders of the anti-imperialist movement began their attack well before the election year. Writing in May, 1899, the Anti-Imperialist League's Secretary, Erving Winslow, in an attempt to influence party leaders and public opinion, stated that "It is already sufficiently obvious to many of us that whatever leader with a single heart opposes imperialism at home and abroad . . . will be the next President of the United States." [1]

The following September William A. Croffut, the Secretary and founder of the Washington Anti-Imperialist League, wrote a fascinating letter on this subject to William Jennings Bryan, the most likely contender for the nomination of the Democratic party. This letter, which displays considerable political sagacity, highlights what was to be the most crucial facet of the election. "Imperialism," Croffut wrote,

---

Material in this chapter is reprinted with permission from the *Pacific Historical Review,* Vol. VI (May, 1967).

1. Erving Winslow, 'The Anti-Imperialist League," *The Independent, op. cit.,* p. 1350.

is certainly to be the great issue next summer. If there were no other issue than that I believe you would be elected, and I beg you to think profoundly before encumbering the platform with anything else. If you will leave in abeyance the definite demand for free silver, I don't believe anything can beat you. If that demand is explicitly reiterated, you cannot carry Massachusetts, Connecticut or New York. You will be fifty electoral votes short and our country will be cursed with a continuation of this monstrous and wicked policy. Let us be politic this time, especially in questions where assertion has been had and where your position can not be doubtful.[2]

This was good advice that Croffut offered, but Bryan would not accept it; and the combination of economic radicalism, egotism and stubbornness, which contributed largely to his rise to national eminence, was also to prove his undoing.

Bryan's economic views, his flamboyance, and his support of the Treaty of Paris caused a great many of the anti-imperialist leaders to distrust him. The choice for these men between Bryan and McKinley was like choosing between Scylla and Charybdis. The anguish which this choice engendered is illustrated in a letter which Carl Schurz wrote to Charles Francis Adams, Jr. in the autumn of 1899: "If a cruel fate should force me to choose between McKinley and the imperialistic policy and Bryan as the anti-imperialist candidate, I should consider it my duty—a horrible duty—to swallow all my personal disgust and to . . . try to defeat imperialism at any cost." [3]

Further evidence that many anti-imperialists, who were disturbed by other facets of Bryan's program, were finding it difficult to accept the Great Commoner as their candidate is provided by remarks made by Erving Winslow at the first annual meeting of the original Anti-Imperialist League. "Our purpose," Winslow said, "should be to maintain an absolute independence of all other issues . . . We must in our organization stand shoulder to shoulder . . . for the one momentous,

---

2. Croffut to Bryan, Sept. 9, 1899, Croffut Papers.
3. Schurz to Adams, Nov. 5, 1899, Schurz Papers.

THE REMNANT COUNTER

Aunty Democracy has a great collection of odds and ends on her bargain table which she hopes to dispose of as a job lot in 1900. Cartoon by Charles L Bartholomew in the *Minneapolis Journal,* December 2, 1899.

vital, paramount issue, Anti-Imperialism and the preservation of the Republic!"[4] Winslow's impassioned plea for solidarity represented the political, or perhaps more accurately apolitical, ideal of the Anti-Imperialist League. However, as so often happens in political matters, the ideal could not be maintained.

Many anti-imperialists desperately sought an alternative which would allow them to express their opposition to imperial-

---

4. *First Annual Meeting of the Anti-Imperialist League,* Nov. 25, 1899, p. 9.

ism without compromising themselves in other areas. After the drastic alternative suggested by General William Birney, President of the Washington Anti-Imperialist League, that formal impeachment proceedings be instituted against McKinley had been rejected,[5] thought then turned to the possibility of forming a strong third party devoted exclusively to anti-imperialism. The first move in this direction came out of a meeting held at the Plaza Hotel in New York on January 6, 1900. Among the influential men present were Richard Pettigrew, Carl Schurz, Andrew Carnegie, John B. Henderson, Brisbane Walker, Gamaliel Bradford, Franklin Giddings, and Edwin Burritt Smith.

Pettigrew wrote that after considering the many complex problems and alternatives posed by the coming election, the group finally decided to organize a third party. He reported that "Mr. Carnegie, in a vigorous speech, urged the necessity of a new political party for the purpose of opposing the imperial policy of both of the old parties, and said that he would give as much money, dollar for dollar, as the rest of us could raise toward the campaign." [6]

E. B. Smith was made chairman of the proposed new party, and the group set forth with high hopes to enlist further support for the movement. Pettigrew stated that the enterprise never really got off the ground because Carnegie subsequently withdrew, thereby taking away its financial angel. He claims that the reason for this was that Carnegie "was waited on by a committee with the ultimatum that they would go no further with the organization of the steel trust unless he abandoned his third party activities and stopped his contributions to the movement." [7]

The withdrawal of Carnegie's financial support, for whatever reason, was a great blow to the third party movement, which almost died aborning. Some men tried to resuscitate it, but the

---

5. See Birney to W. P. Mize, Secretary of the American Anti-Imperialist League (Nov. 10, 1899), and E. B. Smith, Executive Committee Chairman of the American League to Birney (December 7, 1899), Croffut Papers.

6. Richard Pettigrew, *Imperial Washington, op. cit.,* pp. 321-22.

7. *Ibid.,* p. 324.

more practical realized that if anti-imperialism was to have the best chance for success, it must be under the aegis of one of the established parties; and the Democrats were obviously the more likely choice.

This realization was a painful one for many old Republicans. One of the most significant leaders who made his anguished choice apparent at this time was George Boutwell, president of the Anti-Imperialist League. Only five days after the eventually abortive third party movement was launched, Boutwell in a vigorous speech at Washington's Masonic Hall called for the defeat of the Administration's imperialistic policy in the coming election. Although he did not specifically mention Bryan, it is clear from his remarks that Boutwell, who had served the Republican Party ably in so many capacities, was urging the Democrat's election. He said:

> In the month of November, 1900, the future of the nation will be decided. Republic or empire? That is the question, the only question of any importance before the country. If any false financial or industrial policies are entered upon by a new administration, adequate corrections may be applied in four or eight years, but a policy by which Puerto Rico and the Philippines are incorporated in the Union, or attached to it as vassal dependencies, can never be reversed until this republic is numbered among the states that have fallen through an unjust and criminal greed for empire and power.[8]

Many anti-imperialist leaders thought that the best approach to combatting imperialism in the election of 1900 lay in using their influence to try to obtain favorable planks in the platforms of both major parties. Daniel Lord, Chairman of the Finance Committee of the American Anti-Imperialist League, wrote to General Birney on January 13 regarding plans for the coming campaign: "We propose prior to the conventions to reach the

---

8. G. S. Boutwell, *The President's Policy: War and Conquest Abroad, Degradation of Labor at Home* (Chicago, 1900), pp. 7-8.

township workers and doubtful voters of every close state and congressional district throughout the country. We have already found energetic and enthusiastic men in every congressional district ready and willing to aid us." [9]

The most influential man willing to aid them within Republican ranks was Senator George F. Hoar. An interview which he gave on February 15th indicates why he felt that conversion of the Republican party would provide the only desirable solution to the problem. He emphatically rejected the idea of opposing imperialism through the election of Bryan. "His election means," Hoar claimed, voicing the fears and beliefs of many Americans, including a great many anti-imperialists, "the destruction of our unrivaled prosperity, the debasing of our standard of value—tarnishing the national faith, the destruction of credit, the arraying of class against class, bringing into contempt the authority of the Supreme Court, and the undermining of the security of property and values."

Hoar admitted that some very respected men [e.g. Schurz, Boutwell et al.] "say that it is better that all these things should happen than that this policy of imperialism should be persisted in." "But," the Senator contended, "the question is not whether Bryanism or imperialism be the worse for the American people," but rather "whether anything which Mr. Bryan can be trusted to accomplish in opposition to imperialism is worth attaining at the price of all these sacrifices."

Hoar pointed out that the whole question could have been obviated by defeating the Treaty of Paris, but "that purpose . . . was baffled by Mr. Bryan." He noted that even if Bryan's character and vagaries were not a very real part of the equation, and even if he could be elected, Congress would still be in Republican hands for at least four more years. The only solution, therefore, was to "persuade the Republican Party, or a sufficient number of Republicans, to adopt a sound and righteous policy." To that end he pledged to bend his efforts "as long as there is a spark

9. Lord to Birney, January 13, 1900, Croffut Papers.

of hope. I do not see any spark of hope for this cause," he said, "in the election of Mr. Bryan." [10]

The leaders of the anti-imperialist movement hated to lose Hoar's valuable services in this crucial campaign. A fortnight after Hoar's interview in Washington, Moorfield Storey wrote a long and very revealing letter to the Senator which demonstrates so well the basic dilemma facing the great majority of the most influential anti-imperialist leaders.

"I feel with you," he wrote, "that Mr. Bryan and his associates are not the men that I would choose to govern this country." He lamented "that in a crisis like this the country should not have strength enough to present some other candidate than Bryan. I still hope," he said without too much conviction, "that this may be done." [11] "But," Storey said in a statement which was highly significant, "it is clear to me that if President McKinley is reelected on the only issue that is really before the people—that is, whether his policy since the Cuban war is to be sustained—he will feel and his party will feel that they are charged with a mandate as the phrase goes, and will commit this country to dealings with the Philippines and Cuba which it will

---

10. *Boston Herald,* February 16, 1900.

Hoar never wavered from this position. Several years later he wrote in his autobiography: "I have been blamed . . . because with my [anti-imperialistic] opinions I did not . . . help to elect Bryan. I disagreed with him as to every other issue then pending before the American people . . . I found nothing in his attitude or that of his party, to induce me to support him, or even to inspire my confidence in their settlement of the question of imperialism or expansion. In my opinion if he had been elected, he would have accepted the result, have put the blame for it upon his predecessor in office, and matters would have gone on very much as they have under Republican control."—George F. Hoar, *Autobiography, op. cit.,* Vol. II, p. 323.

11. The only real hope, and that was a very slender one, was to put up a third candidate; for as Edward Stanwood has written, and as was clearly evident at the time, "the candidate for President of each of the two great parties was designated in advance without the semblance of opposition."—*A History of the Presidency* (Boston, 1912), Vol. II, p. 30.

be very difficult if not impossible to undo. I feel that every vote cast for McKinley helps to bring this result about. I cannot see how I can give effect to my opposition to the policy of the President except by voting against him . . ." Storey summed up the entire dilemma of the anti-imperialist leadership in this election in a single sentence. "In a word," he said, "I want to vote against imperialism and I do not want to vote for Bryan."

Storey, and many like him, hoped desperately that another alternative could be found. "I wish," he said imploringly to Senator Hoar, "that the large section of the Republican Party which is led by yourself, Mr. Reed, Mr. Edmunds, Governor Boutwell, and others, might in this matter give us a leader." Expressing the view of many people, he anxiously inquired: "Cannot the example of the free soilers be followed again? In the presence of this supreme issue cannot we . . . unite all who believe in American liberty as it was taught by Sumner and Lincoln in some new party of freedom?" [12]

This desire to evoke leadership from the past to help solve this present problem is also reflected in the strenuous activity of the anti-imperialists upon the anniversary of the birth of the man whom they so revered, and whose precepts of foreign policy they so frequently cited. Anti-imperialist orators throughout the nation used Washington's birthday as an opportunity to reiterate his tenets of foreign policy and to attack the McKinley Administration for deviating from them. Thus the Rev. A. A. Berle, speaking on February 22 at Oberlin College, criticized various "fallacies" propounded by the administration and said that "with the great and vexatious problems of American life pressing upon us, here and now, I venture to say we can serve the land of Washington far more acceptably by bracing up the old standards . . . than by scurrying around the earth looking for some vague new duty." [13]

---

12. Storey to Hoar, February 28, 1900, Storey Papers, Library of Congress.

13. A. A. Berle, *Some Popular American Fallacies Refuted* (Chicago, 1900), p. 3.

Washington's birthday also provided the occasion for several important anti-imperialist meetings. The American League of Philadelphia was host to an "Eastern Conference of Anti-Imperialists." George G. Mercer, President of the American League, opened the conference with a notable speech condemning our position in the Philippines. During the following two days of the conference a succession of influential men, including former Senator John B. Henderson, Francis E. Abbot, Herbert Welsh, Carl Schurz, Moorfield Storey, and Gamaliel Bradford, took the rostrum to denounce various aspects of the McKinley administration's policy. Finally, the conference by a unanimous vote passed a significant resolution concerning the coming election which stated that they would not support anyone for the Presidency or Congress who was not completely opposed to the administration's foreign policy, that they would do their utmost to defeat any candidates who favored it, and requested the Executive Committee of the Anti-Imperialist League to call a national convention to unite everyone holding these views.[14]

On the same day that these resolutions were being adopted in Philadelphia, another anti-imperialist meeting at Faneuil Hall in Boston was taking similar action. Bourke Cockran and George S. Boutwell were the principal speakers. Although they touched upon a variety of issues, they ultimately returned to the basic one of the election. Boutwell insisted that "the reelection of McKinley would mean the abandonment of the republic and the acceptance of a colonial empire as the result of his policy." The old Republican leader denied that the organization which he now headed harbored any inherent antipathy toward the Republican party, per se; nor did the League desire to promote any other specific party. "It is not our purpose," he declared, "to advance the interests of any political party. Our purpose, our only purpose, is to defeat the policy of imperialism. If in the execution of our work, parties shall rise or parties shall fall, we shall lament the success of the party of imperialism, and we shall rejoice in

---

14. *New York Evening Post,* "Special Anti-Imperialist Supplement," Feb. 24, 1900, p. 2.

the triumph of any party that shall secure justice to individual men and the full enjoyment of self-government in communities." [15]

Some anti-imperialists were willing to take specific sides even many months before the Republicans and Democrats held their conventions to formally endorse the obvious candidates. Thus on March 16 William James wrote to Carl Schurz from France, and after lavishly praising the latter's anti-imperialist speeches, especially those at Chicago (October 17, 1899) and Philadelphia (February 22, 1900), commented philosophically: "We shall, of course, be beaten; but your warning that we shall never abandon the fight, no matter how many generations it takes, is the right kind of talk for McKinley and the people to hear." He added enthusiastically: "Were I at home I should vote for Bryan with both hands." [16]

Bryan's statements at this time, however, were already dampening the ardor of the more conservative anti-imperialists. It was reported on March 23 that Bryan in a speech in his home city of Lincoln, Nebraska, had announced the platform upon which he desired to stand. The principal elements of this tentative platform were, in order, "money [silver at 16 to 1], trusts and imperialism." One can see that to a certain extent Bryan connected these, for he claimed that "imperialism had its inspiration in the desire of the syndicates to extend their commerce by conquest." [17]

It was just such statements by Bryan which in the estimation of the majority of the anti-imperialist leaders greatly weakened the value of his opposition to imperialism by connecting it with his radical financial theories, and which caused interest in a possible third party movement to be revived sporadically. Schurz wrote to Erving Winslow on March 28 urging the creation of a "third Party composed of old Republicans." Such a ticket, Schurz believed, "would make it easier for many persons of influence

---

15. *Speeches at Anti-Imperialism Meeting, Faneuil Hall, February 23, 1900* (Boston, 1900), pp. 6, 10-11.

16. Schurz Papers.

17. Newspaper clipping (paper unknown), dated March 23, 1900, in "Clippings Relating to the Philippine Question," Widener Library, Harvard University.

who dislike the Democratic candidate . . . to take an active and useful part in the anti-imperialist crusade. It would also open to the anti-imperialist speakers a great many ears which otherwise would be closed to them. I am, therefore, inclined to think that the nomination of such a ticket would tell heavily against McKinley." [18]

Winslow only two days earlier had been sent contradictory advice by another old Republican, ex-Senator John B. Henderson, who interestingly enough was very frequently suggested as the candidate of the proposed third party. Henderson believed it would be best for the anti-imperialists not to take any positive political stand at that particular time, it being his feeling that the uncertainty concerning "the designs of the anti-imperialists bring abundant confusion and trepidation to the enemy. Let them alone to enjoy temporarily the hopes they can never realize, and finally to suffer the despair which will inevitably overtake them." [19]

The majority of anti-imperialists lacked Henderson's faith in Fabian tactics, and felt that demonstrative action was better. One form of this was the mass meeting. A notable one took place on May 24 at Cooper Institute in New York. It was sponsored by the New York Anti-Imperialist League, and its President, Ernest H. Crosby, poet laureate of the Anti-Imperialist cause,[20] presided. The principal speakers, all "old Republicans," were Carl Schurz, Patrick O'Farrell and George Boutwell. They all attacked the "new Republicans" for being false to the traditions of the party and the nation. Boutwell called for the overthrow of the Republicans in the next election, so that the party and nation "might be cleansed of evil influences." [21]

Several resolutions were adopted, as was the usual custom at these anti-imperialist meetings. The most significant one read:

---

18. Schurz papers.

19. Henderson to Winslow, March 26, 1900, Croffut Papers.

20. See especially his *Swords and Plowshares* (New York, 1902), a collection of his anti-imperialist poems.

21. George S. Boutwell, *Republic or Empire* (Boston, 1900), p. 21.

Resolved that the question of imperialism overshadows in importance all other public questions; that the approval or disapproval of the imperialistic policy pursued by the present Administration should be the supreme issue in the coming election; and that all American citizens having the good name and best interests of our free institutions at heart should unite in an earnest effort to secure the condemnation of that policy and the sternest possible rebuke to its authors by a decisive popular vote.[22]

Several days after the Cooper Institute meeting William Croffut wrote to Boutwell praising his speech and commenting, in regard to Senator Hoar's apparently paradoxical support of both anti-imperialism and President McKinley, that "nobody seems to be infringing brother Hoar's patent for denouncing the crime and praising the criminal." [23]

The Republican National Convention, which met in Philadelphia on the 19th of the following month, was, of course, more kindly disposed toward Mr. McKinley. The choice of the presidential candidate simply involved the perfunctory act of renominating the current occupant of the White House. There was some question concerning the nominee for Vice President, but the convention quickly swung to Theodore Roosevelt, and thereby tacitly endorsed imperialism. The platform accorded a blanket endorsement to the policies of the McKinley administration, stating that "its acts have been established in wisdom and in patriotism, and at home and abroad it has distinctly elevated and extended the influence of the American nation." It referred to the annexation of the Philippines as "a new and noble responsibility." It said, furthermore, that "President McKinley has conducted the foreign affairs of the United States with distinct credit to the American people." [24] It specifically approved of the annexation of Hawaii, and of the division of Samoa which had been effected at the end

---

22. Back cover of *ibid.*

23. Croffut to Boutwell, May 27, 1900, Boutwell Papers, Massachusetts Historical Society.

24. Stanwood, *op. cit.,* pp. 49, 50.

of the preceding year.[25] The man chosen for Vice President, as well as the complacency of the platform, applied the coup de grâce to any slight hope that anti-imperialist Republicans might have had that their party would change its ways.

The Republican platform singled out no one issue for special emphasis, nor did the party, unless it was Mark Hanna's blunt admonition to "stand pat." The anti-imperialists, however, continued to insist, perhaps with all the more vehemence because of the studied evasion of the matter by the majority of the McKinley administration's backers, that imperialism was the principal issue facing the electorate.

In the same month as the Republican convention, a choleric article by Frank Parsons on "The Giant Issue of 1900" appeared in *The Arena*. This article, both in tone and content, typified the anti-imperialist writings of the period on the subject. The "giant issue now," Parsons insisted, "is whether the flag shall stand for freedom or oppression." The vital question to be decided is "whether the people approve the policy of abandoning the Declaration of Independence, turning the Republic into an Empire, and transforming a peaceful democracy into an imperial conqueror." [26]

Parsons' views, as those of the anti-imperialists in general, were to be embodied in the Democratic platform, but along with other statements which were to confuse the choice of the voter. The Democratic National Convention convened in Kansas City on the Fourth of July. Bryan's nomination for President was almost as perfunctory as that of McKinley by the Republicans. David B. Hill of New York and Charles A. Towne of Minnesota had fairly substantial backing for the Vice Presidency, but the

---

25. The issue of Samoa, like that of Puerto Rico, was largely swallowed up by the larger question of the Philippines. The anti-imperialists tended to concentrate their attack almost exclusively upon the major Philippine question. One of the few notable exceptions to this was a vigorous speech in the Senate by R. F. Pettigrew denouncing our action vis-à-vis Samoa. See *Congressional Record*, 56th Congress, 1st Session, p. 1295.

26. Frank Parsons, "The Giant Issue of 1900," *The Arena*, Vol. XXIII (June, 1900), p. 561.

nomination went to Adlai E. Stevenson of Illinois, a strong anti-imperialist, who had served as Vice President in Grover Cleveland's second administration.

The real controversy of the convention was over the platform. A great many of the delegates to the convention were opposed to the inclusion of a free silver plank, feeling that it would alienate a great many voters who otherwise would be drawn to the party by the issue of anti-imperialism. Bryan, however, who had risen to national eminence on the silver issue, was adamant in his insistence that the silver plank of 1896 be explicitly reiterated; and, as the party's leader, his view ultimately prevailed.

Most of the platform, nevertheless, was devoted to anti-imperialism. It condemned militarism and denounced the policies and actions of the McKinley Administration vis-à-vis Cuba, Puerto Rico, and the Philippines. It declared, echoing the literature of the various anti-imperialist leagues,

> that all governments instituted among men derive their just powers from the consent of the governed; that any government not based upon the consent of the governed is a tyranny; and that to impose upon any people a government of force is to substitute the methods of imperialism for those of a republic . . . We assert that no nation can long endure half republic and half empire, and we warn the American people that imperialism abroad will lead quickly and inevitably to despotism at home.[27]

In regard to what should specifically be done about the Philippines, the platform stated: "We favor an immediate declaration of the Nation's purpose to give to the Filipinos, first, a stable form of government; second, independence; and third, protection from outside interference such as has been given for nearly a century to the republics of Central and South America.[28] This plan differed somewhat from that favored by the anti-imperialist leagues. They felt that the Philippines should be immediately given independence and that the islands should be neutralized by

---

27. Stanwood, *op. cit.*, p. 58.
28. *Ibid.*, p. 59.

an international convention. The plank in the Democratic platform, while thus not exactly what they wanted, was at least a major step in the right direction.

The most significant element of the Democratic platform was undoubtedly the statement that although there were other issues of importance, "the burning issue of imperialism, growing out of the Spanish war, involves the very existence of the Republic and the destruction of our free institutions. We regard it as the paramount issue of the campaign." [29] If this statement had been the entire Democratic platform, Bryan probably would have received the vote of almost every anti-imperialist in the nation and might possibly even have won the election. As it was, the inclusion of the silver plank and Bryan's vigorous reiteration of his economic views alienated many very influential men who would otherwise have supported him and whose enthusiastic support might have tipped the scales in his favor.

Carl Schurz wrote to E. B. Smith a few days after the Democratic convention, saying that he was afraid that the argument over and subsequent adoption of the free-silver plank "has produced the worst possible impression. Friends of mine . . . who had reconciled themselves to the support of Bryan on the ground that imperialism could not be defeated in any other way are now as profoundly disgusted with the Democrats as they were in 1896. I have no doubt that this feeling is widespread among people who otherwise agree with us on the matter of imperialism." Schurz, in light of the outcome of the Democratic convention, suggested to Smith that the best policy at the forthcoming Liberty Congress might be "to strike out boldly for a new party. There is a very widespread feeling that the people have permitted themselves long enough . . . to be forced by two rotten old party carcases to choose between evils." [30]

Grover Cleveland was so disgusted with his successor as head of the Democratic forces that he wrote a bitter letter to his former Attorney General, Judson Harmon, on July 17, indicating

---

29. *Ibid.*
30. Schurz to Smith, July 8, 1900, Schurz Papers.

that he thought that it would probably be better if Bryan were defeated. "As between imperialism and a continued struggle against sound money," he said, "you and many other good and patriotic Democrats see more danger in the first. The latter and much more trouble we would surely get with Bryan." Cleveland's attitude toward Bryan was much akin to that of Senator Hoar. He asked Harmon: "How certain can you be that he would save you from imperialism? What did he do toward that end when the treaty of peace was before the Senate; and how do you know what such an acrobat would do on that question if his personal ambition was in the balance?" [31]

Bryan, of course, did not think that the reiteration of the silver plank was the great evil that the leaders of the anti-imperialist movement deemed it to be. He wrote to William A. Croffut, who, it will be recalled, had long ago advised him to forgo the silver issue, on July 14, defending the silver plank and insisting that "the anti-imperialist who votes against me on account of my silver views cannot be very strongly opposed to imperialism. The platform opposes imperialism without abandoning silver. I believe that it is the strongest position that could have been taken." [32] Unfortunately for Mr. Bryan, a great many of his countrymen did not agree.

Several of the anti-imperialist mass meetings, as well as many individual anti-imperialist leaders, had called for a national conference of anti-imperialists to decide upon a united policy to pursue in the election. Therefore, on July 20, the Executive Committee of the American Anti-Imperialist League issued a call for a "National Liberty Congress" of representatives of all Leagues in the country to meet at Indianapolis on August 15 "to deliberate and act with reference to the coming campaign." [33]

Carl Schurz, who was one of the prime movers behind the

---

31. *Cleveland Letters,* pp. 532-33.
32. Croffut Papers.
33. Executive Committee of American Anti-Imperialist League to officers of Washington Anti-Imperialist League, July 20, 1900, among *ibid.*

convocation of the Liberty Congress and who was expected to take a leading part in it, was dealt a double blow at this crucial juncture which prevented his attendance at the conference. He was stricken physically by a severe case of food poisoning and emotionally by the death on July 24th of his son Herbert. He wrote to E. B. Smith on August 7, one week before the congress, saying that he would not attend, and urged Smith to try to unite the congress on the nomination of a third ticket. He said that he felt that this would be "the wisest course . . . [it] would prevent a great many voters from drifting to McKinley and give us an absolutely aggressive position in the campaign." He said that he realized that "Mr. Boutwell and Mr. Winslow are strongly opposed to the third ticket plan" and think it best to support Bryan directly; but he still favored the former alternative and recommended that John B. Henderson or Thomas B. Reed be chosen to lead the ticket.[34]

Four days later, Schurz wrote to Moorfield Storey reiterating these views: "My opinion as to the desirability of an independent nomination remains the same." [35] He said, however, that he had talked with Henderson about being the Presidential candidate, but had been told that his health was too precarious. Schurz, therefore, suggested that either Reed or General William Birney should head the proposed new party.

Storey agreed with Schurz, and wrote to him on August 18 regarding the Liberty Congress, saying that there were many others who questioned the wisdom of endorsing Bryan. He pointed out, however, that "the feeling of men like Colonel Codman, [E. B.] Smith, Governor Boutwell and all the prominent leaders was that in this contest there was room for only two sides." Storey said that he, personally, wanted to "stand uncommitted on the question of supporting Bryan," and still favored "a third movement." [36]

Storey apparently convinced himself during the next few

34. Schurz Papers.
35. Schurz to Storey, August 11, 1900, Storey Papers.
36. Schurz Papers.

days that the only practical thing to do was to support Bryan; for he wrote to Schurz on the 21st, saying that

> if a large body of men feeling so strongly on this question of imperialism that they cannot support McKinley, yet tell their fellow countrymen that it is impossible for them to support Bryan, this attitude cannot fail to alienate from Bryan a great many conscientious persons, and the stronger the statement of their reasons, the greater would be its effect. When this body of voters is confronted with the question whether they will indirectly help to elect Bryan by voting for a third candidate, there is very grave danger that they might decline to throw away their votes, and that a considerable portion of them might vote directly for McKinley. In other words, the justification for a third party might prove a justification for supporting McKinley.

Storey, therefore, with regret, concluded that "a third party movement now is not feasible." [37]

This decision must have been especially difficult for Storey, not only because he was opposed to much of Bryan's philosophy and skeptical of his character, but also because he, himself, had been rather actively considered by some people as a likely man to lead a new party. This was bruited about at the Liberty Congress. Storey was even directly approached by a "Third Ticket Movement" headed by J. J. Chapman of New York; but he graciously declined, saying that unfortunately the reversal of our imperialistic policy could only be brought about "by the defeat of McKinley and that means the election of Bryan." [38]

This same ambivalent, and at best lukewarm, attitude toward Bryan is also found in the resolutions passed by the Liberty Congress. These urged the electorate, "without regard to their views on minor questions of domestic policy, to withhold their votes from Mr. McKinley in order to stamp with disapproval what he has done. . . . While we welcome any other method of

---

37. *Ibid.*
38. Storey to J. J. Chapman, Sept. 3, 1900, Storey Papers.

opposing the re-election of Mr. McKinley, we advise direct support of Mr. Bryan as the most effective means of crushing
imperialism." [39]

Bryan's speech accepting the nomination for President by
the Democratic Party, delivered at Indianapolis one week before
the Liberty Congress, probably did much to swing the congress
and the anti-imperialist leagues formally to his side; for it was
entitled "Imperialism" and was devoted almost entirely to a
lengthy attack upon its evils. He echoed many of the salient points
made in the literature of the anti-imperialist leagues. He considered the principal arguments of the imperialists and offered
refutations of them. He pointed out that imperialism ran counter
to the fundamental principles and traditions of American government and policy. He warned that "if we have an imperial policy
we must have a great standing army," and insisted that "the
spirit which will justify the forcible annexation of the Philippine
Islands will justify the seizure of other islands and the domination
of other people. . . ." [40]

If Bryan had continued in this vein, the anti-imperialists
would certainly not have had any cause for complaint with his
campaign. However, in the majority of his speeches economic
matters were given precedence. The leaders of the anti-imperialist
movement were naturally disappointed and discouraged. Carl
Schurz, who just a few days earlier had given a stirring anti-
imperialist oration at Cooper Union,[41] wrote on October 7 to
Edward M. Shepard, another active publicist for the cause, com-
plaining that Bryan "had strangely neglected" the issue of imperialism. Schurz offered his "private opinion" that if "the elec-

---

39. *Address to the Voters of the United States, Adopted by the
National Congress of Anti-Imperialists at Indianapolis, Indiana,
August 15-16, 1900* (Liberty Tract No. 13) (Chicago, 1900), pp.
3-4. See also *Report of the Second Annual Meeting of the New
England Anti-Imperialist League* (Boston, 1900), p. 7.

40. William Jennings Bryan, Speeches of *William Jennings Bryan*
(New York, 1909), Vol. II, pp. 27-39.

41. See *Springfield Republican,* Oct. 5, 1900.

tion were to take place tomorrow, McKinley would be elected by a strong majority." [42]

The leaders of the anti-imperialist movement were quick to censure Bryan for his inability to swing enough of the nation's independent voters to his side because he would not forget other matters and stress only anti-imperialism. They themselves, however, were partly to blame, and for the same reason. They could not put aside their inherent economic conservatism, and they felt constrained each time they urged support for Bryan to add a personal disclaimer for the Great Commoner's economic views. Thus the American Anti-Imperialist League's *Address to Independent Voters*, which was signed by a host of influential men, stated: "We have not prior to this year supported the candidacy of Mr. Bryan. We do not now concur in certain of his views on minor issues. Yet . . . we now favor his election as the most effective way of showing disapproval of Mr. McKinley's course." One will also note that they were not so much urging a vote for Bryan, about whom they candidly admitted they had reservations, as they were urging a vote against McKinley. This attitude crops up again and again in the literature of the leagues. Another notable example of it is found in *Anti-Imperialist Broadside No. 12*, which consisted of an "open letter" by D. H. Chamberlain, quondam Governor of South Carolina, to Andrew D. White, current U.S. Ambassador to Germany. Chamberlain said that he did not support Bryan's financial theories or principles, nor did he approve "all he represents or all items of the Kansas platform," but favored him as "the least objectionable of the two candidates to whom our choice is limited." [43]

If one admires the honesty of the leaders of institutional anti-imperialism, he is appalled at their salesmanship. In advocating anti-imperialism they had enough of a problem in that they were supporting a self-abnegating and negative doctrine. But when they compounded this by constantly excusing their candidate's

---

42. Schurz Papers.

43. *Anti-Imperialist Broadside No. 12* (Boston, n.d., but undoubtedly October, 1900).

views on other issues, and urged a vote, not *for* him, but *against* his opponent, it is little wonder that they were not as successful as they would have wished.

It was an agonizing decision for the leaders of the anti-imperialist movement. "Bryanism and McKinleyism!" Grover Cleveland ranted, "What a choice for a patriotic American!" [44] Cleveland's former Secretary of Agriculture, J. Sterling Morton, expressed the matter even more vividly when he wrote to his erstwhile chief on November 2: "It is a choice between evils, and I am going to shut my eyes, hold my nose, vote, go home, and disinfect myself!" [45]

Even that most loyal of anti-imperialists, Carl Schurz, on the eve of the election gave vent to his misgivings in a letter to C. F. Adams:

> For a considerable time I have not expected Mr. Bryan to succeed. The Kansas City Convention gave my hopes the first shock. Still, if after his splendid Indianapolis speech against imperialism, Bryan had retired, resting his case on that speech, he might have had a chance. But when he then went into the field and indulged in all sorts of loose talk which sounded far more dangerous than it really was, thus bringing various other things, especially the money question, into the foreground, I became more and more confirmed in the belief that he would not be elected. [46]

Schurz' forebodings concerning the election were substantiated the following day when the people went to the polls; for McKinley received 7,219,530 popular and 292 electoral votes

---

44. Cleveland to Charles S. Hamlin, Sept. 13, 1900, *Cleveland Letters,* p. 536.

45. Cleveland Papers.

46. Schurz to Adams, Nov. 5, 1900, Schurz Papers.

A week after the election, Schurz wrote much the same thing to Louis R. Ehrich, the leading anti-imperialist in Colorado. He said: "Bryan's fine Indianapolis speech would, perhaps, have given him a chance if he had rested his case upon it and then retired in dignified silence. When he again launched out in his campaign of small talks all hope was gone. . . . Almost every one of his speeches lost him votes."

to Bryan's 6,351,071 popular and 155 electoral votes. The anti-imperialists had wanted the election to be Armageddon—the final all-out battle against the imperialists, but Bryan had discomfited them. They, therefore, refused, and rightly so, to feel that it was their cause that had been defeated. The Executive Committee of the New England Anti-Imperialist League stated that the League, "in view of the fact that the anti-imperialists of the country were divided in sentiment as to the candidates in the recent Presidential election, does not and can not recognize that the question of Anti-Imperialism was settled by that election." [47]

The individual leaders of the anti-imperialist movement concurred in this feeling and were glad to sever quickly any relationship with Bryan. Carl Schurz wrote to E. B. Smith: "I am *very* glad you did not attend the Bryan dinner. Whatever good qualities Bryan may possess, I have always considered him the evil genius of the anti-imperialist cause. To vote for him was the most distasteful thing I ever did. . . . I did it . . . because I wanted to make on my part the strongest imaginable protest against the policy of the Administration." Schurz added that he thought that it would be very "unwise for the anti-imperialists . . . to identify themselves [further] with Bryan in any manner." [48] The anti-imperialists were only too happy to follow this advice, for it removed them from the terrible dilemma in which Bryan's candidacy in the election of 1900 had placed them.

---

47. *Report of the Second Annual Meeting of the New England Anti-Imperialist League* (Boston, 1900), p. 10.
48. Schurz to E. B. Smith, Nov. 17, 1901, Schurz Papers.

CHAPTER 15

The White Man's Burden

The election of 1900 marked the apogee of the debate over imperialism in the United States. It was to continue, but with gradually and steadily diminishing intensity. On the anti-imperialist side, each year after the turn of the century witnessed the demise of an increasing number of the original leaders of the movement; and their places were not filled with men of comparable stature and devotion to the cause. Moreover, the infirmities and lessening vigor of advancing years reduced the contribution made by those of the original leaders who did survive. The number and strength of the anti-imperialist organizations also steadily declined after 1900. The weaker ones, naturally, dissolved first; but by 1904 the original league would be the only viable organization left in the field. It would, however, continue its work, although on a much diminished scale, until the end of the second decade of the new century.

Although the anti-imperialists were not successful in preventing the nation from treading the imperialist path, their efforts were very valuable in helping to keep the country from proceeding further along this thorny route than otherwise would have been the case. The critiques which the anti-imperialists offered, and the probing questions they asked about our present policy in relation to our traditions and basic principles eventually proved quite effective. Also, that bitter teacher—experience—was to inculcate in a demonstrative way the truth of the theoretical lessons which the anti-imperialists sedulously and selflessly tried to teach their countrymen. The American people were to learn that the "white man's burden" was indeed a heavy one.

This last phrase, itself, was a significant source of contention between the imperialists and anti-imperialists at the turn of the century. The majority of American imperialists were uneasy about the use of the word "imperialism"; for it had always had a vaguely unpleasant connotation for most Americans. They, therefore, from the very beginning utilized more pleasing euphemisms like "expansion," "extension," "territorial growth," or such nebulous but powerful phrases as "Manifest Destiny." They were very fond of talking of the dictates of "destiny," "duty," "Providence," etc. Thus, when at a particularly difficult period for the imperialists—February, 1899—Rudyard Kipling came forth with his poem, "The White Man's Burden," the American imperialists eagerly adopted it. After the poem had been published in the February issue of *McClure's Magazine*, it "circled the earth in a day and by repetition became hackneyed within a week." [1]

The imperialists, however, really seized only the mellifluous and righteous-sounding title and not the meaning of the poem. In fact, one wonders how many of the American imperialists who so glibly employed the phrase had ever read the poem. Had they read it carefully, they might have realized that the title and repeated opening line of each stanza, which they employed as a euphemism for imperialism, was actually rather ironical. The poem, itself, really carried no optimistic exhortation to go forth and fondly aid one's "little brown brother" with the expectation of reproducing Western civilization in the Philippines within a decade. The entire tone of the poem, rather, is distinctly pessimistic and lugubrious from the very first stanza:

> Take up the White Man's burden—
> Send forth the best ye breed—
> Go bind your sons to exile
> To serve your captive's need;

---

1. Cited by Mark Sullivan, *Our Times* (New York, 1928), Vol. I, p. 6.

> To wait in heavy harness
>> On fluttered folk and wild—
> You new-caught, sullen peoples
>> Half devil and half child.[2]

And what will be the result of the expense, the trouble, the sickness, and "the savage wars of Peace?" "All your hope" will simply be brought "to nought." Granting that Kipling's aim was not simply irony, why, then, did he exhort the United States (the poem is pointedly subtitled "The United States and the Philippine Islands") to "take up the white man's burden?" The answer lies in the final stanza:

> Take up the White Man's burden—
>> Have done with childish days—
> The lightly proffered laurel,
>> The easy, ungrudged praise.
> Comes now, to search your manhood
>> Through all the thankless years,
> Cold-eyed with dear-bought wisdom,
>> The judgment of your peers.

Kipling urged the United States to take up the burden not for the benefit of the Filipinos, but to prove that its "childish days" were past and that it had attained "manhood" and could bear the solemn and heavy responsibilities, as well as the prestige, of a world power.

Interestingly enough, the anti-imperialists largely seemed to accept the imperialists' interpretation of the poem, if arguing vehemently against the validity of the implied theory. Two men, however, noted well the warning of tribulation, frustration, and failure which the poem presented. Senator Benjamin R. Tillman, in a notable speech in the Senate, insisted that the American people should heed not the exhortation but the admonition which Kipling—a man who "knows whereof he speaks"—offered to them.[3]

---

2. *Rudyard Kipling's Verse: Definitive Edition* (Garden City, Doubleday, 1940), p. 321.

3. See *Congressional Record,* 55th Congress, 3rd Session, pp. 1531-1532.

Winslow Warren, another one of the original officers of the Anti-Imperialist League, presented the most perceptive contemporary commentary upon the poem. In a letter to the *Boston Evening Transcript* he observed that "a singular phase of the inverted Americanism of the present time is the reception given by the press, and many of our public speakers, to Kipling's latest poem, 'The White Man's Burden.' He astutely pointed out that "if taken as a timely warning, it is forceful and happy, but accepted, as it apparently is by many, as an invocation to what is called duty, the words and spirit are simply brutal." Warren decried the imperialists' "perversion of humanity and civilization to cover our greed and selfishness. We say this has been thrust upon us as a 'duty.' Never was there such a case of a nation's blindly assuming as a right and duty something which had no foundation but in our own lust for domain and power." Warren demonstrated that this sort of rationalization through the use of specious terminology was not a new phenomenon. "People's memories," he said, "must be short if they do not run back to times before the Civil War when the slave masters of the South talked of manifest destiny, of the white man's burden, and of the benefits of the white man's rule in promoting the happiness and civilization of the Negroes in slavery." [4]

Many anti-imperialists sought to weaken the support which the imperialists derived from their interpretation of this controversial and widely quoted poem by penning parodies of it. These began to appear amazingly quickly after the publication of the original version. Henry Labouchère on February 12, 1899 cabled his version from London to the *New York World* and *Chicago Tribune*. Many of the nation's anti-imperialist journals published Labouchère's parody, "The Brown Man's Burden," side by side with the original poem. It read in part:

> Pile on the brown man's burden,
>   to gratify your greed;
> Go clear away the "niggers"
>   Who progress would impede;

---

4. *Boston Evening Transcript,* Feb. 18, 1899.

Be very stern, for truly
   'Tis useless to be mild
With new-caught sullen peoples
   Half devil and half child.

Pile on the brown man's burden
   And if ye rouse his hate,
Meet his old-fashioned reasons
   With maxims up to date.
With shells and dumdum bullets
   A hundred times made plain
The brown man's loss must ever
   Imply the white man's gain.

And if by chance ye falter
   Or lag behind the course
If, as the blood flows freely
   Ye feel some slight remorse,
Hie ye to Rudyard Kipling,
   Imperialism's prop,
And bid him, for your comfort
   Turn on his jingo stop.[5]

Herbert Welsh's newspaper, *City and State*, which along with many others published Labouchère's poem, printed another parody by one "W.P.G." entitled "Beware of the Lion When He Talks Like a Man." This poem which implies that Great Britain wanted a partner to help in exploiting backward peoples to increase British trade, reads in part:

Take up the white man's burden,
   That's how they talk to you;
'Tis the hand of merry England,
   But the voice of Gunga Dhu.

Take up the white man's burden
   Exploit the brown man's land,
Like Clive and Warren Hastings
   With altruistic hand.

---

5. *City and State,* Feb. 16, 1899, Welsh Papers, Pennsylvania Historical Society.

> The brown man bears the burden
>> Whether he will or no;
> But the white man takes the guerdon
>> As British coffers show.
>
> So take the white man's burden
>> In philanthropy arrayed;
> Take the sympathy of England
>> And she will take the trade.[6]

Perhaps the best known parody of Kipling's "White Man's Burden" was a sardonic poem of the same title written by the president of the New York Anti-Imperialist League, Ernest H. Crosby. It first appeared in *The New York Times* of February 15, 1899, and reads in part:

> Take up the White Man's burden;
>> Send forth your sturdy sons,
> And load them down with whiskey
>> And Testaments and guns.
> Throw in a few diseases
>> To spread in tropic climes
> For there the healthy niggers
>> Are quite behind the times.
>
> Take up the White Man's burden,
>
> .   .   .   .   .
>
> Then learn that if with pious words
>> You ornament each phrase,
> In a world of canting hypocrites
>> This kind of business pays.[7]

Increasingly after 1900, not only the anti-imperialists, but the American people in general began to ask searching questions concerning American imperialism. E. C. Tompkins' poem "By Whose Command?" inquired:

---

6. *Ibid.*
7. *New York Times,* February 15, 1899.

> *Who* kens the White Man's Burden
> > *Where* is it writ or said
> Go across the seas to seek it
> > And strike the Brown Man dead?
>
> *Why* bind our sons in exile?
> > *What* captives pray have we?
> Our one-time human chattels
> > Were long ago set free.[8]

A somewhat less grave and more witty writer in the *New York World* commented:

> We've taken up the white man's burden
> > Of ebony and brown
> Now will you kindly tell us Rudyard,
> > How we may put it down? [9]

The burden rapidly became a very onerous one, and, for whatever reason it was assumed, the mass of the American people soon grew tired of it. The anti-imperialists continued to insist in both poetry and prose that "the pretense that we are to hold the Philippines for the moral, political, or spiritual benefit of their inhabitants is fraudulent and hypocritical." [10] Philippine expert John Foreman observed that "the U.S. campaign in the Philippine Islands, originally proclaimed to have been undertaken 'for the sake of humanity,' has, so far, conferred no benefits on the Filipinos in particular, nor on mankind in general. After eighteen months' trial, American Imperialism has achieved nothing of advantage to anyone concerned in those islands. . . ." [11]

By 1901 the anti-imperialists' position was beginning to be more widely accepted. An increasing number of Americans were

---

8. *Anti-Imperialist Leaflet No. 20* (Washington; n.d., but probably late in 1900).

9. Cited by Thomas A. Bailey, *The Man in the Street* (New York, 1948), p. 275.

10. H. D. Money, "Expansion—Past and Prospective," *The Arena,* Vol. XXIII (April, 1900), p. 339.

11. John Foreman, *Will the United States Withdraw from the Philippines?* (Liberty Track No. 14) (Chicago, 1901), p. 3.

coming to agree with Grover Cleveland that "a strange voyage has been entered upon without count of cost and without chart and compass;" [12] and to ask, like Congressman Seth Brown: "If we hold the Philippine Islands perpetually . . . what will be the effect of our action on the people of the United States and their free institutions, and on the people of these islands?" [13]

In the same month (February, 1901) that Brown was asking his searching questions in Congress, a man whose fame rested upon his penchant for humor excoriated the imperialists in an exceedingly sardonic and scathing essay—"To the Person Sitting in Darkness." Mark Twain, who ultimately served as an officer of several anti-imperialist organizations, mocked the imperialists with a bitter sarcasm, which is reminiscent of Voltaire, concerning the U.S. role in the Philippines:

> There have been lies, yes, but they were told in a good cause. We have been treacherous, but that was only in order that real good might come out of apparent evil. True, we have crushed a deceived and confiding people; we have turned against the weak and the friendless who trusted us; we have stamped out a just and intelligent and well-ordered republic; we have stabbed an ally in the back and slapped the face of a guest; we have bought a shadow from an enemy that hadn't it to sell; we have robbed a trusting friend of his land and his liberty; we have invited our clean young men to shoulder a discredited musket and do bandits' work under a flag which bandits have been accustomed to fear, not to follow; we have debauched America's honor and blacked her face before the world; but each detail was for the best.[14]

When the most renowned and beloved author in the United States wrote something like the foregoing, the American people

---

12. Holland Society Address, January 17, 1901, *New York Times*, January 18, 1901.

13. *Speech in House of Representatives,* February 9, 1901, reprinted by the New York Anti-Imperialist League (New York, 1901), p. 4.

14. Mark Twain, "To the Person Sitting in Darkness," *North American Review,* Vol. CLXXII (February, 1901), p. 175.

listened. This was no Boston Brahmin preaching abstract theory; this was Mark Twain, sage of the people, speaking bitterly in language that all could and did understand, as much as they might not like what they heard.

If Mark Twain had been aware at the time of the casuistry of the Supreme Court's decision in the "Insular Cases" this too would have probably elicited a scornful commentary. As we have noted, the annexation of the various islands raised complicated constitutional questions. After the question of the constitutionality of the annexations themselves had been disposed of, there still remained the issue of whether all aspects of the Constitution pertained to the new possessions and the population thereof—that is whether, in popular parlance, "the Constitution followed the flag." The imperialists claimed, in general, that it did not and the anti-imperialists that it did.

The matter was vigorously debated for several years, and was eventually taken before the Supreme Court, which decided, in effect, that it did and it didn't. To be more precise, which the Supreme Court was not, the McKinley administration claimed that the Constitution did not apply to our new possessions until extended to them by Congress, and, furthermore, that Congress in legislating for them was not necessarily bound by all the provisions of the Constitution. The Supreme Court in the late spring of 1901, by a five to four decision, backed up the administration and Congress by deciding that Puerto Rico and the Philippines were not a part of, but merely appurtenant to, the United States; and that, therefore, Congress might legislate for them accordingly. Justice Brown's reasoning in the majority opinion was so tortuous that none of the other four justices (White, Gray, McKenna, and Shiras) who concurred in his conclusion agreed with the method by which he reached it.

The important thing is that a decision, and the one that the administration wanted, was reached. The decision pleased some, disturbed others, but for the most part simply confused the American people. Finley Peter Dunne in his own inimitable way commented:

Some say it laves the flag up in th' air an' some say that's where it laves th' constitution. Annyhow, something's in the air. But there's wan thing I'm sure about."

"What's that?" asked Mr. Hennessy.

"That is," said Mr. Dooley, "no matter whether th' constitution follows th' flag or not, th' supreme coort follows th' illiction returns." [15]

The "Insular Cases" constituted the most important feature in 1901 of the continuing debate over American imperialism. In a document signed by representatives of all the major anti-imperialist leagues in the country (e.g. the American Anti-Imperialist League, and the New England, New York, Philadelphia, Washington, Cincinnati, and Minneapolis Leagues), the anti-imperialist leaders stated that "they had hoped that the Supreme Court would with no uncertain voice declare that no human being under our control could be without the rights secured by our Constitution." Unfortunately, this hope was not realized. They complained that "the Supreme Court has spoken, but left the law in doubt." The proclamation of the leagues emphasized the views in Justice Harlan's dissenting opinion that the decision would yield "a radical and mischievous change in our system of government" and was "wholly inconsistent with the spirit and genius as well as the words of the Constitution." [16]

The matter was also taken up at the annual meeting of the New England Anti-Imperialist League in November. The League's Secretary, Erving Winslow, pointed out that the decision had been a divided opinion which not only did not settle the legal questions but which also "confused the perturbed public opinion still further." He praised the opinions of the four dissenting justices, which "fully sustain and justify our position, so persistently maligned and denied for the last three years by the supporters of the colonial policy." Again evincing the constant

---

15. Finley Peter Dunne, *Mr. Dooley's Opinions* (Boston, 1901), p. 71.

16. *To the American People,* Anti-Imperialist Broadside No. 15 (Boston, 1901).

connection in the minds of the League's leaders between the erstwhile anti-slavery crusade and the present anti-imperialist crusade, Winslow predicted that "as the dissenting opinion in the Dred Scott case became the platform of the Republican Party, it may well be that the dissenting opinions in the Insular Cases will become the most important plank of the party of liberty." [17]

While the Insular Cases constituted the cynosure of the debate over imperialism in 1901, the anti-imperialists also busied themselves with other matters. One of the most basic of these was simply to keep interest in the anti-imperialist cause from flagging. Colonel Charles R. Codman, who was chairman of the principal anti-imperialist mass meeting of the spring (held in Boston on March 30) said: "One of our objects in meeting here tonight is to give information to anxious inquirers. We will continue the work of our League; we will spread the information we have over the country wherever it is asked for, and sometimes where it is not asked for." [18]

One of the items about which they spread the information was the censorship of news emanating from the Philippines. They were aided in this campaign against censorship by Harold Martin, who had represented the Associated Press in the Philippines. Martin, in a revealing article in *The Forum* of June, 1901, protested against the continuing military censorship, which "throughout has been absurd and unreasonable." Martin claimed that the censorship was maintained "to prevent the people of the United States from being informed of what was happening in the islands; its keynotes being partisan politics and military pride." [19] The anti-imperialists asserted that this represented one more example of the oppression and curtailment of freedom inherent in imperialism. They also pointed out that while the citizens of a free country had a right to know all the news, the mere fact that

---

17. *Report of the Third Annual Meeting of the New England Anti-Imperialist League,* Nov. 30, 1901 (Boston, 1901), p. 6.

18. *Free America, Free Cuba, Free Philippines* (Speeches at Faneuil Hall, March 30, 1901) (Boston, 1901), p. 6.

19. Harold Martin, "The Manila Censorship," *The Forum,* Vol. XXXI (June, 1901), p. 463.

American soldiers were engaged in a colonial war against a people whose only transgression was the desire to be free and independent was a damning commentary in itself.

The Administration's Cuban policy also came under strong attack from the anti-imperialists during 1901. The suggestion that the United States might actually continue to rule Cuba was, of course, vehemently assailed. Representative Brown (Republican of Ohio) demanded: "What more miserable, more inhuman, more unpatriotic course could be advocated? It is the acme of avarice, without a single redeeming feature." [20]

The eventual compromise that was decided upon between retaining actual control of Cuba and truly letting the island republic go its own way—the Platt Amendment [21]—also incurred the wrath of the anti-imperialists. A joint statement of the nation's leading anti-imperialist leagues charged that the Platt Amendment had violated the nation's solemn pledge given in the Teller Amendment and made "the stain on our national record indelible." [22] Nevertheless, as unjust as the anti-imperialists felt the terms of the Platt Amendment to be, they conceded that the Cubans at least were better off than the Puerto Ricans and the Filipinos, to whom the United States was denying entirely the right of self-government.

The anti-imperialists were frequently accused of offering only negative strictures in regard to American policies for Puerto Rico and the Philippines. However, it was simply their feeling that the only completely desirable policy was one that provided for immediate independence for the islands.

There were four logical courses of action available to the United States in regard to its insular possessions. First, they could

---

20. Seth W. Brown, *op. cit.*, p. 2.

21. The Platt Amendment was attached to the Army Appropriation Bill of March 2, 1902. The official text of the amendment appears in *U.S. Statutes at Large*, Vol. XXXI, Part II, pp. 895-898; for a more convenient source, see Ruhl J. Bartlett, *The Record of American Diplomacy* (New York, 1954), pp. 535-537.

22. *To the American People*, Anti-Imperialist Broadside No. 15, *op. cit.*

continue to be held in subjugation and governed by alien masters without governmental representation, but the anti-imperialists pointed out that this was completely in opposition to America's principles and traditions and contravened the Declaration of Independence and the Constitution. Second, the islands' inhabitants could be granted full American citizenship with all its attendant rights and privileges, but the imperialists claimed that they were unfit for American citizenship and the anti-imperialists conceded that this course of action did present some very real practical problems. Third, the islands could be held indefinitely but with the understanding that they would very gradually be granted a greater measure of autonomy. This is, of course, what actually happened, but the anti-imperialists insisted that in the school of self-government experience was the best teacher, and that this simply postponed interminably what was the right decision. The fourth, and the anti-imperialists argued only proper, alternative was to grant the islands immediate freedom, and to provide for their independence by securing international treaties to this effect.

E. B. Smith, in an important speech at the National Social and Political Conference in Detroit on June 29, 1901, called for immediate action to implement this last solution to the nation's increasingly complex and distasteful colonial imbroglio. He also gave some tacit advice to his fellow anti-imperialists, as well as explicit counsel to the opposition, when he said that "whether we should have acquired Puerto Rico and the Philippines, it is now too late to discuss. If we are to remain a free people, it can never be too late to believe and proclaim that the United States ought not to acquire or hold any territory anywhere that may not be governed by American methods." [23] He was, thus, saying that although the anti-imperialists certainly felt that it was wrong for the United States to have ever acquired any colonial possessions, the fact of the matter was that we had done so. The important thing at this juncture was to see, first, that it did not happen again, and second, what could be done

23. Edwin Burritt Smith, *Shall the United States Have Colonies?* (Anti-Imperialist Broadside No. 14) (Boston, 1901).

about hastening the independence of the islands. The anti-imperialists were largely successful in the former—the United States never again engaged in the type of insular expansion of 1898–99—but were to be frustrated in regard to the latter endeavor.

Just five days after Smith's speech in Detroit, the anti-imperialist leagues of the nation issued their most important joint policy statement since the election of 1900. The date of July 4th was, of course, deliberately chosen for its symbolic significance and presaged the themes that would be emphasized in the document. It was certainly ironic that on this day when the United States celebrates its freedom from colonial status the nation should be in the process of subduing a colony of its own.

Aside from the continuing war in the Philippines, the two most important foreign policy issues at this time were the administration's Cuban policy and the Supreme Court's handling of the Insular Cases, and both of these received severe censure. The anti-imperialists warned that if the nation was despotic in its foreign policy, its domestic policy would soon be adversely affected, for "indifference to liberty anywhere breeds indifference to liberty everywhere." They maintained that the nation could not have both citizens and subjects and retain its democratic form of government. Citing the patron saint of the movement, they pointed out that on July 4, 1776 the nation was "conceived in liberty and dedicated to the proposition that all men are created equal" and they warned that a "house divided against itself cannot stand." They insisted that the real division now was between the people and the imperialistic administration, and they presented their fervent appeal for the abandonment of colonialism to those "who for the moment exercise the power of the nation from the people who are the nation." [24]

This position was reiterated at the annual meeting of the New England Anti-Imperialist League, where Erving Winslow stated: "Our appeal lies to the American people that the questions which have arisen concerning the possessions which have come under

---

24. *To the American People,* Anti-Imperialist Broadside No. 15 (Boston, 1901).

our control in consequence of the Spanish War shall be rightfully settled in obedience and conformity to the Constitution." [25] This theme was repeated over and over again, it being the sincere belief of the anti-imperialists that there was a real dichotomy between the feelings of *the people* and their representatives in the government.

There is no doubt that popular disenchantment with imperialism had grown considerably as the cost in men and dollars of subduing the Philippine insurrection mounted. More and more people began to feel that the whole venture was ill-fated. A. A. Berle, who gave the principal address at the New England Anti-Imperialist League's meeting in November, voiced the undoubtedly correct belief that if the question of United States foreign policy could be submitted to the people "dissociated from all other complicating and confusing questions, they would give their overwhelming approval for free government for Filipinos." [26] However, as the election of 1900 should have taught the anti-imperialists, matters simply do not exist in such pristine isolation in American politics.

There were other reasons in addition to the obfuscation and conflicting currents of politics why the anti-imperialists had not been more successful in influencing the mass of the American people. Their arguments tended to be too academic and their speeches perhaps too erudite for widespread popular consumption. They had failed to convey their ideas in a meaningful way to the average man. One of their principal problems was that their position was negatory and people respond much more to a positive program. Part of the real strength of the imperialist's program was that it was positive and dynamic, while the anti-imperialist's position was negative, restrictive, and self-denyng. It added an eleventh negative commandment when the people already had a difficult time adhering to the first ten. The more perceptive of the anti-imperialist leaders realized this and resolved at the annual meeting in 1901 to devote themselves to

25. *Report of the Third Annual Meeting of the New England Anti-Imperialist League, op. cit.,* p. 11.
26. *Ibid.,* p. 18.

"a positive purpose," [27] but this was more easily enunciated than carried out, and the anti-imperialist position, as its very name implied, remained basically a negative one.

The activities of the anti-imperialists in 1902, other than an abortive attempt to make anti-imperialism a significant issue in the congressional elections, centered on criticism of allegedly unnecessarily cruel methods of dealing with the Filipinos. Although George S. Boutwell had said at the previous annual meeting of the New England League that the anti-imperialists "dealt with the course of affairs in our insular possessions . . . for purposes of illustration only," [28] it is clear that cruelty or injustice anywhere offended their strong humanitarian sensibilities and influenced their view of imperialism and the stand they took upon our early handling of matters in the Philippines.

The anti-imperialists were especially quick to point out any similarities between our policy and the frequently harsh methods used by Spain. For example, the *Chicago Public* in January, 1902, published an item headed "Reconcentration—Condemned by the American People in 1898, Sanctioned by the American Government in 1902," which noted that on December 8, 1901, General Bell had issued a reconcentration edict at Batangas in the Philippines. There then followed a poem by Bertrand Shadwell, who composed much inept anti-imperialist poetry, entitled "Reconcentration," which read in part:

> So we must doff our caps to Weyler now
> > Whom late we railed at as a fiend accurst—
> Of Tyrant's tools the vilest and the worst
>
> .   .   .   .   .
>
> Thus have we cursed what now we justice call
> > So high we seemed to stand, so low we fall.[29]

---

27. *Ibid.*, p. 22.
28. *Ibid.*, p. 4.
29. Clipping among Croffut Papers. There is also an interesting letter from Shadwell to Croffut, dated December 10, 1901, asking Croffut to send Shadwell the names of any newspapers and periodicals which might publish his anti-imperialist verses.

The anti-imperialists also continued their campaign against excessive cruelty in the prosecution of the war in the Philippines. This agitation eventually contributed to a senatorial investigation of affairs in the islands in the spring of 1902. Erving Winslow, in the annual report of the New England League, stated that in his capacity as the League's Secretary he had visited Washington and "supplied the defenders of liberty in the Senate committee with such of our documents and collections as might be useful to them in their investigation." [30]

The imperialists at first denied that the charges of cruelty had any foundation. Secretary of War Elihu Root stated that "the war in the Philippines has been conducted by the American army with scrupulous regard for the rules of civilized warfare; with careful and genuine consideration for the prisoner and non-combatant; with self-restraint, and with humanity never surpassed, if ever equaled, in any conflict, worthy only of praise and reflecting credit upon the American people." [31] Unfortunately this was not the case. Root's sophistry was exposed not only by the anti-imperialists but also by others who would have been glad if they could have supported him without making an obvious travesty of bitter truth. The Commander in Chief of the U.S. Army at the time, Nelson A. Miles, in his autobiography, says of his visit to the Philippines in 1902: "I received a number of complaints of . . . unwarranted acts of the military toward prisoners in their hands in order to obtain information concerning arms, numbers and disposition of Filipino troops, and I issued rigid orders prohibiting such unjustifiable acts." [32] Even the pro-Administration *Outlook*, which had originally printed Root's statement as an answer to anti-imperialist charges, later admitted that "there is no doubt that acts of cruelty and oppression, some of them truly characterized as atrocities, have been perpetrated by members of the U.S. army in the Philippines." [33]

---

30. *Report of the Fourth Annual Meeting of the New England Anti-Imperialist League* (Boston, 1903), p. 11.

31. *The Outlook,* Vol. LXX (March 22, 1902), p. 711.

32. Nelson A. Miles, *Serving the Republic* (New York, 1911), p. 307.

33. *The Outlook,* Vol. LXXII (May 9, 1903), p. 100.

The venerable Carl Schurz joined in the agitation and sought
to persuade others to do so. On May 8 he wrote to Jacob Gould
Schurman,[34] who had served on several governmental commis-
sions in the Philippines, and urged him to aid in investigating
the charges of barbarism. He said that "in such a crisis I think
we have to do what we can. The first thing necessary is that we
discover the truth and let the people know it. I cannot give up
the hope that when the American people know the truth, they
will do what is right." [35] This was also the philosophy of the
"Muckrakers" of the Progressive Era which was now dawning,
with whom the anti-imperialist publicist had much in common.
Schurz later (August 2, 1902) wrote to Andrew Carnegie [36]
urging him to use his influence ("you have his ear") with the
man who named the Muckrakers—Theodore Roosevelt—to elicit
a statement in favor of Philippine independence. Schurz pointed
out that "new evidence of . . . barbarities is constantly cropping
out as officers and soldiers come back from the Philippines . . .
and to aggravate it all, we have done this, as the case now stands,
in furtherance of a policy of conquest." [37]

This phase of the anti-imperialists' critique of the manifestations of imperialism continued throughout the summer of 1902.
In June Benjamin Flower, the crusading editor of *The Arena*,
presented a long exposé of the brutality accompanying the war
in the Philippines. He gave a detailed account of the horrors of

34. For an analysis of Schurman's role in Philippine affairs, see
Kenneth E. Hendrickson, "Reluctant Expansionist—Jacob Gould
Schurman and the Philippine Question," *Pacific Historical Review,*
vol. XXXVI (Nov., 1967), pp. 405-421.

35. Schurz Papers.

36. Carnegie, himself, had recently written an article criticizing
American policy in the Philippines, in which he pointed out that
"we prohibited the reading of the Declaration of Independence in
the Philippines last 4th of July. To the incredulous reader let me
repeat this fact. It is on record and acknowledged by our officials.
. . . We are engaged in work which requires suppression of American
ideas hitherto held sacred."—*The Opportunity of the United States*
(New York, 1902), pp. 6-7. (The citation is from the reprint in
booklet form by the New York Anti-Imperialist League; the essay
originally appeared in the *North American Review,* May, 1902).

37. Schurz Papers.

the "water cure," and the wanton and indiscriminate slaughter of noncombatants, including women and children. He went into the case of Major Littleton Waller, who, when court martialed for cruelty, testified that he was merely carrying out the orders of General Jacob H. Smith, who told him to "kill and burn" and that "the more he killed and burned the better he would like it." Flower stated, in concluding his essay of horrors, that "the fact that our soldiers are becoming familiar with despotic acts and savage practices, and that they see on every hand a disregard for the very things our fathers held most fundamental and essential to a republic—such as freedom of the press, respect for civil authority and the rights of man—should be the subject of the gravest concern to thoughtful lovers of free government everywhere." [38]

A symposium sponsored by *The Arena* in July on "Why I Oppose Imperialism" reiterated many of the same points which Flower had emphasized. Brutality in the prosecution of the war was deplored and censorship and the suppression of news was strongly criticized. Bolton Hall expressed great concern about the excesses of the military spirit, "with its glorification of brute force, threatening the gag and the noose for those who voice humanity's sighs, and branding as traitors those who protest against the betrayal of our allies." [39]

In a notable article in August the Reverend Robert E. Bisbee demonstrated that the anti-imperialists felt that the evidence of cruelty was simply a symptom of the greater disease of imperialism: "The cost, the hardships, the slaughter, the unspeakable personal crimes . . . I do not dwell upon; for great as they are, they are of slight importance compared with the destruction of our ideals and the suppression of the spirit of independence among millions of people." [40] Erving Winslow at the fourth an-

---

38. Benjamin O. Flower, "Some Dead Sea Fruit of Our War of Subjugation," *The Arena,* Vol. XXVII (June, 1902), p. 653.

39. Bolton Hall, et al, "Why I Oppose Imperialism: A Symposium," *The Arena,* Vol. XXVIII (July, 1902), p. 6.

40. Robert E. Bisbee, "Why I Oppose Our Philippine Policy," *The Arena,* Vol. XXVIII (August, 1902), p. 117.

nual meeting of the New England Anti-Imperialist League stated the precise position of the anti-imperialist movement on the matter: "The Anti-Imperialist Leagues as such have upheld and encouraged the efforts which have been made and will still be made to make public the treatment which the Filipinos have received at the hands of subjugating armies, as only a corroborating evidence of the evils of imperialism." [41]

Several incidental factors about the fourth annual meeting of the New England League indicate that the anti-imperialist movement had begun to lose some of its vitality. First, it was no longer held in one of Boston's large public halls as in the past, but rather was moved to the small, august rooms of the Twentieth Century Club. Second, it would seem to have become to a large degree a social meeting, for it included a luncheon and the invitation stated that "the presence of ladies is especially desired." Third, the organization, in a literal sense, was losing some of its vitality as well as significant financial support, for the Secretary reported that death had removed two generous benefactors of the League—F. A. Brooks and Dr. F. E. Potter. In spite of this lessening of the movement's vigor, its leaders vowed to continue the fight, "to keep this great question constantly before the eighty million people of the nation; to educate the minds and awaken the consciences of the voters; and to teach them that the principles of our Declaration of Independence apply to Malays in the East as well as to Anglo-Saxons here." [42]

The League's persistent agitation, combined with the bitter experience of the war in the islands with its distressing concomitants of disease, destruction, and death, greatly diminished the people's enthusiasm for imperialism. By 1903 our imperial adventure in the Philippines no longer seemed so romantic. The American soldier had never been too fond of the notion of international uplift and tramped, disgustedly, through the enervating islands singing:

---

41. *Fourth Annual Meeting of the New England Anti-Imperialist League, op. cit.,* p. 11.

42. *Ibid.,* p. 18.

Damn, damn, damn the Filipino
Pock-marked khakiac ladrone
Underneath the starry flag
Civilize him with a Krag
And return us to our beloved home.

When the soldiers returned home in 1903, all they wanted was to forget about the Philippines, and the general populace concurred; for most Americans the glorious White Man's Burden had become simply a burden.

CHAPTER 16

The Battle Rejoined

Theodore Roosevelt's virtual seizure of the Panama Canal Zone in 1903 focused national attention once more on the issue of imperialism. The United States had been interested in an isthmian canal since the middle of the nineteenth century. As early as 1846, the United States had signed a treaty with New Granada (Colombia) granting the United States the right of transit across the isthmus of Panama. Four years later in the Clayton-Bulwer Treaty the United States agreed that any future canal would be undertaken jointly with Great Britain. American Secretaries of State attempted on numerous occasions before the 1890's to have this abrogated, so that the United States could have exclusive control of the canal. The writings of Alfred Thayer Mahan throughout the 1890's, combined with the dramatic race of the U.S.S. *Oregon* around the Horn during the Spanish American War, emphasized the need for a canal. Then when we obtained our insular possessions in the Caribbean and the Pacific in 1898-99, the American imperialists insisted that the canal project could wait no longer.

The Roosevelt administration finally succeeded in having the Clayton-Bulwer Treaty set aside in the second Hay-Pauncefote Treaty, which was approved by the U.S. Senate on February 21, 1902. The Hay-Herran Treaty (signed January 22, 1903) was then negotiated with Colombia, giving the United States control of a strip of land across the Panamanian isthmus. When the Colombian Senate refused to ratify the treaty, Roosevelt was greatly displeased.

The Administration quietly let it be known that it would not be at all adverse to the secession of Panama from Colombia, and when a revolt conveniently ensued on November 3, 1903, the United States insured its success by having its warships prevent Colombian troops from putting down the revolt. Seventy-two hours after the revolt, the United States officially recognized the new nation of Panama and on November 18 signed a treaty with the fledging republic for the canal zone. Roosevelt at the time denied complicity in the revolution, but he was obviously pleased by the whole affair and some years later boasted that he "took the Canal Zone."

The anti-imperialists, for their part, had no doubt who "took Panama;" and they roundly denounced both the act and the man. The entire "Panama affair" was criticized by several speakers at the fifth annual meeting of the New England Anti-Imperialist League, which took place at the end of the same month as the coup d'état. The League's Treasurer, David Greene Haskins, Jr., said indignantly:

> The criminal blunder in the Philippines is bearing its natural fruit in a more lordly and overbearing attitude toward our weaker neighbors in this hemisphere. Events passing before our eyes this present month show it. The Administration has approved and aided, if it has not instigated, a revolt in Panama against a friendly power. It has forcibly prevented that power from suppressing the revolt; and with indecent haste has signed a treaty for the coveted canal with the agent of an irresponsible revolutionary committee.[1]

Winslow Warren, who presided at the annual meeting, also equated the Panamanian incident with our imperialism in the Pacific, saying melodramatically that "having begun with murder and outrage in the Philippines, so soon have [we] come to burglary and common stealing in Panama." [2]

---

1. *Report of the Fifth Annual Meeting of the New England Anti-Imperialist League* (Boston, 1903), p. 17.
   The "agent" about whom Haskins speaks was Philippe Bunau-Varilla, who was actually a French citizen.
2. *Fifth Annual Meeting, op. cit.,* p. 5.

Robert L. Bisbee felt that our actions in both the Philippines and Panama were simply manifestations of an even more fundamental evil. "The question of the Philippines," he insisted, "is a subordinate question. It is merely the symptom of a disease which is very deep-seated. So, also, of this Panama question. We have bad blood in this nation. Ours is an era when original genuine democracy is making the struggle of its life against an overwhelming oligarchy of power." Bisbee's speech, as those of many other anti-imperialists at this time, illustrates the fact that anti-imperialism was beginning to merge with the broad reform sentiments of the Progressive Era. Bisbee even went so far as to suggest that they "ought to enlarge the scope of this League and make it a great, general, deep-seated movement in the interests of genuine democracy." [3]

Erving Winslow, in his usual optimistic way, felt that this latest incident in the long run might prove beneficial by stimulating interest in the anti-imperialist cause. He and his fellow anti-imperialists hoped that the Panama affair might shock the American people so profoundly that they would be led "back to the ways of sanity, peace, and humanity." [4]

The anti-imperialist forces in the Senate were also quick to question and criticize the Panama affair. On December 9, Senator Hoar offered a resolution inquiring into American participation in the revolution. On the 17th he supported his own resolution, saying that there was a "suspicion of national dishonor" in the matter and that the Senate and the American people were "entitled to know the whole truth." The following day, Senator Edmund W. Pettus of Alabama censured the Administration for "bullying" Colombia. He inquired: "Now, have we gotten to be so great, has all this power been entrusted to us by our Master that we should abuse it like a bully? I fear we are doing it." [5]

Senators Gorman of Maryland and Daniel of Virginia, who had also been strong critics of the Treaty of Paris, soon joined Hoar and Pettus in the attack. Hoar called upon the President

3. *Ibid.,* p. 37.
4. *Ibid.,* p. 7.
5. M. M. Miller, *op. cit.,* Vol. III, pp. 422, 426, 434.

to provide any information which might cast light on the relation of the U.S. government to the secession movement in Panama. *Harper's Weekly* correctly observed that Hoar and the others "seemed disposed to condemn our Federal Executive in advance, for [they] insinuated that the facts would not justify President Roosevelt and Secretary Hay in asserting, as they have asserted categorically, that they were entirely blameless as regards the charge of promoting the Panama revolution." [6]

Others, both inside and outside of the Senate, concurred with the suspicions of the above Senators. Professor Theodore Woolsey of Yale, who more than a decade previously was one of the first to note and criticize the drift of the United States toward imperialism, presented a strong critique of the administration's actions vis-à-vis Panama. Even leaving aside the controversial issue of whether the Administration tacitly or otherwise contributed to the revolution, he felt that there was much that was undesirable in the undisputed facts of the Panama situation. He claimed that our military intervention was not justified by the treaty of 1846, under which it was invoked, and that "to prevent Colombia's coercion of Panama was an act of war." He asserted that "the hasty recognition of a new State in Panama was not in accordance with the law of Nations," and that "the canal treaty, negotiated and ratified by the [Panamanian] Junta, with no constitutional authority or other authorization, is of doubtful validity." [7] Nevertheless, once the United States had recognized Panama, the other nations soon followed suit.

As far as the Hay-Bunau-Varilla Treaty was concerned, the anti-imperialists fulminated in vain; for after a certain amount of acrimonious debate, it was approved on February 23, 1904, by a vote of 66 to 14. The Senatorial opposition to the treaty really had been in an awkward position. The canal,

---

6. *Harper's Weekly,* Vol. XLVIII, No. 2454 (Jan. 2, 1904), p. 8.

7. *The Outlook,* Vol. LXXVI (Jan. 30, 1904), pp. 248-9.
For a similar indictment, see J. P. Gordy, "The Ethics of the Panama Case," *The Forum,* Vol. XXXVI (July, 1904), pp. 15-24.

if not the means by which the United States acquired the right to construct it, was a highly worthwhile and popular project. Then, too, once the matter had gone so far, the possible alternatives were rather limited. The editor of *Harper's Weekly* commented that those men who opposed the treaty failed "to explain what they would have us do hereafter?" He pointed out, moreover, that "should the inhabitants of the isthmus find that President Roosevelt is unable for the moment to secure a ratification of the treaty, they may demand admission to our Union, either as a State or as a Territory." [8] The alternative possibility that the United States might annex all of Panama was, of course, even more distasteful to the anti-imperialists and served to mitigate their opposition to the treaty. Although the anti-imperialists never mustered really formidable opposition to the treaty, the administration's aggressive and overbearing tactics in the Panama affair did give them a new issue, which they utilized to reawaken interest in the anti-imperialist cause.

The other factor which served temporarily to revivify the movement was the advent of the election of 1904. Feeling that their cause had not had a chance to be really judged by the electorate in 1900 because of a variety of conflicting issues and loyalties, the anti-imperialists looked forward hopefully to the election of 1904. They began quite early to give the matter consideration in their public utterances. Thus Charles A. Towne, who was considered by some to be a likely candidate for the Democratic Party, in an anti-imperialist speech in New York on July 4, 1903, said: "Let us go before the people with the truth [about imperialism]. Let us not confuse them with too many issues. Let us draw the line firm and plain between those who, on one side, would violate the Declaration of Independence and evade the Constitution, and those who, on the other, find still an essential truth in the former and believe in maintaining the authority of the latter." [9]

8. *Harper's Weekly, op. cit.,* pp. 8-9.
9. Charles A. Towne, *The Continental Republic: A Protest Against Colonialism* (Boston, 1903), p. 16.

At the annual meeting of the New England Anti-Imperialist League in November of 1903, the forthcoming election was discussed by several speakers. One would expect a philosopher like William James, who had become an officer of the League, to have some interesting comments to make upon the subject. The Harvard professor, who gave the principal address at the meeting, said: "The Democrats have already espoused our principles, and many of us think, therefore, that the only thing left for us is to espouse the Democratic cause." James, however, like many old Republicans among the anti-imperialists, questioned this move. "Against it," he observed, "there is the objection that the Democrats are only half sincere in the matter—it is largely an opposition issue to gain the independent vote—and there is the still stronger objection that the Republicans themselves have not half made up their minds that the islands ought to be retained."

In a statement that sounds like Madison Avenue jargon of the 1960's, he remarked that "the better self of the Republicans, their subliminal consciousness, so to speak, is already on our side." James contended that the Republican party "was railroaded into its conquistador career by the McKinley administration. The war short-circuited political reflection. . . . But we may be sure that the state of mind, even of our leaders, is full of misgivings, and that if we don't put them too much on the defensive, time will do our work." [10] Many of the League's leaders did not agree with the characteristic pragmatism of James's advice, and favored instead George S. Boutwell's insistence that the destruction of "the policy of Empire introduced by President McKinley [can] be accomplished only by and through the overthrow of the Republican Party." [11]

Winslow Warren felt that the salvation of their cause lay in particular men and ideas rather than in one party or the other. He said that he looked forward to the time when the

---

10. *Fifth Annual Meeting, op. cit.*, pp. 23-24.
11. *Ibid.*, p. 25.

Republican party would again be led by men like Edmunds, Sherman and Hoar instead of Roosevelt, Beveridge, and Lodge, and the Democrats would realize that "there is a surer stay in the principles of their grand old man at Princeton [12] . . . than in the vagaries of those who lead them to unutterable defeat." [13] If such a time came, he was certain that the League's cause would be safe in the hands of either party and their work would be done. Warren got half of his wish; for although the Republicans did not forsake Roosevelt, the Democrats chose as their standard-bearer in 1904 a man—Judge Alton B. Parker—who was a true Cleveland Democrat, i.e. forthright, conservative, and anti-imperialistic.

Before the conventions even met the anti-imperialists sought to influence the platforms by circulating a paper requesting the parties to come out in favor of independence for the Philippines. The petition was enthusiastically received by the intelligentsia, being signed by scores of college professors and prominent clergymen. Carl Schurz commented upon the paper, saying that he supposed the Republicans would ignore it, but adding that he would not be surprised if it would "encourage the Democratic Convention to put forth some energetic pronouncement." [14]

Schurz's predictions turned out to be quite accurate. The Republican convention nominated Roosevelt and Charles Fairbanks on a platform which endorsed the policy of the previous four years. The plank concerning the Philippines praised the "effective and strong administration" of the islands and ignored the matter of independence completely.

The Democratic convention convened in Chicago on July 6. After a brief boom for the publisher William Randolph Hearst subsided, Judge Parker, as anticipated, was nominated

---

12. The reference is to Grover Cleveland, who had retired to Princeton, N.J. He had recently published in the *Saturday Evening Post* a strong anti-imperialist article which was very well received.

13. *Fifth Annual Meeting, op. cit.,* p. 27.

14. Bancroft, *op. cit.,* Vol. VI, p. 349.

for President and Henry Davis for Vice President. A delegation from the New England Anti-Imperialist League conferred with the Democratic platform committee and endeavored to have a plank inserted calling for immediate freedom for the Philippines. The actual statement in the platform, while acceptable to the League's delegates, was less demonstrative. It stated: "We insist that we ought to do for the Filipinos what we have already done for the Cubans, and it is our duty to make that promise now, and . . . set the Filipino people upon their feet free and independent to work out their own destiny." [15]

The anti-imperialists were pleased with the candidacy of Judge Parker and the Democratic platform. Schurz in a letter to Erving Winslow stated the anti-imperialist view that Parker was a "leader . . . deserving and possessing the confidence of the people," and that the Philippine plank in the platform was "the voice of right, of justice, of genuine Americanism and of true statesmanship." [16]

Schurz and many other anti-imperialist leaders labored in behalf of Parker and Davis. Indeed, they seemed to do more than the candidates themselves, who conducted a very sedentary (which was understandable in Davis' case—he was eighty-two years old!) and lackluster campaign. There is a lengthy document by Schurz among his papers entitled "An Open Letter to the Independent Voter." Like the efforts of most anti-imperialists, it is characteristically negative. Almost the entire "Letter" is spent deprecating the Republican party and Roosevelt; relatively little is said about the Democratic party, and that is not very forceful. This is, however, probably to be expected when the writer is a former Republican.

Schurz complained that many of the leaders of his erstwhile party "treat the principles of the Declaration of Independence— once its Magna Carta—with supercilious contempt." He said that the Republican party no longer stood for democracy, liberty, and

---

15. Stanwood, *op. cit.,* p. 120.
16. Bancroft, *op. cit.,* Vol. VI, p. 356.

peace. "Its ideal is now /to be/ a great 'world-power' governing foreign lands and alien populations by arbitrary rule, and asserting its position among the other powers of the world by the number of its battle-ships." Schurz insisted, rather, that the way for a nation to be a truly great world power was not through armaments and bullying, but by presenting to the world "the most encouraging example of a great people governing themselves in liberty, justice, and peace," and by being eminently fair in "its dealings with all other nations great and small, strong and weak."

Schurz condemned Roosevelt's handling of the Panama affair, stating that, in addition to being intrinsically wrong, it would certainly arouse the distrust of the other Latin American nations. He said, furthermore, that what later came to be known as the Roosevelt Corollary to the Monroe Doctrine was absolutely "incredible . . . the task thus mapped out for us is so unreasonable in itself, so adventurous, fraught with such arbitrary assumptions of power, with so many complications and with responsibilities so incalculable, that any statesmanship which proposes it may well be thought capable of any eccentricity ever so extravagant." [17]

Schurz's pronouncement was, as usual, thoughtful, cogent, and eloquent; and if he had been running instead of Parker, the Republicans might have been more concerned. The fact was, however, that Parker and Davis were barely running at all; and they were attempting, if terribly passively, to oppose a man who was so dynamic that he appeared to be running even when he was standing still, which for the author of "the strenuous life" was a rare condition.

The anti-imperialists did their utmost, although it was to prove in vain, to make anti-imperialism "the great issue" of the campaign. With this in mind, Charles R. Codman, a vice presi-

---

17. Schurz Papers.

J. P. Gordy offered a similar critique of the Roosevelt policy—"a more dangerous doctrine than this would be difficult to conceive"—in "The Ethics of the Panama Case," *The Forum,* Vol. XXXVI (July, 1904), p. 117.

dent of the New England Anti-Imperialist League, led a delegation representing the Parker Independent Clubs to the Judge's home at Esopus, New York, on the ides of October of 1904. Although the die of American public opinion had by this time, undoubtedly, been irrevocably cast against the Democratic candidate, Codman and Henry W. Hardon issued forceful public statements; and Parker, who was not a very able extemporaneous speaker, read a prepared reply. Codman said that many people of various political persuasions—Republican, Democratic, and Independent—were banding together to support Parker, "because they are convinced that, at this time, higher considerations than any involved in the ordinary political questions demand the cordial and effective union of those who place the honor and good name of the Republic, and the necessity of maintaining the principles upon which it was founded, above all other issues." [18]

Judge Parker replied to Codman and Hardon, by saying that the importance of anti-imperialism could not be overestimated. "It is attracting the attention of the thoughtful and patriotic men all over the country." He recalled the statement concerning the Philippines in the Democratic platform. "Here," he said, "we have the issue clearly defined. The Republican Party stands for the subjugation of defenseless foreign peoples. Democracy [i.e. the Democratic Party] stands for freedom."

Actually, however, Parker's own position on the issue was closer to the one toward which the Republicans were moving than it was to the position of the organized anti-imperialists. He stated: "I have said before that we may not disregard the responsibility imposed by possession of the Philippines, and [this] responsibility will be best subserved by preparing the islands as rapidly as possible for self-government, and giving them the assurance that it will come as soon as they are reasonably prepared for it." [19] The Anti-Imperialist League, on the other hand, consistently maintained that self-government was best learned by experience and that the Filipinos should be given their

18. Charles R. Codman, Henry W. Hardon, and Alton B. Parker, *Anti-Imperialism: The Great Issue* (Boston, 1904), p. 3.

19. *Ibid.,* pp. 9-11.

independence immediately and be allowed to work out their destiny in their own way.

Nevertheless, Parker's position was considered to be definitely a step in the right direction, and the leaders of the anti-imperialist movement did what they could in his behalf. Unfortunately for them, Parker did too little in his own behalf. His campaign really never got off the ground; in fact, it rarely got off his front porch at Esopus. This lethargy, combined with his lack of personal appeal and T. R.'s possession of it in plenitude, led to a landslide victory for Roosevelt. The anti-imperialist leaders realized this themselves. George S. Boutwell commented that "while the Democratic Party in its platform and candidate was acceptable to the Anti-Imperialists, it is to be said that Judge Parker was deficient in the personal and individual characteristics which were attractive and commanding in President Roosevelt." [20]

Although the Anti-Imperialist League would courageously, if with steadily diminishing vigor, carry on for sixteen more years, the election of 1904 virtually marked the last time in which anti-imperialism would be a really active and vital force on a broad national scale. In this election they were able, if unsuccessfully, to rally the anti-imperialist forces behind a man, who, in spite of his inability to stir the masses, was a person whom they respected. In 1908 the Democrats would again bring forth that faded rose who had never smelled fragrant to the leaders of the anti-imperialist movement—William Jennings Bryan —against William Howard Taft, who at worst was a reluctant, benign, and passive imperialist, and whose other characteristics were not unappealing to the remaining members of the anti-imperialist old guard. By 1912 anti-imperialism was dead and beyond resuscitation as a viable political issue; and the victory of the Democratic candidate, Woodrow Wilson, although it led to a somewhat greater measure of self-government for the Filipinos, did not win the anti-imperialists' desired goal of independence for the islands.

---

20. *Report of the Sixth Annual Meeting of the Anti-Imperialist League* (Boston, 1904), pp. 4-5.

The outcome of the election in 1904 was certainly disappointing to the anti-imperialists, but a small hard core vowed to carry on the fight. The League's loyal treasurer, David Greene Haskins, Jr., commented: "The defeat in an election of a political party that has bravely, and, I believe, honestly advocated our principles is regrettable, but it is a mere passing incident. . . . Victory will come, and it may be nearer than we think." [21]

---

21. *Ibid.,* pp. 16, 17.

CHAPTER 17

Taps

The anti-imperialists' victory was coming, but the majority of the men who formed the backbone of institutional anti-imperialism would not live to see it. The inexorable force of time took its toll of the movement, and the necrology of anti-imperialists lengthened with each passing year. Erving Winslow, secretary of the Anti-Imperialist League, stated truly at the annual meeting in 1904 that there had been "irreparable breaches" in the ranks of the League's supporters.[1]

The movement was losing, through constant attrition not only its most influential members, but also its monetary support. Thus Winslow remarked when Henry Brewer Metcalf died that the League had lost "a generous giver of time and money. His place can scarcely be supplied." [2] The financial condition of the various leagues would never have impressed Dun and Bradstreet, but with the death of certain key individuals the pecuniary picture became even darker.[3]

By the end of 1904 many of the prominent men who had been among the early officers of the Anti-Imperialist League had died. Among them were John Sherman, John C. Bullitt, Hazen

---

1. *Sixth Annual Meeting, op. cit.,* p. 11.
2. *Ibid.*
3. *Report of the Seventh Annual Meeting of the Anti-Imperialist League* (Boston, 1905), p. 18.
For an interesting financial commentary on one of the other leagues, see the letter (Feb. 2, 1900) from Henry Hallam, Treasurer of the Washington Anti-Imperialist League to William Croffut. Croffut Papers, Library of Congress.

S. Pingree, John J. Valentine, Charlton T. Lewis, and Hermann Von Holst. The following year saw the death of such irreplaceable anti-imperialist crusaders as George S. Boutwell, Edward Atkinson, James Coolidge Carter, Emil Preetorius, and Patrick A. Collins.

These men and others like them, who had led the anti-imperialist forces in the thick of the fight in 1899, in most cases steadfastly maintained their faith to the end. George F. Hoar, who died September 30, 1904, literally carried his faith in the cause to the grave: The ivy-fringed monument where he is buried in Sleepy Hollow Cemetery in Concord, Massachusetts, bears the following characteristic epitaph:

> I have no faith in fatalism, in destiny, in blind force. I believe in God, the living God. I believe in the American people, a free and brave people, who do not bow the neck or bend the knee, and who desire no other to bow the neck or bend the knee to them. I believe that a republic is greater than an empire. I believe, finally, whatever clouds may darken the horizon that the world is growing better, that today is better than yesterday, and that tomorrow will be better than today.

The remaining leaders of the anti-imperialist movement shared Hoar's credo and only hoped that his optimism would prove to be justified. Moorfield Storey became the titular head of the movement when he replaced George S. Boutwell as president of the Anti-Imperialist League [4] upon the latter's death. [5] On May 29, 1905, Carl Schurz wrote to Storey concerning his new position. "I think," he said, "that you have done well in accepting the presidency of the Anti-Imperialist League, for I am sure that you will keep it within the lines of real usefulness. . . . It is undoubtedly true," Schurz remarked, "that the people generally are very tired of the possession of the Philippines. The

---

4. As was mentioned previously, the New England Anti-Imperialist League at the annual meeting in 1904 re-assumed its original designation as *the* Anti-Imperialist League, since it was, for all intents and purposes, the only really viable organization still left in the field.

5. Boutwell died at Groton, Massachusetts on Feb. 27, 1905.

trouble is that they are so tired of it that they lose all interest in the matter." [6]

Schurz's observation points up the fact that one of the League's greatest problems at this juncture was that the public was simply apathetic about anti-imperialism. It was no longer the vital question that it had been five years earlier. This doubtless prompted Erving Winslow to insist at the seventh annual meeting that "agitation is our imperative duty, agitation and still more agitation, though it may sometimes seem out of season to the mere politician." [7]

Most of the League's present "agitation" consisted of the reiteration of arguments which were by now rather hoary. The principal project of this period involved a proposal for the neutralization of the Philippines, which had originally been suggested by Carl Schurz several years earlier. A resolution on the subject was prepared and forwarded to Washington,[8] but nothing substantial came of the proposal.

In another indignant resolution the League denounced President Roosevelt's custom house intervention in the Dominican Republic. In his annual message of December, 1904, Roosevelt had outlined the controversial policy known as the "Roosevelt Corollary to the Monroe Doctrine." He had said, in part, that

chronic wrongdoing, or an impotence which results in a general loosening of the ties of civilized society, may in America, as elsewhere, ultimately require intervention by some civilized nation, and in the Western Hemisphere the adherence of the United States to the Monroe Doctrine may force the United

---

6. Storey Papers.

7. *Seventh Annual Meeting, op. cit.,* p. 3.

8. *Ibid.,* p. 12.
The resolution read: "Whereas, it is frequently urged as a reason for refusing their independence to the Philippine Islands that some other nation would take the Islands if the United States abandoned them . . . the President is requested to open negotiations with the other nations for the purpose of securing neutralization of the Philippine Islands and recognition of their independence whenever same shall be granted to them by the United States."

States, however reluctantly, in flagrant cases of such wrongdoing or impotence to the exercise of an international police power.[9]

Under this self-imposed obligation the United States early in 1905, to forestall possible European intervention to collect debts, took over the Dominican custom house and administered it. The anti-imperialists felt that this action was "quite beyond the authority of law, foreign to the legitimate business of popular government, and fraught with dangerous precedents as regards our relations to the peoples of Central and South America." [10]

Roosevelt had prefaced his corollary by saying that "it is not true that the United States feels any land hunger or entertains any projects as regards the other nations of the Western Hemisphere save such as are for their welfare." [11] The anti-imperialists, however, were skeptical concerning such disclaimers, because they had heard similar ones propounded just as righteously in the case of the Philippines.

The anti-imperialists feared that the current intervention might turn out to be merely a prelude to annexation. But Roosevelt, who was becoming increasingly disenchanted with the realities of colonial administration in the Philippines, insisted, and probably sincerely, that "as for annexing the island [i.e., Santo Domingo], I have about the same desire to annex it as a gorged boa constrictor might have to swallow a porcupine wrong-end-to." [12] Roosevelt's interest in Santo Domingo was undoubtedly motivated by a desire to protect the strategic approaches to the Panama Canal Zone rather than by a desire for further territorial expansion. In fact, Roosevelt's attitude toward foreign affairs, in general, was shifting to one of concern for simply strategic, rather than broadly imperialistic, ends.

By 1905 imperialism had lost most of its tinseled appeal for the American people. This was in no small measure due to the vigorous, persistent anti-imperialist agitation of the preceding

9. *Congressional Record,* 58th Congress, 3rd Session, p. 19.

10. *Seventh Annual Meeting, op. cit.,* pp. 50-51.

11. *Congressional Record, loc. cit.*

12. Cited by James Ford Rhodes, *The McKinley and Roosevelt Administrations* (New York, 1922), p. 318.

years, combined with a growing appreciation of the validity of the anti-imperialists' fundamental position. Moorfield Storey commented that "the wave of imperialism which reached this country in 1898 and for a while threatened to drown our people's faith in the great principles of free government has spent its force, and the tide is ebbing fast." [13]

The current of public opinion was drifting more strongly in the direction that the anti-imperialists desired. Carl Schurz, writing to Erving Winslow on February 20, 1906, less than three months before his death, commented on this trend. "It will," he said, "move slowly and try our patience." [14] But Schurz and his fellow anti-imperialists were confident that they would ultimately be completely victorious.

Anti-imperialist activities naturally subsided further with the passing of more of the movement's principal spokesmen. Schurz, the foremost publicist of the anti-imperialist movement, died in 1906, as did George G. Mercer, President of the American League of Philadelphia, and Edwin Burritt Smith. Smith had been an indefatigable supporter of the cause, especially through the American Anti-Imperialist League. The following year witnessed the demise of, among many, Donelson Caffery, a staunch opponent of imperialism for more than a dozen years and one of the most steadfast supporters of anti-imperialism in the Senate; General William Birney, president of the Washington Anti-Imperialist League; Ernest Crosby, first president of the New York Anti-Imperialist League and one of the cause's leading poets; and Leonard Woolsey Bacon, one of the early and extremely loyal officers of the Anti-Imperialist League, who was especially active in combatting the support of imperialism by the Protestant clergy.

The other principal reason for the gradual decline of anti-imperialist agitation is that there was considerably less need for it. The cumulative effect of their past propaganda and vigorous activity, plus the actual arduous experience of colonial administration, was now bearing results in a changed public attitude.

---

13. *Seventh Annual Meeting, op. cit.,* p. 21.
14. Bancroft (ed.), *op. cit.,* Vol. VI, p. 443.

The Nation, in commenting upon an anti-imperialist rally held at Faneuil Hall on November 25, 1907, observed: "Originally a very unpopular cause, anti-imperialism has, within a remarkably short period, been strikingly vindicated." [15] Erving Winslow at the Anti-Imperialist League's ninth annual meeting pointed out that for the first time in years the League was finding support among the leading papers of New York. He remarked that this could not "fail to be agreeable to our members after long years of injustice and misrepresentation," and he quoted with obvious pleasure from a recent editorial of one of the League's former detractors:

> The Anti-Imperialist League is considerably more respected, and its proposals are likely to be much more generally heeded today than at any time since it was started nearly ten years ago. . . . Today the air is surcharged with weariness and disgust toward the whole Philippines experiment. The cost in money is excessive; the cost in trouble, present and prospective, far greater; the profit, material, moral, or national, non-existent. Men who, but yesterday, were boasting that "trade follows the flag," and talking of "duty and destiny" are today advocating that we get rid of the Islands on almost any feasible basis or bona fide proposition whatsoever.[16]

This feeling had apparently even become widespread in Congress. The *New York Herald* early in September of 1907 published a report which stated that only 27 out of 138 members of Congress interviewed favored retention of the Philippines. *The Nation* observed that a surprising number of Republicans now opposed retention of the Philippines and commented that "some declare themselves ready to support any reasonable way of getting rid of our Oriental burden." This sentiment was not localized; Republican Congressmen from seventeen states favored it. Indeed, it was noted that "enough Republican Representatives are desirous of leaving the Philippines now, or at some future

---

15. *The Nation,* Vol. LXXXV, No. 2212 (Nov. 28, 1907), p. 483.

16. *Report of the Ninth Annual Meeting of the Anti-Imperialist League* (Boston, 1907), pp. 13-14.

date, to hold the balance of power in the House, and, if they are willing to act with the Democrats, to outvote the imperialists."

The really interesting fact is that the leading figures of the Republican party were now willing to depart from the Philippines. *The Nation* quoted Speaker of the House Joseph G. Cannon as saying that he "would be in favor of getting out tomorrow if there was any honorable way of getting out." [17] Moreover, *mirabile dictu,* even Theodore Roosevelt the previous month in a letter to William Howard Taft had said that he now favored Philippine independence. He had come to feel that the islands were a nuisance and a strategic liability. "The Philippine Islands," he asserted, "form our heel of Achilles." He said that he "should be glad to see the Islands made independent, with perhaps some kind of international guarantee for the preservation of order." [18]

The very strong indication of a changed attitude on Roosevelt's part toward the Philippines reflected in his letter to Taft was corroborated by Andrew Carnegie. He reported that when he was having dinner at the White House in 1907, Roosevelt had said to him, referring to Secretary of War Taft and himself: "If you wish to see the two men in the United States who are the most anxious to get out of the Philippines, here they are." [19]

Although these statements by Roosevelt were influenced by a temporary fear of possible conflict with Japan in an area which was militarily indefensible and were private and not public ones, there is little doubt that the Republican leadership was moving away from a strong imperialist position. They were gradually coming to accept the idea of Philippine independence, although maintaining the view that the Filipinos should be thoroughly prepared for self-government before it was granted—a position which prompted Andrew Carnegie to observe wryly: "This is the policy of 'Don't go into the water until you learn to swim.' " [20]

17. *The Nation,* Vol. LXXXV (Sept. 17, 1907), p. 219.

18. Roosevelt to Taft, Aug. 21, 1907; cited by Pringle, *op. cit.,* pp. 408-409.

19. Carnegie, *Autobiography, op. cit.,* p. 365.

20. *Ibid.*

It was the feeling of the anti-imperialists that self-government could only really be learned by the actual, completely independent practice of it.

By the time of the 1908 presidential election the positions of the Republican and Democratic parties and their candidates on the Philippine question were not really too divergent. The Republican nominee, William Howard Taft, actually had a rather reluctant relationship to American colonialism. His views, in fact, had originally been somewhat anti-imperialistic. He had opposed the acquisition of the Philippines; and when President McKinley asked him to head the Second Philippine Commission, he had candidly replied: "But Mr. President I am sorry we have got the Philippines. I don't want them and think you ought to have someone who is more in sympathy with the situation." [21] Taft, furthermore, even had a kind word for the Anti-Imperialist League, saying that its work had been "of value in upholding the standard of the government in the Islands because it has put that government on trial and has made every member of it strain himself to make it worthy of support." [22] This is not to say that Taft held anti-imperialist views in 1908, but his position on the subject was certainly a moderate one.

The Democrats again trotted out the aging "Boy Orator" of Nebraska, whose appeal to the Eastern intellectuals who led the anti-imperialist movement had never been great. Imperialism was not an important factor in the campaign. Moorfield Storey, speaking at the League's annual meeting just a few weeks after the election, remarked pointedly that it could not be said that the people really expressed a decided opinion on any issue, "save that they preferred Mr. Taft to Mr. Bryan."

---

21. J. F. Rhodes, *op. cit.,* p. 197. Jacob Gould Schurman, the head of the First Philippine Commission, had similar reservations about the wisdom of American policy. See Kenneth Hendrickson's recent article "Reluctant Expansionist: Jacob Gould Schurman and the Philippine Question," *Pacific Historical Review,* Vol. XXXVI (November, 1967), pp. 405-421.

22. *Sixth Annual Meeting of the Anti-Imperialist League, op. cit.,* p. 8.

This meeting marked the tenth anniversary of the founding of the Anti-Imperialist League. The occasion was naturally a nostalgic one for the League's leaders, who had labored so long and assiduously. Erving Winslow felt that real progress had been made, but regretted that the "harvest had not yet been garnered." David Haskins, more optimistically, hailed the "trend of the world in favor of the cause" and looked forward "with full confidence to victory." The third member of the League's faithful triumvirate of principal officers, Moorfield Storey, concluded the meeting in Churchillian terms. "We must," he said, "continue the contest without faltering. The end of the contest may come soon or late, but whether we live to see the end or not, the fight for freedom must never be abandoned." [23] The fight was maintained, but taps was to be sounded for the League and all of its loyal supporters before the goal of actual Philippine independence was attained.

However, even in 1908 it was evident, as David Haskins remarked, that the "enthusiasm for colonies is dead;" and its demise was hastened by men like Haskins, Winslow, and Storey and their indefatigable anti-imperialist colleagues. Only a decade earlier—certainly a brief span of years when one thinks of the empires of previous centuries—Admiral Dewey had returned to a nation filled with intense pride in its newly acquired imperial glory and had ridden while thousands cheered beneath a beautiful triumphal arch, which had been built by popular subscription in New York's Madison Square. The arch, made of wood and plaster—designed merely as a model for a later marble one—was truly a symbol of American imperialism, for, like what it represented, it weathered rapidly and crumbled before it could ever be made permanent.

The goal of Philippine independence, nevertheless, proved to be highly elusive. As Erving Winslow pointed out at the League's annual meeting in 1909, the work of the anti-imperialists at this point was "not so much a fight against an open enemy, but

---

23. *Tenth Annual Meeting of the Anti-Imperialist League* (Boston, 1908), p. 21.

against a silent and hidden force upon which that enemy relies
—inertia—the indifference to the whole matter among the mass
of the people." [24]

One of the reasons for this popular indifference was the lack
of a new and exciting issue to stimulate the people's interest. The
anti-imperialists themselves realized this. Winslow remarked at
the thirteenth annual meeting that "now that our sympathies are
no longer aroused and our emotions excited by 'Marked Severities,' by the 'Water Cure' or by 'Reconcentration,' it is very
probable that the evidence of some economic abuses, of grave
defects in Philippine administration, of social discontent, and of
the deep but ever reverberating demand for independence may
fall on deaf or indifferent ears, even among ourselves." [25]

The principal campaign of the anti-imperialists in the years
between 1909 and 1912, subsidiary of course to their continued
agitation for Philippine independence, per se, was one of opposition to the economic exploitation of the islands. One aspect of
this was analyzed by W. Cameron Forbes, a wealthy Bostonian
and friend—if an ideological opponent—of the officers of the
Anti-Imperialist League, who served as Governor General of the
Philippines.[26] Forbes observed that "fear of the trusts was played
upon by the officers of the Anti-Imperialist League, who, honestly
believing, as they did, that American capital would militate
against the realization of Philippine independence, encouraged

---

24. *Report of the Eleventh Annual Meeting of the Anti-Imperialist League* (Boston, 1909), p. 13. For an interesting and sympathetic contemporary commentary upon this meeting of the League
see Robert E. Bisbee, "The Democracy of Anti-Imperialism," *The
Arena,* Vol. XLI (Feb., 1909), pp. 231-233.

25. *Report of the Thirteenth Annual Meeting of the Anti-
Imperialist League* (Boston, 1912), p. 28.

26. Moorfield Storey pointed out that he had known Forbes
"from his infancy. He is as sincere in his beliefs as we in ours, and
if we criticize him, it is not on personal grounds, but because he
represents a policy which we believe to be wrong; because he is engaged in a hopeless undertaking." *Eleventh Annual Meeting, op. cit.,*
p. 32.

among the Filipinos the opposition to the coming of capital." [27]

Moorfield Storey insisted that "every American dollar which is planted in the Philippines is a rivet in the chain which binds them to us." [28] This belief led the Anti-Imperialist League to oppose vigorously the sale of large parcels of "friar lands" (the very extensive former landholdings in the Philippines of various Catholic monastic orders now held by the government) to American syndicates and corporations. The League supported a campaign in Congress led by John A. Martin of Colorado, James L. Slayden of Texas, and J. Harry Covington of Maryland to investigate and, if possible, curtail foreign exploitation of these lands. Moorfield Storey, who aided the Congressmen with his vast legal acumen, also discussed the controversy in some detail at the League's annual meeting in 1910. He pointed out that the government's policy was, paradoxically, "establishing in these unhappy islands the very trusts which we are seeking to break up in the United States." [29]

The debate over the "friar lands" continued into 1911 and became increasingly bitter. The League accused the Secretary of the Interior of the Philippines, Dean C. Worcester, of misconduct and nepotism in the apparently unauthorized sale and lease (for extremely low prices) of large tracts of public lands to certain

---

27. W. Cameron Forbes, *The Philippine Islands* (Boston, 1928), Vol. II, p. 28. Much of this very extensive work is given over to cataloguing and praising the many, and very real, material improvements which the United States made in the Philippines. Forbes felt that the Filipinos were very ungrateful to criticize the Americans who had done so much for them. It is especially interesting to read this in light of the statement which Moorfield Storey made at the outset of Forbes' administration: "Mr. Forbes has a great opportunity. If he uses it to cover the islands with . . . material improvements in the largest sense his time will have been wasted. Let us hope that he will realize how little material benefits weigh in the scale against human liberty."—*Eleventh Annual Meeting, op. cit.*, p. 35.

28. *Ibid.*, p. 33.

29. *Report of the Twelfth Annual Meeting of the Anti-Imperialist League* (Boston, 1910), p. 41.

favored individuals, including his own nephew. Worcester was so incensed by the charge that he had published in various newspapers on March 13, 1911, "An Open Letter to the Officers and Members of the Anti-Imperialist League," in which he defended his actions and especially attacked the League's Secretary, Erving Winslow.[30]

The matter was eventually taken up by the House Committee on Insular Affairs. Jackson H. Ralston prepared a brief for the League which he submitted to the committee. He complained about the specific matter at issue—the allegedly improper transfer of lands to American citizens, syndicates, and corporations, but then broadened his attack in a sharp peroration: "While we have enumerated those things which seem most immediately pressing, we should not for a moment be unconscious of the infinite egotism of Americans in assuming that they, who are as yet but learning to govern themselves,[31] are competent to rule a people of another language, customs, traditions, ideals, and mode of thought. Rather than continue to display our necessary incompetence, we should permit the Filipinos, in their own way, learning by their own mistakes, to develop for themselves that system of government and that civilization which shall prove most nearly in accord with their own aspirations." [32]

The anti-imperialists felt that this goal—Philippine Independence—could only be reached under a Democratic administration. They pointed out that although President Taft was "a benevolent and sincere imperialist," [33] he was still an imperialist,

---

30. David Greene Haskins, Jr., in turn, vigorously condemned "the attack made by Mr. Worcester on our Secretary."—*Thirteenth Annual Meeting of the Anti-Imperialist League* (Boston, 1912), p. 58.

31. This is probably an oblique reference to the scandals in municipal and state governments being brought to light at this time by muckraking journalists. It will be recalled that a frequent anti-imperialist argument was that the United States should solve its problems of government at home before seeking to govern a colonial empire. See for example *Eleventh Annual Meeting, op. cit.*, p. 30.

32. *Thirteenth Annual Meeting*, op. cit., p. 9.

33. *Eleventh Annual Meeting, op. cit.*, p. 19.

and, therefore, by definition, a foe. The anti-imperialists believed, and correctly so, that most of the leaders of the Republican party were tired of the Philippine experiment and would be happy to be rid of the burden, but that "party pride and consistency will necessarily prevent their making any move themselves in favor of Philippine independence." [34]

The members of the League, therefore, put their faith in the Democratic party, and when the Democrats gained control of the House in 1910 they were elated. Their elation was logical. The Democratic party had now been opposing imperialism for almost twenty years—since the beginning of the debate over Hawaiian annexation in the early '90's. A majority of Democratic Senators, in spite of great pressure to the contrary, had opposed the Treaty of Paris which definitely established the U.S. empire overseas. In 1900 the Democratic platform had called imperialism the paramount issue and in every subsequent national convention the party had taken an anti-imperialist position. The Anti-Imperialist League's officers naturally believed that if the Democrats came into power, they could "hardly discard such a cardinal and long-maintained article of their faith." [35]

Taking the Democrats at their word, a risky practice with a political party, the anti-imperialists decided to support the Democratic party once again in 1912. They received further encouragement to this end. It was reported at the annual meeting in 1911 that "several candidates for the Democratic nomination for the presidency have more or less specifically pledged themselves to the cause of Philippine independence." [36] On June 20, 1912, the Executive Committee of the Anti-Imperialist League drew up a suggested plank for insertion in the platform of the Democratic Party which was to meet at Baltimore five days later. The actual plank adopted by the party turned out, interestingly, to be a more sweeping denunciation of imperialism than that submitted by the League. It read:

---

34. *Twelfth Annual Meeting, op. cit.*, p. 22.

35. David Greene Haskins at the *Twelfth Annual Meeting, ibid.*, p. 23.

36. *Thirteenth Annual Meeting, op. cit.*, p. 21.

We reaffirm the position thrice announced by the Democracy in national convention assembled against a policy of imperialism and colonial exploitation in the Philippines and elsewhere. We condemn the experiment in imperialism as an inexcusable blunder, which has involved us in enormous expense, brought us weakness instead of strength, and laid our nation open to the charge of abandonment of the fundamental doctrine of self-government. We favor an immediate declaration of the nation's purpose to recognize the independence of the Philippine Islands as soon as stable government can be established,[37] such independence to be guaranteed by us until the neutralization of the islands can be secured by treaty with other powers.[38]

The members of the Anti-Imperialist League were naturally very pleased with the Democratic platform. Also, with Taft and Roosevelt, who were both so closely associated with imperialism, as the other two principal candidates, running on platforms which in the case of the former reaffirmed the present policy and in the latter simply ignored the matter, the League had little hesitancy in giving its wholehearted support to Woodrow Wilson. Thus on October 30, the Executive Committee, acting on behalf of the League, issued a public statement strongly urging a vote for Wilson.

Although imperialism was not a significant issue in the campaign, for the first time in a dozen years the anti-imperialists' man won, and they were jubilant. Erving Winslow said: "We are now congratulating ourselves upon the accomplishment of Governor Boutwell's condition precedent to the success of our cause, the destruction of the Republican Party. It is a singular illustration of the unexpected results brought about by the political whirligig, that the prognostication of the sage of Groton

---

37. This was the principal point upon which the anti-imperialists diverged from the Democratic platform; they wanted the Filipinos to have immediate independence and be their own judge of the stability of their own government.

38. Kirk H. Porter, *op. cit.*, p. 332.

has virtually been fulfilled by the agitator of Oyster Bay, the imperialist of imperialists."

It must, indeed, have been especially sweet for the anti-imperialists to have the Democratic candidate's victory brought about by two of their oldest foes—Roosevelt and Taft—restaging the celebrated encounter of the Kilkenny cats. David Haskins said that he was happy to be able to "congratulate the members of the League on the remarkable improvement in the political situation and prospects of the cause. For twelve years we carried on our work under great difficulties." While this last statement is true, it should also be pointed out that the difficulties gave them a martyr's cause which they relished, a definite enemy, and missionary zeal, which they lost when the Democrats came into power.

At the time, however, they viewed the Democratic landslide, which yielded not only the presidency but also control of both Houses of Congress, as an unqualified blessing. David Haskins observed that the election had certainly put the Democrats in a perfect "position to perform their pledges, four times solemnly given in national conventions." [39]

The officers of the Anti-Imperialist League were not alone in their elation and expectation of the imminent consummation of their work for Philippine independence. In 1913 scores of letters poured in from prominent men all over the United States and even from abroad, praising the League for its steadfast devotion to a cause which had now apparently triumphed.

Waldo R. Browne, editor of *The Dial*, offered his "hearty felicitations on the promises in the political sky of an early fulfillment of the League's noble work. At this time, when the sought for end is at last in sight, it is the duty of every liberty-loving American to express to the officers . . . of the League something at least of the debt of pride and honor that he must feel in their achievement." E. G. Kohnstamm of New York

---

39. *Report of the Fourteenth Annual Meeting of the Anti-Imperialist League* (Boston, 1913), pp. 3, 23.

echoed Browne's sentiments and said that "when the Filipino people put up monuments, commemorative of the success of their cause, the officers of the Anti-Imperialist League should have the first and the greatest." [40] Warren Olney of California wrote that "it is a cause of rejoicing that the American people have so quickly outgrown the lust of conquest that ushered in the twentieth century," and correctly observed that the "continual hammering of the Anti-Imperialist League has helped the growth of a sentiment that will no doubt in the future control the policy of the United States." Sigmund Zeisler's letter of commendation actually constitutes an excellent succinct summary of the efforts of the League since its inception:

> For fifteen years the Anti-Imperialist League . . . has aroused our people to a realization of the crime not less than the folly of our horribly expensive experiment in colonial government; has furnished the friends of liberty in Congress with ammunition of facts and arguments; has driven the loud-mouthed champions of the original Philippine program to take the defensive. Its views have become the views of the overwhelming majority of the people, and what it has been clamoring for these fifteen years has become the policy of the National Administration, with the result that the day of freedom and independence of the Philippines is dawning.[41]

Zeisler and the officers of the Anti-Imperialist League, of course, could not realize in the heady atmosphere of apparent victory in early 1913 that the coming of the actual dawn would be so protracted. They could not conceive at this juncture that Wilson would fail to honor the pledge of his party's platform, which he had sworn to uphold, to issue "an immediate declaration of the nation's purpose to recognize the independence of the Philippine Islands."

They felt with the election of a Democratic President, House, and Senate on a platform which was certainly demonstrative in

---

40. It is interesting that the square in front of the Malacanan Palace, the Philippine equivalent of the White House, in Manila, is called "La Liga Anti-Imperialista."

41. *Fifteenth Annual Meeting* (Boston, 1913), pp. 10-18.

its opposition to imperialism and the former Philippine policy that their work would soon be triumphantly finished. The subsequent inaction on the part of Wilson and Secretary of State William Jennings Bryan—who had so frequently and ostentatiously denounced imperialism and the Republican policy for years—must have seemed almost perfidious to the devoted anti-imperialists.

Soon they realized that Wilson was not going to carry out the Philippine plank of the Democratic platform. The anti-imperialists, in one of the League's earliest annual reports, had castigated Mark Hanna for being wickedly cynical when he had observed that a political platform was like a railway platform —something to get in on, not stand on. The anti-imperialists now learned that the Republican party did not have a monopoly on Machiavellian politics.

Moorfield Storey contacted President-elect Wilson and Secretary of State Bryan about the Philippine issue, but got nowhere. He wrote to Charles Francis Adams on May 16, 1913, expressing his profound disappointment that "Wilson takes no position on the Philippine question." [42]

By the time of the sixteenth annual meeting, the Anti-Imperialist League's officers were thoroughly disillusioned with the Democratic party. The Democrats' refusal to pass the Jones Bill, which promised "definite and absolute independence" to the islands and their substitution of a bill which contained only a nebulous academic statement on the subject was a very great disappointment to them.

Other facets of the Democrats' foreign policy also came in for censure by the League during the next several years. The dealings of the United States with Mexico, Santo Domingo, Nicaragua, and Honduras were criticized. The League asserted that they demonstrated that "the imperialistic spirit still prevails in less aggressive form." [43] On October 22, 1915, the Executive

---

42. Howe, *op. cit.,* p. 305. Storey was, in fact, so disgusted with Wilson that he voted for Hughes in 1916.

43. *Report of the Seventeenth Annual Meeting of the Anti-Imperialist League* (Boston, 1916), p. 14.

Committee of the League forwarded a memorandum to President Wilson and Congress, which stated:

> The Anti-Imperialist League maintains with faith and courage its special work of obtaining, by the establishment of Philippine independence, relief from the anomalous and dangerous responsibility of holding and defending remote 'possessions.' But the situation calls for the application to affairs in the Western Hemisphere of the doctrines which the League upholds, and demands a protest against a drift which menaces the peace and safety of the Republic. No spheres of influence, protectorates, or trusteeships should be undertaken here by the United States . . .[44]

The League urged that strong support be given the Pan-American Union in dealing with problems in Central and South America. Many people seem to think that because the anti-imperialists opposed American imperial expansion they were thoroughgoing isolationists. This is inaccurate. The leaders of the movement felt firmly that their beliefs—in freedom, democracy, self-government, and peace—had universal validity. They, therefore, energetically upheld any and all multi-national bodies which favored these ends. They supported the Pan-American Union and were early and vigorous advocates of a League of Nations. On December 18, 1916, the Executive Committee of the Anti-Imperialist League sent a communication to President Wilson saying: "The World War has borne in upon our minds the enormity of violation of treaty obligations and oppression of small states by powerful ones; and it shows that it is indispensable for the maintenance of civilization that some peaceful international league should be formed." [45]

A few months earlier—on August 29, 1916—the Jones Bill (The Organic Act of the Philippine Islands) was enacted, which, more than three years after the anti-imperialists had expected it, partially honored the pledge of the Democratic platform of 1912.

---

44. *Ibid.*, p. 10.
45. *Report of the Eighteenth Annual Meeting of the Anti-Imperialist League* (Boston, 1916), p. 30.

It gave the Filipinos a greater measure of self-government and affirmed the intention of the United States to give the Filipinos their independence upon the establishment of a stable government. The anti-imperialists had hoped for an outright grant of independence, but greeted this as at least a step in the right direction, and voiced the hope that independence, per se, would soon be granted. [46]

The nation at large, however, was absorbed at this time in the events of "the great war." The Anti-Imperialist League, itself, had taken an early and abiding interest in the conflict. On September 16, 1914, the Executive Committee sent a missive to the Belgian delegation to the United States, which said that "the Anti-Imperialist League, believing that the neutralization of small countries is a very long step toward the preservation of international peace, and an important curb upon aggressive imperialism, desires to express the indignation and horror with which it has seen Belgium and Luxembourg invaded." [47]

Unlike many individuals and organizations in the United States, the League immediately took sides in the war. Moorfield Storey said that Germany was entirely at fault. He asserted that the Kaiser upholds "the example of Attila; and today on the plains of Belgium and France . . . we see the sure fruit of imperialism." The anti-imperialists felt, nevertheless, that good would eventually come out of the war. "The cause of Democracy," Storey said, "grows stronger every day that this war lasts, and imperialism is doomed." [48] David Haskins declared that the "developments of the war have indeed tended to strengthen our cause. Never within the memory of any man now

---

46. President Wilson during the time that he had Democratic majorities in both houses of Congress and was in firm control failed to take demonstrative action in this regard. Not until December, 1920, when his party had been routed in the past election and he faced a hostile Congress, did he come out strongly in favor of Philippine independence. The result of this terribly belated gesture was negative. Various vicissitudes were to postpone the independence of the Philippines for more than two decades.

47. *Sixteenth Annual Meeting, op. cit.,* pp. 13-14.

48. *Ibid.,* pp. 26, 34.

living has there been such a widespread hatred in this country for the two accursed twins—militarism and imperialism." [49]

The anti-imperialists saw their cause becoming part of one great, triumphal, universal movement. Moorfield Storey said that "now substantially the whole world outside of Germany and its subjects, Austria, Bulgaria, and Turkey, is united in a great anti-imperialist league, and is bending all its energies to maintain the principles which our league was formed to assert and defend." Storey connected the long battle which the League had waged with the present contest. "The people of the Philippine Islands," he stated, "are as numerous as the Belgians, and have the same right to work out their destiny, 'unhindered, unthreatened, and unafraid.' When peace comes it will find the whole world an 'anti-imperialist league,' and then, our task accomplished, we can dissolve our association and depart in peace. But till that hour comes we must not lay aside our armor but must still fight on, sure that in the long run our cause will triumph though we, like our comrades who have left us, may not live to see it." [50]

When the League assembled for its next annual meeting the war had terminated. "Thank God," Haskins exclaimed, "the great war is over at last! Thank God democracy has triumphed and the ill-omened monster Imperialism is overthrown! . . . The millennium seems almost in sight. Never during the twenty years in which this League has worked and struggled for what is now called 'the right of self-determination' has the principle found such widespread and hearty sympathy as today. It would seem as if the whole world were engaging in forming a huge Anti-Imperialist League." [51]

The annual report ends with the statement; "The meeting was dissolved." This is how all of the first twenty annual reports of the Anti-Imperialists League concluded; but this time the organization as well was just about dissolved. Although there were to

---

49. *Report of the Nineteenth Annual Meeting of the Anti-Imperialist League* (Boston, 1917), p. 16.

50. *Ibid.*, pp. 23, 29.

51. *Report of the Twentieth Annual Anti-Imperialist Meeting* (Boston, 1919), p. 24.

be two more annual meetings, they were brief and perfunctory, and the remaining members of the League felt that their work was done. They had fought a good fight; they had finished their course; they had kept the faith. They were very old men now and they longed to rest. Symbolically, perhaps, a great part of the League's last two annual reports was devoted to necrology. The final meeting of the Anti-Imperialist League was held November 27, 1920; its report ends: "The meeting was adjourned, subject to the call of the Secretary." It never came. The Anti-Imperialist League, and with it the great debate which had engendered it and to which it had contributed so much, had passed into history.

CHAPTER 18

Retrospect and Prospect

By the time of the Anti-Imperialist League's demise in 1920, the question of American imperialism had long since ceased to be a vital national issue. The League's president, Moorfield Storey, would, characteristically, have the last word on the subject in a book which he was preparing with a young Filipino lawyer, Marcial Lichauco.[1] But it had all been said before more cogently and eloquently and when more people were listening.

The year before, the most dynamic and colorful of the imperialists, the irrepressible Theodore Roosevelt, had died quietly in his sleep at his home at Oyster Bay—far from the tumult of San Juan Hill and Luzon. Rudyard Kipling, who had urged his friend Theodore to take up the "white man's burden," appropriately sang him to his rest in a moving poetic eulogy;[2] but even Roosevelt had changed his mind about Philippine independence.

The anti-imperialists' other arch-foe, the urbane and erudite Henry Cabot Lodge, still occupied his accustomed seat in the Senate and eminent place in national affairs. But he was now more intent on warning of the dangers of international entanglements in the affairs of the League of Nations, while the few remaining anti-imperialists, ever at odds with their fellow Bosto-

---

1. Moorfield Storey and Marcial P. Lichauco, *The Conquest of the Philippines by the United States,* 1898-1925 (New York, 1926.)

2. See "Great Heart"—Kipling's final tribute to Theodore Roosevelt. *Rudyard Kipling's Verse: Definitive Edition* (Garden City, N.Y., 1940), p. 579-580.

nian, viewed the new League as an extension of many of their own principles and gave the fledging organization their strong support.

The current occupant of the White House insisted that what the nation really needed was a return to "normalcy," and whatever Warren Harding's tortuous semantics implied, it was certainly not imperialist expansion. The anti-imperialists had adequately demonstrated that imperialism was not consonant with America's traditional standards and values and should be forever renounced.

While a great deal that was exciting and meaningful had occurred in the interim, at the end of the period under consideration, the American position on colonial expansion had reverted to its stand of three decades earlier. Before 1890 attempts to expand the territory of the United States beyond its continental limits had always failed. During the final frenzied decade of the nineteenth century a variety of economic, political, strategic, intellectual, and psychological factors coalesced to give support to a policy of imperialism. Among these elements were the need and desire for new and wider markets for the burgeoning output of the nation's farms and factories, the example of European imperialism, the influence of Social Darwinism, the theoretical closing of the frontier, the missionary impulses of the Protestant churches, and the resurgence of Manifest Destiny.

The writings of theorists prepared the way for political activists, who were essentially more interested in international power and prestige than in other considerations and who wished to see the United States embark upon an imperial course. The growing influence of imperialist sentiments in the 1890's filled those who supported the nation's traditional anti-colonial policy with great anxiety. Their fears were confirmed when the initial involvement of the United States in Samoa was followed in 1893 by the attempt to annex the Hawaiian Islands. It was then that the great debate over imperialism, which was to be a significant part of national affairs for the ensuing decade, began in earnest.

Anti-imperialists countered the demands for the annexation of Hawaii in 1893 with multifarious arguments. Indeed, the anti-imperialist position was quite fully developed at this time—many years before the period in which context it is usually discussed. Many prominent men, who would remain steadfastly opposed to overseas acquisitions for the rest of their lives, voiced strong objections to imperialism at this time.

The Harrison administration, besides facing the barrage of practical and philosophical arguments launched by the anti-imperialists against overseas expansion, was embarassed by the complicity of Minister Stevens and the involvement of U.S. Marines in the revolutionary imbroglio, the question of the legitimacy of the pro-annexationist Hawaiian government, and the charges of chicanery and bulldozing tactics leveled by the opposition.

Although Harrison could not effect annexation, and Cleveland would not, with the return of the Republicans to power in 1897 and the ascendancy in the party of such dedicated imperialists as Lodge and Roosevelt, imperialism took on new vigor. The outbreak of the Spanish-American War, which was as strongly opposed by the majority of anti-imperialists as it was supported by the imperialists, provided the decisive imperialist catalyst.

The lengthy and bitter debate over Hawaii ended in a victory for the annexationists, and the islands became an American possession and eventually an integral part of the United States. Hawaii could probably have existed as an independent entity, as indicated by its experience in the period from 1893 to 1898 and the more recent example of many small nations throughout the world, and its annexation in the context of the times was an imperialist venture. Also at that juncture the arguments of the anti-imperialists vis-à-vis the Hawaiian Islands were at least as valid and in some ways more cogent than those of the imperialists. Nevertheless, the passage of the years and ensuing significant changes lend a different perspective on Hawaii. Improvements in transportation and communication largely nullified the critiques based on the Islands' distance from the U.S. mainland. Hawaii has been quite viable economically rather than being a burden. The Islands have been more of an asset than a liability from a strategic standpoint. Far from being a racial battleground, it has proven to be an unusually successful example of cultural pluralism. Most important, however, the granting of full rights of citizenship and eventual statehood, with complete incorporation into the American political system and every other major area of national life, eliminated the strongest congeries of anti-imperialist arguments.

The Philippines were quite a different case. They had no extensive history of contact with the United States as did Hawaii, nor was there any desire on the part of even a minority, as in the case of Hawaii, for annexation by the United States. They had a much larger and more diverse indigenous population. Not only were they geographically very far removed from the United States, but also the cultural gap was enormous. Unlike Hawaii, relatively few Americans settled permanently in the Philippines during the period in which they were under United States control. They were, as even the imperialists soon admitted, a burden militarily and strategically. They were not a great asset economically, nor did they open any vast Asian market, as some imperialists had hoped and claimed they would. Unlike the annexation of Hawaii, the takeover of the Philippines was very difficult and entailed a major war, which in its duration and cost of life and money dwarfed the Spanish-American War. This was no "splendid little war"; it was a large, inglorious, vicious conflict. The suppression by the United States of the Filipinos' just aspiration for freedom and independence was tragic. Whether viewed from a contemporary or historical vantage point, whether considered pragmatically, philosophically, or morally, the acquisition and retention of the Philippine Islands by the United States was a grave mistake. The position of the United States in contemporary international affairs would certainly be stronger, especially with the people of the crucial Third World, if the nation had never become an imperialist power.

Once the United States had become involved, however, there was really no easy way out. Few Americans would have countenanced the return of the Philippines to Spain. Even the anti-imperialists, since they were opposed to imperialism per se (although they primarily stressed their concern with American imperialism) would not have approved this; nor would they have liked to see the islands taken over by another imperial power. If the Philippines had been given immediate independence and left completely on their own, this might have caused a scramble for possession by other nations, and possibly even a general war in Asia, which would have benefited no one.

Three steps, however, could have been taken which might have provided an acceptable solution to the complex Philippine problem. First, the American government might have clearly stated in January, 1899, its sincere intention to grant the Filipinos independence as soon as even a modicum of order was restored in the islands. This would have allayed the fears of the Filipinos, who rightly suspected they were just trading one imperialist master for another, and avoided the very unfortunate war that ensued. Second, immediate steps could have been taken to help the Filipinos set up their own independent government. Objective observers maintained at the time that the Filipinos were at least as capable of self-government as the Cubans. Even if that government had been unstable or inefficient, as the imperialists argued—perhaps with good reason—that it would be, it still would have been preferable to foreign domination and rule. Third, as was frequently suggested by the anti-imperialists at the time, the United States could have guaranteed Philippine independence, either unilaterally or by a larger international agreement. Although this solution also has its difficulties, it would have been better than simply setting the islands adrift in very troubled waters: and it certainly would have been more desirable —both for the Filipinos and the United States—than holding them as an imperial possession for many decades.

The United States did become a rather benevolent ruler and was more enlightened in this regard than other colonial powers. The Filipinos benefited materially in many ways. However, if America's interests there were simply altruistic, as some imperialists claimed, much of the same material assistance could have been given without ruling the islands.

Although Hawaii precipitated the great debate over American imperialism, it was the question of the Philippines which really gave anti-imperialism impetus as a movement, and it was on this issue that the anti-imperialists took their strongest stand. They would have liked to block the takeover of the Philippines at the outset by defeating the Treaty of Paris. Frustrated in this attempt, they sought to turn the election of 1900 into a referendum on imperialism, but the candidacy of William Jennings Bryan, whom many anti-imperialists disliked because of his flamboyant style, economic views, and curious behavior regarding the treaty, split their ranks. Nevertheless, they carried on courageously, and their steadfast opposition to imperialism was eventually to be rewarded.

At a time when the United States was initiating a major change in its foreign policy—a change fraught with far-reaching consequences, the anti-imperialists insisted, in the best democratic tradition, that the matter should be thoroughly debated and all its problems and ramifications completely explored. To further this end, a significant movement was started. Its formal embodiment—the Anti-Imperialist League—was a remarkable organization in many ways. It was composed of a group of eminent and gifted men, who in speeches, meetings, and voluminous writings raised many crucial questions and contributed importantly to public thinking on the subject.

Their constant agitation, which they maintained even after the period of greatest national concern with the question, had a cumulative effect—especially when combined with the bitter practical experience of imperialism. In a way, their experience was like that of a number of minor parties in American history which have been rejected by the voters but whose ideas have ultimately won large acceptance. The fact is that after the turn of the century the United States never again engaged in the type of imperialism which characterized this period and eventually granted the Philippines their independence. Although, as in almost every historical question, multiple factors were involved, the contributions of the anti-imperialists must be given their full measure of credit. Certainly in the light of later history their basic stand against imperialism has been completely vindicated.

While the anti-imperialists pointed out the many of grave

problems stemming from the adoption of an imperialist policy, they especially emphasized that imperialism was morally wrong and an inherent negation of the American ethos. At a time when much of the nation was temporarily intoxicated by the exotic elixir of imperialism, the anti-imperialists soberly called for a rededication to the timeless principles of liberty and self-government upon which the true greatness of the United States rests.

Bibliography

PRIMARY MATERIALS

I ARTICLES

Adams, Charles Francis. "Mr. Cleveland's Tasks and Opportunities," *The Forum*, XV (May, 1893), 298-303.

————. "What Mr. Cleveland Stands For," *The Forum*, XIII (July, 1892), 662-670.

Adams, George Burton. "A Century of Anglo-Saxon Expansion," *The Atlantic Monthly*, LXXIX (April, 1897), 528-538.

Adler, Felix. "Parting of the Ways in the Foreign Policy of the United States," *Review of Reviews*, XVIII (November, 1898), 586-588.

Agnew, Daniel. "Unconstitutionality of the Hawaiian Treaty," *The Forum*, XXIV (December, 1897), 461-470.

Alverez, Don Segundo. "The Situation in Cuba," *North American Review*, CLXI, No. 466 (September, 1895), 362-365.

Atkins, Edwin F. "The Commercial Arguments for Cuban Annexation," *The Independent*, L, Part III (December 1, 1898), 1568-1569.

Atkinson, Edward. "How Distrust Stops Trade," *North American Review*, CLVII, No. 440 (July, 1893), 25-29.

————. "Jingoes and Silverites," *North American Review*, CLXI, No. 468 (November, 1895), 554-560.

Baldwin, Simeon E. "The Constitutional Questions Incident to the Acquisition and Government by the United States of Island Territories," *American Historical Association Annual Report*, 1898 (United States Government Printing Office, Washington, 1899), 313-343.

————. "The Historic Policy of the United States as to Annexation," *Yale Review*, II (August, 1894), 133-158.

Bancroft, Frederick. "Seward's Ideas of Territorial Expansion," *North American Review,* CLXVIII (July, 1898), 79-89.

Barrett, John. "Admiral George Dewey," *Harper's New Monthly Magazine,* XCIX (October, 1899), 799-813.

———. "America in the Pacific and Far East," *Harper's New Monthly Magazine,* XCIX (November, 1899), 917-926.

———. "America's Interest in Eastern Asia," *North American Review,* CLXII, No. 472 (March, 1896), 257-265.

———. "The Cuba of the Far East," *North American Review,* CLXIV, No. 483 (February, 1897), 173-180.

———. "The Paramount Power of the Pacific," *North American Review,* CLXIX (August, 1899), 165-179.

———. "The Problem of the Philippines," *North American Review,* CLXVII (September, 1898), 259-267.

———. "Some Phases of the Philippine Situation," *Review of Reviews,* XX (July, 1899), 65-74.

Becker, Carl. "Law and Practice of the United States in the Acquisition and Government of Dependent Territory," *Annals of the American Academy of Political and Social Science,* XVI (November, 1900), 404-420.

Besant, Walter. "The Future of the Anglo-Saxon Race," *North American Review,* CLXIII, No. 477 (August, 1896), 129-143.

Bisbee, Robert E. "The Democracy of Anti-Imperialism," *The Arena,* LI (February, 1909), 231-233.

———. "Why I Oppose Our Philippine Policy," *The Arena,* XXVIII, No. 2 (August, 1902), 113-118.

Bourne, Henry E. "Lessons from the Recent History of European Dependencies," *American Historical Association Annual Report, 1898* (Government Printing Office, Washington, 1899), 301-312.

Boyd, Carl Evans. "Our Government of Newly Acquired Territory," *The Atlantic Monthly,* LXXXII (December, 1898), 735-742.

Bridge, James Howard. "A Fresh View of Manifest Destiny," *Overland Monthly,* XXXI Second Series (February, 1898), 115-119.

Bridgman, R. L. "Brute or Man—the Annexation Problem," *New England Magazine,* XIX New Series (September, 1898), 82-93.

Brooks, Sydney. "America and the War," *North American Review,* CLXX (March, 1900), 337-347.

———. "American Imperialism," *The Fortnightly Review,* LXXVI (August, 1901), 226-238.

———. "A Colonial Career for Americans," *Harper's Weekly,* XLVIII (July 2, 1904), 1012-1013.

———. "An Englishman on the Philippines," *Harper's Weekly,* XLVIII (June 11, 1904), 900-901.

————. "A Glance at World Politics," *North American Review,* CLXXIX (August, 1904), 269-281.

————. "The Monroe Doctrine," *Fortnightly Review,* LXXVI (December, 1901), 1013-1026.

————. "President Roosevelt," *Fortnightly Review,* LXXXI (February, 1904), 290-307.

Bryan, William Jennings. "The Election of 1900," *North American Review,* CLXXI, No. 529 (December, 1900), 788-801.

————. "How Could the United States, If Necessary, Give Up Its Colonies," *The World Today,* XIV, No. 2 (February, 1908), 151-154.

Bryce, James Lord. "The Policy of Annexation for America," *The Forum,* XXIV (December, 1897), 385-396.

Burgess, John William. "How May the United States Govern Its Extra-Continental Territory?" *Political Science Quarterly,* XIV (March, 1899), 1-18.

Carlisle, John Griffin. "Our Future Policy," *Harper's New Monthly Magazine,* XCVII (October, 1898), 720-728.

————. "Our Policy of Expansion—Cuba and the Philippines," *Harper's Weekly,* XLII (October 22, 1898), 1027.

————. "The Recent Election," *North American Review,* CLI, No. 409 (December, 1890), 641-649.

Carnegie, Andrew. "The ABC of Money," *North American Review,* CLII, No. 415 (June, 1891), 723-750.

————. "Americanism Versus Imperialism," *North American Review,* CLXVIII, Part I and Part II (January, 1899), 1-13; (March, 1899), 362-372.

————. "As Others See Us," *Fortnightly Review,* CLXXII, New Series (February 1, 1882), 156-165.

————. "Distant Possessions—The Parting of the Ways," *North American Review,* CLXVII (August, 1898), 239-248.

————. "Do Americans Hate England?" *North American Review,* CL (June, 1890), 752-760.

————. 'Mr. Bryan the Conjurer," *North American Review,* CLXIV, No. 482 (January, 1897), 106-118.

————. "A Look Ahead," *North American Review,* CLVI, No. 439 (June, 1893), 685-710.

————. "The Ship of State Adrift," *North American Review,* CLXII, No. 475 (June, 1896), 641-648.

————. "The Silver Problem," *North American Review,* CLVII, No. 442 (September, 1893), 354-370.

————. "Summing Up the Tariff Discussion," *North American Review,* CLI, No. 404 (July, 1890), 47-74.

————. "The Venezuelan Question," *North American Review,* CLXII, No. 471 (February, 1896), 129-144.

Cassatt, Alfred C. "The Monroe Doctrine: Defence, Not Defiance," *The Forum,* XX (December, 1895), 456-464.

Chamberlain, Eugene Tyler. "The Invasion of Hawaii," *North American Review,* CLVII, No. 445 (December, 1893), 731-735.

Chapman, Edward Mortimer. "The Menace of Pseudo-Patriotism," *North American Review,* CLXIV, No. 483 (February, 1897), 250-252.

Chetwood, John. "Monroe Doctrine Repeal and 'Our Next War,'" *The Arena,* XXIII (March, 1900), 245-253.

Clarke, George Sydenham. "Captain Mahan's Counsels to the United States," *Nineteenth Century,* XLIII (February, 1898), 292-300.

————. "Imperial Responsibilities A National Gain," *North American Review,* CLXVIII (February, 1899), 129-141.

————. "A Naval Union with Great Britain," *North American Review,* CLVIII, No. 448 (June, 1893), 353-365.

Clemenceau, Georges. "The French Navy," *North American Review,* CLXIV, No. 483 (February, 1897), 181-192; No. 484 (March, 1897), 305-317.

Clowes, William L. "American Expansion and the Inheritance of the Race," *The Fortnightly Review,* LXX (December, 1898), 884-892.

Cockran, W. Bourke. "The Financial Outlook," *North American Review,* CLVI, No. 439 (June, 1893), 739-749.

Coggins, Albert H. "The Menace of Imperialism," *The Arena,* XXIV (October, 1900), 345-350.

Cohen, Solomon Solis. "The Spectre of Imperialism," *The Arena,* XX (October, 1898), 445-452.

Colomb, P. H. "The Battle-Ship of the Future," *North American Review,* CLVII, No. 443 (October, 1893), 412-422.

Conant, Charles A. "The Economic Basis of 'Imperialism,'" *North American Review,* CLXVII (September, 1898), 326-340.

Cooley, Thomas M. "Grave Obstacles to Hawaiian Annexation," *The Forum,* XV (June, 1893), 389-406.

Coudert, Frederic R. "The Hawaiian Question," *North American Review,* CLVIII, No. 446 (January, 1894), 57-63.

Coudert, Frederic R.; Evans, John Gary; Oates, William C., *et al.* "Ought We to Annex Cuba: A Symposium," *The American Magazine of Civics,* VII, No. 1 (July, 1895), 37-49.

Cramp, Charles H. "Sea Power of the United States," *North American Review,* CLIX, No. 453 (August, 1894), 137-149.

Currier, Charles W. "Why Cuba Should be Independent," *The Forum,* XXX (October, 1900), 139-146.

Curtis, George Ticknor. "Can Hawaii Be Constitutionally Annexed to the United States?" *North American Review,* CLVI, No. 436 (March, 1893), 282-286.

Curtis, Henry G. "Government of Our New Possessions," *The Outlook,* LXIV (February 10, 1900), 353-356.

Davies, Theophilus H. "The Hawaiian Revolution," *The Nineteenth Century,* XXXIII (May, 1893), 830-835.

————. "The Hawaiian Situation," *North American Review,* CLVI, No. 438 (May, 1893), 605-610.

Davis, C. Wood. "The Exhaustion of the Arable Lands," *The Forum,* IX (July, 1890), 461-474.

Davis, Cushman K. "Two Years of Democratic Diplomacy," *North American Review,* CLX, No. 460 (March, 1895), 270-284.

Davis, Mrs. Jefferson. "The White Man's Problem," *The Arena,* XXIII (January, 1900), 1-4.

Davis, William H. "The National Duty Delusion," *The Arena,* XXI (June, 1899), 736-740.

DeKalb, Courtenay. "The Nicaragua Canal—Ours or England's," *The Forum,* XVI (February, 1894), 690-695.

DeLaneleye, Emile. "The Division of Africa," *The Forum,* X (January, 1891), 479-496.

Denby, Charles. "The Constitution and the Flag," *The Forum,* XXIX (May, 1900), 257-262.

————. "Criticisms of Our Philippine Policy," *The Independent,* LIII (March 21, 1901), 649-651.

————. "Do We Owe Independence to the Filipinos," *The Forum,* XXIX (June, 1900), 401-408.

————. "The Philippine Question," *The Independent,* LII (March 8, 1900), 582-585.

————. "The Present Political Aspect of the Philippine Question," *Harper's Weekly,* XLIV (August 4, 1900), 721.

————. "The Question of the Hour," *The Independent,* LII (April 5, 1900), 805-806.

————. "The Rights of the United States in the Philippines," *The Independent,* LI (December 7, 1899), 3263-3268.

————. "Shall We Keep the Philippines?" *The Forum,* XXVI (November, 1898), 278-281.

————. "What of the Democratic Party?" *The Forum,* XXXI (March, 1901), 15-22.

Dicey, Edward. "After the Present War," *Nineteenth Century,* XLVI (November, 1899), 693-707.

————. "New American Imperialism," *Nineteenth Century,* XLIV (September, 1898), 487-501.

————. "Rival Empires," *Nineteenth Century,* LIV (December, 1903), 885-902.

Dick, Charles. "Why the Republicans Should Be Endorsed," *The Forum,* XXX (November 1900), 257-274.

Dilke, Charles W.; Barrett, John; Lusk, Hugh H., "The Problem of the Philippines," *North American Review,* CLXVII (September, 1898), 257-277.

Doane, William Croswell. "Follies and Horrors of War," *North American Review,* CLXII, No. 471 (February, 1896), 190-194.

Dolliver, J. P. "The Work of the Next Congress," *North American Review,* CLXI, No. 469 (December, 1895), 453-457.

Doster, Frank. "Will the Philippines Pay?" *The Arena,* XXV (May, 1901), 465-470.

Douglass, Frederick. "Haiti and the United States: The Inside History of the Negotiations for the Mole St. Nicholas," *North American Review,* CLIII, No. 458 (September, 1891), 337-345; No. 459 (October, 1891), 450-459.

E.K.F. "Imperialism, Nationalism, and Internationalism," *Westminster Review,* CLXV (March, 1906), 240-248.

Eddy, Ulysses D. "Our Chance for Commercial Supremacy," *The Forum,* XI (June, 1891), 419-428.

Edmonds, Richard H. "Unparalleled Industrial Progress," *The Forum,* XIII (August, 1892), 673-685.

Edmonds, Thomas F. "Is Our Nation Defenseless?" *North American Review,* CLII, No. 412 (March, 1891), 381-384.

Ellan, John E. "Imperialism and the Coming Crisis for Democracy," *The Westminster Review,* CLVI (September, 1901), 237-252.

Estenanez, Nicolas. "What Spain Can Teach America," *North American Review,* CLXVIII (May, 1899), 563-569.

Faraday, Ethel R. "Some Economic Aspects of the Imperial Idea," *Fortnightly Review,* LXX (December, 1898), 961-967.

Farrar, F. W. "Imperialism and Christianity," *North American Review,* CLXXI, No. 526 (September, 1900), 289-295.

Fleming, John S. "Are We Anglo-Saxons?" *North American Review,* CLIII, No. 418 (August, 1891), 253-256.

Flower, Benjamin Orange. "Some Dead Sea Fruit of Our War of Subjugation," *The Arena,* XXVII, No. 6 (June, 1902), 647-653.

Foster, Burnside. "Leprosy and the Hawaiian Annexation," *North American Review,* CLXVII (September, 1898), 300-306.

Gannet, H. "Annexation Fever," *National Geographic,* VIII (December, 1897), 354-358.

Garnett, Lucy M. J. "The Philippine Islanders," *The Fortnightly Review*, LXX (July, 1898), 72-87.

Giddings, Franklin H. "Destinies of Democracy," *Political Science Quarterly*, XI (December, 1896), 716-731.

————. "Imperialism?" *Political Science Quarterly*, XIII (December, 1898), 585-605.

Gladden, Washington. "The Issues of the War," *The Outlook*, LIX (July 16, 1898), 673-675.

Godkin, E. L. "The Absurdity of War," *Century Magazine*, LIII (January, 1897), 468-470.

————. "Accountability," *The Nation*, LXIII (December 10, 1896), 433.

————. "Americanism," *The Nation*, LVI (February 23, 1893), 136-137.

————. "Apropos of the Philippines, " *The Nation*, LXVII (September 22, 1898), 216.

————. "Carl Schurz," *The Nation*, LXVIII (March 9, 1899), 179.

————. "The Cause of Peace," *The Nation*, LXVIII (April 20, 1899), 289-290.

————. "The Church in the War," *The Nation*, LXVI (May 19, 1898), 377.

————. "Cleveland's Hawaiian Message," *The Nation*, LVII (December 21, 1893), 460.

————."The Condition of Good Colonial Government," *The Forum*, XXVII (April, 1899), 190-203.

————. "Democratic Wars," *The Nation*, LXVIII (January 5, 1899), 4.

————. "Destiny and Duty," *The Nation*, LXVII (October 27, 1898), 306-307.

————. "Development of the Monroe Doctrine," *The Nation*, LXII (January 2, 1896), 4.

————. "Diplomacy and the Newspaper," *North American Review*, CLX (May, 1895), 570-579.

————. "Education of War," *The Nation*, LXVI (April 21, 1898), 296.

————. "The End of the Beginning: The Outbreak at Manila," *The Nation*, LXVIII (February, 1899), 102.

————. "Expansionist Dreams," *The Nation*, LXVIII (January 26, 1899), 61.

————. "The Growth and Expression of Public Opinion," *The Atlantic Monthly*, LXXXI (January, 1898), 1-15.

————. "Hawaii," *The Nation*, LVI (February 9, 1893), 96.

————. "Hawaiian News," *The Nation*, LX (February 14, 1895), 121.

————. "Imperial Policy," *The Nation*, LXVI (May 26, 1898), 396.

————. "Imperialism," *The Nation*, LXV (December, 1897), 511-512.

————. "Imperium et Libertas," *The Nation*, LXVIII (May 18, 1899), 368-369.

————. "Latest Hawaiian Phase," *The Nation*, LXVI (January 20, 1898), 42.

————. "Militarism in a Republic," *The Nation*, LXII (March 5, 1896), 190.

————. "Military Morality," *The Nation*, LXIX (October 12, 1899), 273-274.

————. "Military and Warlike Nations," *The Nation*, LXIX (October 26, 1899), 309.

————. "Navalism," *The Nation*, LIV (January 21, 1892), 44.

————. "New American Doctrine," *The Nation*, LXII (January 23, 1896, 70-71.

————. "New Diplomacy and War," *The Nation*, LXIX (December 7, 1899), 421.

————. "New Duties and New Relations," *The Nation*, LXVII (September 29, 1898), 234.

————. "The Next Step," *The Nation*, LXVIII (February 2, 1899), 81-82.

————. "Old Constitution," *The Nation*, LXVIII (January 12, 1899), 22.

————. "Our Samoan Trouble," *The Nation*, LVIII (June 28, 1894), 480-481.

————. "Patriotism," *The Nation*, LIV (February 4, 1892), 82-83.

————. "The Policy of Isolation," *The Nation*, LXVI (April 28, 1898), 319.

————. "Real Mischief of Jingoism," *The Nation*, LXI (November 7, 1895), 322.

————. "Revolutionary Imperialism," *The Nation*, LXVII (July 28, 1898), 69.

————. "Samoan Troubles," *The Nation*, LVIII (May 17, 1894), 358-359.

————. "Signs of a Halt," *The Nation*, LXVIII (January 19, 1899), 40.

————. "The War and After," *The Nation*, LXVI (April 28, 1898), 316.

————. "The War and Foreign Trade," *The Nation*, LXVI (April 14, 1898), 279-280.

————. "War and Peace," *The Nation*, LXVI (April 21, 1898), 296.

————. "What If the Treaty Is Not Ratified?" *The Nation*, LXVIII (February 2, 1899), 80.

————. "What To Do with Hawaii," *The Nation,* LVIII (January 18, 1894), 42.

————. "What To Do with the Philippines," *The Nation,* LXVII (October 6, 1898), 253-254.

Gordy, J. P. "The Ethics of the Panama Case," *The Forum,* XXXVI (July, 1904), 115-124.

Gray, George. "Two Years of American Diplomacy," *North American Review,* CLX, No. 461 (April, 1895), 409-424.

Groff, George G. "Porto Rico Today," *The Independent,* L, Part III (October 6, 1898), 964-966.

Grosvenor, Charles Henry. "A Republican View of the Presidential Campaign," *North American Review,* CLXXI, No. 524 (July, 1900), 41-54.

Halstead, Murat. "American Annexation and Armament," *The Forum,* XXIV (September, 1897), 56-66.

Hawley, Joseph R. "Mr. Harrison's Sound Administration," *The Forum,* XIII (July, 1892), 650-661.

Hazeltine, Mayo W. "The Foreign Policy of the New Administration," *North American Review,* CLXIV, No. 485 (April, 1897), 479-486.

————. "Possible Complications of the Cuba Question," *North American Review,* CLXII, No. 473 (April, 1896), 406-413.

————. "What Is To Be Done with Cuba," *North American Review,* CLXVII (September, 1898), 318-325.

————. "What Shall Be Done about Cuba," *North American Review,* CLXIII, No. 481 (December, 1896), 731-742.

————. "What Shall Be Done about the Philippines," *North American Review,* CLXVII (October, 1898), 385-392.

Herbert, Hilary A. "Porto Rico, Cuba, and the Philippines," *The Independent,* L, Part III (December 8, 1898), 1646-1651.

Hollis, Ira Nelson. "The War with Spain and After," *The Atlantic Monthly,* LXXI (June, 1898), 721-727.

Howard, George E. "British Imperialism and the Reform of the Civil Service," *Political Science Quarterly,* XIV (June, 1899), 240-250.

Howard, William W. "Cuban Relief: A Practical Plan," *The Outlook,* LXI (April 29, 1899), 963-966.

————. "A Practical Plan of Relief in Cuba," *The Outlook,* LVIII (April 9, 1898), 916-919.

Hubbard, James M. "Warlike Europe," *North American Review,* CLI, No. 404 (July, 1890), 125-127.

Hudson, Thomas Jay. "Evolution and the Spanish-American War," *National Magazine* (February, 1899), 435-447.

Johnston, Joseph F. "Development of Our Own Territory," *The Independent*, L, Part I (June 16, 1898), 779.

Jordan, Thomas. "Why We Need Cuba," *The Forum*, XI (July, 1891), 559-567.

Judson, H. P. "Our Federal Constitution and the Government of Tropical Territories," *Review of Reviews*, XIX (January, 1899), 67-75.

Kaine, John Langdon. "The Cuban War," *The Independent*, L, Part I (April 28, 1898), 536-538.

Kenney, George Warren. "The Place of Imperialism in Historic Evolution," *The Arena*, XXIV (October, 1900), 350-357.

King, Clarence. "Shall Cuba Be Free?" *The Forum*, XX (September, 1895), 50-65.

Labouchere, Henry. "The Foreign Policy of England," *North American Review*, CLV, No. 431 (October, 1892), 430-445.

Latane, John H. "Intervention of the United States in Cuba," *North American Review*, CLXVI (March, 1898), 350-361.

Lathrop, George Parsons. "How a War Begins," *North American Review*, CLXII, No. 471 (February, 1896), 195-200.

Lecky, W. E. H. "The Relations between the United States and Other Powers," *The Independent*, L, Part II (July 7, 1898), 15-17.

Leedon, James. "The Fallacy of Patriotism," *North American Review*, CLIII, No. 419 (October, 1891), 509-512.

Lodge, Henry Cabot. "American Policy of Territorial Expansion," *The Independent*, L, Part I (January 13, 1898), 41.

———. "Our Blundering Foreign Policy," *The Forum*, XIX (March, 1895), 8-17.

———. "Our Duty to Cuba," *The Forum*, XXI (April, 1896), 278-287.

———. "Washington's Conception of America's Future," *Magazine of American History*, XXIII (February, 1890), 160-161.

Long, E. V. "The Menace of Imperialism," *The Arena*, XXIV (October, 1900), 337-345.

Lopez, Sixto. "The Philippine Problem," *The Outlook*, LXVII (April 13, 1901), 857-859.

Lord, W. F. "The Creed of Imperialism," *The Nineteenth Century*, LXVI (July, 1909), 29-37.

Lorne, The Marquis of. "The Partition of Africa," *North American Review*, CLI, No. 409 (December, 1890), 701-712.

Low, Seth. "The United States in 1899," *University [of Pennsylvania] Bulletin*, III, No. 5 (February, 1899).

Lowell, A. Lawrence. "The Colonial Expansion of the United States," *The Atlantic Monthly*, LXXXIII (February, 1899), 145-154.

Luce, S. B. "The Benefits of War," *North American Review,* CLIII (December, 1891), 672-683.

Ludlow, William. "The Military Systems of Europe and America," *North American Review,* CLX, No. 458 (January, 1895), 72-84.

MacDonald, William. "The Dangers of Imperialism," *The Forum,* XXVI (October, 1898), 177-187.

———. "Expansion as an Issue," *The Nation,* LXIX (July 27, 1899), 64-65.

———. "Imperialism Versus the Constitution," *The Nation,* LXVIII (January 12, 1899), 25-26.

———. "The Needs of Imperialism," *The Nation,* LXIX (August 10, 1899), 104.

———. "Relations of Civil and Military Power," *The Nation,* LXIX (August 3, 1899), 85.

Mahan, Alfred Thayer. "Hawaii and Our Future Sea-Power," *The Forum,* XV (March, 1893), 1-11.

———. "Possibilities of an Anglo-American Reunion," *North American Review,* CLIX, No. 456 (November, 1894), 551-563.

Marble, John Hobart. "The American Attempt at Conquest," *The Arena,* XXII (November, 1899), 554-570.

Marshall, Newton H. "Empires and Races," *Contemporary Review,* XCVI (September, 1909), 304-316.

Martin, Bradley, Jr. "American Imperialism," *The Nineteenth Century,* XLVIII (September, 1900), 393-406.

Martin, Harold. "The Manila Censorship," *The Forum,* XXXI, No. 4 (June, 1901), 462-471.

Matheson, Fred J. "United States and Cuban Independence," *The Fortnightly Review,* LXIX (May, 1898), 816-832.

Mayo-Smith, Richmond. "Theories of Mixture of Races and Nationalities," *Yale Review,* III (August, 1894), 166-186.

McCord, Myron H. "The United States Should Not Shrink from Its Responsibilities," *The Independent,* L, Part I (June 16, 1898), 780.

Mead, E. D. "British and American Imperialism," *New England Magazine,* XIX, new series (October, 1899), 244-256.

Medley, George W. "A New Era for the United States," *The Forum,* XV (March, 1893), 24-31.

Melville, R. D. "Aspects of Empire and Colonization: Past and Prospective," *Westminster Review,* CL (October, 1899), 244-256.

Merrill, George B. "Thirty Years After: A Protest against Hawaiian Annexation," *Overland Monthly,* XXXII, second series (July, 1898), 64-65.

Merry, William L. "The Nicaragua Canal: Its Political Aspects," *The Forum,* XII (February, 1892), 721-728.

Miles, Nelson A. "Our Acquisition of Territory," *North American Review,* CLXI, No. 468 (November, 1895), 561-565.

———. "The War with Spain," *North American Review,* CLXVIII, Part I and Part II (May, 1899), 513-529; (June, 1899), 749-760.

Miller, George McA.; Will, Thomas E.; Hall, Bolton; Crosby, Ernest. "Why I Am Opposed to Imperialism: A Symposium," *The Arena,* XXVIII, No. 1 (July, 1902), 1-11.

Miller, Warner. "The Nicaragua Canal and Commerce," *The Forum,* XII (February, 1892), 714-720.

Money, H. D. "Expansion—Past and Prospective," *The Arena,* XXIII (April, 1900), 337-342.

Morgan, John T. "The Territorial Expansion of the United States," *The Independent,* L, Part II (July 7, 1898), 10-12.

Olney, Richard. "The Growth of Our Foreign Policy," *Atlantic Monthly,* LXXXV (March, 1900), 293-301.

———. "The International Isolation of the United States," *The Atlantic Monthly,* LXXXI (May, 1898), 577-588.

Palmer, William J. "The United States and Cuba: Arguments for Neutrality," *The Outlook,* LVIII (April 23, 1898), 1014-1015.

Parks, Samuel C. "Causes of the Philippine War," *The Arena,* XXVII, No. 6 (June, 1902), 561-572.

———. "Imperialism," *The Arena,* XXV (June, 1901), 577-587.

Parrish, Samuel L. "American Experience Considered as Historical Evolution," *Journal of Social Science,* XXXVII (1899), 99-110.

Parsons, Frank. "The Giant Issue of 1900," *The Arena,* XXIII (June, 1900), 560-565.

Peffer, W. A. "Imperialism, America's Historic Policy," *North American Review,* CLXXI, No. 525 (August, 1900), 246-258.

———. "A Republic in the Philippines," *North American Review,* CLXVIII (March, 1899), 310-320.

Perez, Antonia G. "The Independence of Cuba," *The Contemporary Review,* LXXVI (July, 1899), 118-131.

Petersen, George D. "Germany and the Spanish-American War," *The Independent,* L, Part I (June 16, 1898), 782-783.

Porter, Robert P. "The Future of Cuba," *North American Review,* CLXVIII (April, 1899), 418-423.

Potter, H. C. "National Bigness or Greatness—Which?" *North American Review,* CLXVIII (April, 1899), 433-444.

Powers, Frederick Perry. "The United States as a Colonial Power," *Lippincott's Magazine* (August, 1898), 255-261.

Powers, H. H. "The Ethics of Expansion," *The International Journal of Ethics,* X (April, 1900), 288-306.

———. "War as a Suggestion of Manifest Destiny," *Annals of the American Academy of Political and Social Science* (September, 1898), 173-192.

Pratt, Dwight Mallory. "Patriotism and the Flag," *The Independent,* L, Part II (July 7, 1898), 26-27.

Pratt, Harry Judson. "Can We Give Up Our Colonies?" *The World Today,* XIV, No. 4 (April, 1908), 367-370.

Prince, Leon C. "The Passing of the Declaration of Independence," *The Arena,* XXV (April, 1901), 353-364.

Proctor, John R. "Hawaii and the Changing Front of the World," *The Forum,* XXIV (September, 1897), 34-45.

———. "Isolation or Imperialism?" *The Forum,* XXVI (September, 1898), 14-26.

Reinsch, Paul S. "Can the United States Americanize Her Colonies?" *The World Today,* XV, No. 3 (September, 1908), 950-953.

———. "Colonial Government," *The Nation,* LXXV (July 31, 1902), 99.

———. "The New Conquest of the World," *World's Work* (February, 1901), 425-431.

———. "Problems of Government in the Philippines," *The Arena,* XXIV (September, 1900), 281-292.

———. "The Positive Side of the Monroe Doctrine," *The Independent,* LV (January 1, 1903), 9-11.

———. "Representation and Colonial Government," *The Forum,* XXXIII (June, 1902), 281-292.

Richardson, George A. "The Subjugation of Inferior Races," *Overland Monthly,* XXXV, new series (January, 1900), 49-60.

Ridpath, John C. "The Republic and the Empire," *The Arena,* XX (September, 1898), 344-363.

Robinson, Charles. "The Hawaiian Controversy in the Light of History," *American Journal of Politics,* IV, No. 5 (May, 1894), 477-490.

Robinson, Edward Van Dyke. "The Caroline Islands and the Terms of Peace," *The Independent,* L, Part III (October 13, 1898), 1044-1046.

Roman, S. Rhett. "American Chauvinism," *North American Review,* CLV, No. 433 (December, 1892), 756-759.

Roosevelt, Theodore. "True American Ideals," *The Forum,* XVIII (February, 1895), 743-750.

———. "What 'Americanism' Means," *The Forum,* XVII (April, 1894), 196-206.

Sanford, Henry S. "American Interests in Africa," *The Forum,* IX (June, 1890), 409-429.

Schurz, Carl. "Imperialism," *The Independent,* L, Part II (July 14, 1898), 83.

———. "Manifest Destiny," *Harper's* LXXXVII (October, 1893), 737-746.

———. "Thoughts on American Imperialism," *The Century Illustrated Monthly Magazine,* LVI (September, 1898), 781-788.

Schouler, James. "Mr. Cleveland and the Senate," *The Forum,* XXIII (March, 1897), 65-74.

———. "A Review of the Hawaiian Controversy," *The Forum,* XVI (February, 1894), 670-689.

Scott, I. M. "Philippine Annexation Justified by Our History, Constitution and Laws," *Overland Monthly,* XXXIV, second series (October, 1899), 310-318.

Seaman, Louis L. "Native Troops for Our Colonial Possessions," *North American Review,* CLXXI (December, 1900), 847-860.

Shepard, Edward M. "Support of Mr. Bryan by Sound-Money Democrats," *North American Review,* CLXXI, No. 528 (October, 1900), 446-455.

Sherman, John. "The Nicaragua Canal," *The Forum,* XI (March, 1891), 1-9.

Shibley, George H. "Is the Republic Overthrown?" *The Arena,* XXII (October, 1899), 443-453.

Smith, Charles Emory. "Vital Issues of the Campaign," *North American Review,* CLXXI (October, 1900), 468-473.

Smith, George H. "Puerto Ricans and the Constitution," *The Arena,* XXIII (June, 1900), 626-634.

Smith, Goldwin. "Anglo-Saxon Union," *North American Review,* CLVII, No. 441 (August, 1898), 170-185.

———. "Imperialism in the United States," *The Contemporary Review,* LXXV (May, 1899), 620-628.

———. "The Moral of the Cuban War," *The Forum,* XXVI (November, 1898), 282-293.

Smith, Robert B. "The Policy of Isolation Is Wrong," *The Independent,* L, Part I (June 16, 1898), 779.

Sobral, Jose Guitierrez. "A Spanish View of the Nicaragua Canal," *North American Review,* CLXIV, No. 485 (April, 1897), 462-471.

Solomon, A. "Porto Rico as a Field for Investors," *The Independent,* L, Part II (September 29, 1898), 903-905.

Spreckels, Claus. "The Future of the Sandwich Islands," *North American Review,* CLII, No. 412 (March, 1891), 287-298.

Springer, William M. "The Hawaiian Situation: Our Present Duty," *North American Review,* CLVII, No. 445 (December, 1893), 745-752.

Steckel, Amos. "The Natural Right of Self-Government," *The Arena,* XXIII (May, 1900), 458-463.

Stevens, John L. "A Plea for Annexation," *North American Review,* CLVII, No. 445 (December, 1893), 736-745.

Stevenson, Adlai E. "The Issue of the Campaign," *North American Review,* CLXXI, No. 528 (October, 1900), 433-439.

Steward, T. G. "A Plea for Patriotism," *The Independent,* L, Part II, (September 29, 1898), 887-888.

Stewart, Freeman. "Christianity and Imperialism," *The Arena,* XXIII (June, 1900), 565-577.

Stone, William J. "The Campaign of 1900 from a Democratic Point of View," *The Forum,* XXX (October, 1900), 99-108.

Sumner, William Graham. "The Fallacy of Territorial Expansion," *The Forum,* XXI (June, 1896), 414-419.

Taylor, Hannis. "The Study of War," *North American Review,* CLXII, No. 471 (February, 1896), 181-189.

———. "England's Colonial Empire," *North American Review,* CLXII, No. 475 (June, 1896), 682-697.

———. "Pending Problems," *North American Review,* CLXVII (November, 1898), 609-624.

———. "The Work of the Peace Commission," *North American Review,* CLXVII (December, 1898), 744-751.

Taylor, Rebecca J. "Disposition of the Philippine Islands," *The Arena,* XXIX, No. 1 (January, 1903), 48-52.

Thorpe, Francis N. "The Civil Service and Colonization," *Harper's New Monthly Magazine,* XCVIII (May, 1899), 858-862.

Thurston, Lorrin A. "President Dole and the Hawaiian Question," *The Outlook,* LVIII (February 5, 1898), 316-320.

———. "The Sandwich Islands: The Advantages of Annexation," *North American Review,* CLVI, No. 436 (March, 1893), 265-281.

Tillman, Benjamin Ryan. "Causes of Southern Opposition to Imperialism," *North American Review,* CLXXI, No. 528 (October, 1900), 440-446.

Towne, Charles A. "Campaign Issues from a Democratic Standpoint," *The Outlook,* LXVI (October 13, 1900), 403-409; (October 20, 1900), 449-457.

———. "Reasons for Democratic Success," *The Forum,* XXX (November, 1900), 275-285.

Trent, W. P. "In Re Imperialism," *The Sewanee Review,* VI (October, 1898), 479-499.

Tucker, J. Randolph. "Our New Colonial Policy," *The Arena*, XXI (January, 1899), 84-90.

Twain, Mark. "To the Person Sitting in Darkness," *North American Review*, CLXXII (February, 1901), 161-176.

Van Dyke, Henry. "The American Birthright and the Philippine Pottage," *The Independent*, L, Part III (December 1, 1898), 1579-1585.

Vest, G. G. "Objections to Annexing the Philippines," *North American Review*, CLXIX (October, 1899), 564-576.

Viallete, Achille. "Les Preliminaires de la Guerre Hispano-Americaine et l'Annexion des Philippines par les Etats-Unis," *Revue Historique* (Juillet-Aout, 1903), 282-283.

Villard, O. G. "Another Weary Titan," *The Nation*, LXXXVI, No. 2236 (May 7, 1908), 415-416.

Von Holst, Hermann E. "Some Expansionist Inconsistencies and False Analogies," *University of Chicago Record*, III, No. 50 (March 10, 1899), 339-345.

———. "Some Lessons We Ought to Learn," *University of Chicago Record*, III, No. 46 (February 10, 1899), 299-304.

Watson, J. "The Restless Energy of the American People," *North American Review*, CLXIX (October, 1899), 564-576.

Weed, Elbert D. "Our Duty in the Philippines," *The Arena*, XX (October, 1898), 453-459.

West, Henry L. "The Republican and Democratic Platforms Compared," *The Forum*, XXX (October, 1900), 86-98.

White, Arthur Silva. "Our Benefits from the Nicaragua Canal," *North American Review*, CLXI, No. 469 (December, 1895), 720-725.

White, Stephen M. "The Proposed Annexation of Hawaii," *The Forum*, XXIII (August, 1897), 723-736.

Whitmarsh, H. Phelps. "The Situation in the Hawaiian Islands," *The Outlook*, LXIII (October 28, 1899), 489-493.

———. "Through Filipino Eyes," *The Outlook*, LXIII (December, 2, 1899), 835-839.

Whittle, J. Lowry. "Bryan and McKinley—The Parting of the Ways," *The Forthnightly Review*, LXXIX (November, 1900), 778-789.

Wilcox, Marion. "The Filipino's Vain Hope of Independence," *North American Review*, CLXXI, No. 526 (September, 1900), 333-347.

Willis, Henry Parker. "Can the United States Administer Colonies?" *The World Today*, XIV, No. 3 (March, 1908), 315-319.

Willis, S. T. "Cuba as a Mission Field," *The Independent*, L, Part III (December 1, 1898), 1608-1609.

Winslow, Erving. "The Anti-Imperialist League," *The Independent,* LI, Part II (May 18, 1899), 1347-1351.

————. "The Anti-Imperialist Position," *North American Review,* CLXXI, No. 528 (October, 1900), 460-468.

Woolsey, Theodore S. "An Inquiry Concerning Our Foreign Relations," *Yale Review,* I (August, 1892), 162-174.

————. "Cuba and Intervention," *The Independent,* L, Part I, (March 17, 1898), 337-338.

————. "The Law and the Policy for Hawaii," *Yale Review,* II (February, 1894), 347-355.

————. "The President's Monroe Doctrine," *The Forum,* XX (February, 1896), 705-712.

Wyatt, H. F. "Ethics of Empire," *Nineteenth Century,* XLI (April, 1897), 516-530.

Young, John Russell. "American Influence in China," *North American Review,* CLI, No. 405 (August, 1890), 192-200.

Zendrini, Paolo. "The Spanish Decline," *The Westminster Review,* CLI (February, 1899), 172-181.

Anonymous ("A Filipino"). "Aquinaldo's Case Against the United States," *North American Review,* CLXIX (September, 1899), 425-432.

Anonymous ("A Foreign Naval Officer"). "Can the United States Afford to Fight Spain?" *North American Review,* CLXIV, No. 483 (February, 1897), 208-214.

II NEWSPAPERS

Boston Evening Transcript
Boston Herald
New York Evening Post
New York Herald
New York Sun

The New York Times
New York Tribune
Philadelphia Press
Pittsburgh Dispatch
Springfield Republican

III GOVERNMENT DOCUMENTS AND RELATED MATERIALS

Congressional Globe

Congressional Record

Foreign Relations of the United States, 1894, Appendix II, "Affairs in Hawaii" (Washington: U.S.G.P.O., 1895).

Foreign Relations of the United States, 1898 (Washington: U.S.G.P.O., 1901).

House of Representatives

 House Document 1, part 3, 56 Cong., 1 Sess. "Preliminary Statement of Commissioners Appointed by President to Investigate Affairs in Philippine Islands" (Washington: U.S.G.P.O., 1899).

House Executive Document 47, 53 Cong., 2 Sess. "Report of Special Commissioner James H. Blount re Affairs in the Hawaiian Islands" (Washington: U.S.G.P.O., 1893).

House Document 230, 55 Cong., 2 Sess. "Report from Committee on Foreign Affairs Adverse to H. R. 175" (re U.S. assumption of certain Hawaiian Debts) (Washington: U.S.G.P.O., 1898).

House Document 233, 55 Cong. 2 Sess. "Report from Committee on Foreign Affairs Adverse to H. R. 162" (Treaty for Hawaiian Annexation) (Washington: U.S.G.P.O., 1898).

House of Representatives (Document) *1355*, part 2, 55 Cong., 2 Sess. "Views of Minority of Committee on Foreign Affairs, Adverse to H. J. R. 259 for Annexing the Hawaiian Islands" (Washington: U.S.G.P.O., 1898).

McKee, Thomas H. (ed.). *The National Conventions and Platforms of All Political Parties, 1789–1904* (Baltimore: Friedenwald Co., 1906).

Malloy, William (ed.). *Treaties, Conventions, International Acts, Protocols, and Agreements between the United States of America and Other Powers*, 2 vols. (Washington: U.S.G.P.O., 1910).

Miller, Marion Mills (ed.). *Great Debates in American History* (14 vols.), Vol. III, Foreign Relations, Part Two (New York: Current Literature Publishing Co., 1913).

Porter, Kirk H. (ed.). *National Party Platforms* (New York: Macmillan Co., 1924).

Richardson, James D. (ed.). *A Compilation of the Messages and Papers of the Presidents, 1789–1897*, 10 vols. (Washington: U.S.G.P.O., 1899).

Senate

Senate Document 214, 55 Cong., 2 Sess. "Argument Favoring Annexation of Hawaii" (by J. D. Caton) (Washington: U.S.G.P.O., 1898).

Senate Document 62, 55 Cong., 3 Sess. "In Re Hawaiian Annexation" (Washington: U.S.G.P.O., 1898).

Senate Document 82, 55 Cong., 2 Sess. "Lecture against Annexation of Hawaii" (by F. T. DuBois) (Washington: U.S.G.P.O., 1898).

Senate Document 29, 55 Cong., 3 Sess. "Memorial in Relation to (Philippine) Islands" (Washington: U.S.G.P.O., 1899).

Senate Document 55, 55 Cong., 2 Sess. "Memorial Remonstrating Against Annexation of Hawaii" (Washington: U.S.G.P.O., 1898).

Senate Executive Documents 76 and 77, 52 Cong., 2 Sess. "Papers Relating to the Annexation of the Hawaiian Islands to the United States" (Washington: U.S.G.P.O., 1893).

Senate Document 148, 56 Cong., 2 Sess. "Papers Relating to the Treaty with Spain" (Washington: U.S.G.P.O., 1900).

Senate Report 227, 53 Cong., 2 Sess. "Report of Senate Committee on Foreign Relations, John T. Morgan, Chairman, re Affairs in the Hawaiian Islands" (Washington: U.S.G.P.O., 1894).

Senate Report 681, 55 Cong., 2 Sess. "Report of Committee on Foreign Relations upon the Joint Resolution for Hawaiian Annexation" (Washington: U.S.G.P.O., 1898).

Senate Executive Document 132, 53 Cong., 2 Sess. Re Samoa (Washington: U.S.G.P.O., 1894).

Senate Executive Document 93, 53 Cong., 2 Sess. Re Samoa (Washington: U.S.G.P.O., 1894).

Senate Document 62, Parts 1 and 2, 55 Cong., 3 Sess. "Treaty of Peace Between United States and Spain; with Accompanying Papers" (Washington: U.S.G.P.O., 1899).

Senate Document 188, 55 Cong., 2 Sess. "Views as to Strategic and Commercial Value of Nicaraguan Canal, Future Control of the Pacific Ocean, Strategic Value of Hawaii and Its Annexation" (Washington: U.S.G.P.O., 1898).

Senate Document 221, 56 Cong., 1 Sess. "War Investigating Commission: Correspondence Re Campaigns in Philippine Islands and Puerto Rico" (Washington: U.S.G.P.O., 1900).

United States Supreme Court. *Opinions Delivered in the Insular Tariff Cases* (Washington: U.S.G.P.O., 1901).

IV BOOKS, BOOKLETS, AND PAMPHLETS

Adams, Brooks. *America's Economic Supremacy* (New York: The Macmillan Co., 1900).

——. *The New Empire* (New York: The Macmillan Co., 1902).

Adams, Charles Francis. *An Autobiography* (Boston: Houghton-Mifflin Co., 1916).

——. *Imperialism and the Tracks of Our Forefathers* (Boston: Dana Estes and Co., 1899).

American Anti-Imperialist League. *Address to the Voters of the United States* (Liberty Tract No. 13) (Chicago: American Anti-Imperialist League, 1900).

Americus Free (pseudonym). *The Coming Empire: A Political Satire* (New York: Patriotic Publishing Co., 1900).

Anti-Imperialist League, *Arguments Against a So-Called Imperial*

Policy (Anti-Imperialist Broadsides Nos. 1, 2 and 3), (Washington: Anti-Imperialist League, n.d., but probably December, 1898).

————. *In the Name of Liberty: Protest Against the Philippine Policy* (Boston: Rockwell and Churchill Press, 1899).

————. *The Moral and Religious Aspects of the So-Called Anti-Imperial Policy* (Anti-Imperialist Broadsides Nos. 5 and 6) (Washington: Anti-Imperialist League, n.d., but probably January, 1899).

Atkins, Edwin F. *Sixty Years in Cuba* (Boston: Houghton Co., 1926).

Atkinson, Edward. *The Anti-Imperialist* (Brookline: Edward Atkinson, 1899).

————. *The Imperial Chain* (Brookline: Edward Atkinson, 1899).

Bancroft, Frederick (ed.). *Speeches, Correspondence, and Political Papers of Carl Schurz,* six volumes (New York: G. P. Putnam's Sons, 1913).

Berle, A. A. *Some Popular American Fallacies Refuted* (Chicago: Pilgrim Press, 1900).

Bingham, Harry. *The Annexation of Hawaii: A Right and a Duty* (Concord, N.H.: The Rumford Press, 1898).

Blount, James H. *The American Occupation of the Philippines, 1898–1912* (New York: G. P. Putnam's Sons, 1912).

Boutwell, George S. *Address at Faneuil Hall, Boston, February 23, 1900* (Boston: New England Anti-Imperialist League, 1900).

————. *Hawaiian Annexation* (Boston: Anti-Imperialist League, 1898).

————. *In the Name of Liberty* (N.C.: Anti-Imperialist League, 1899).

————. *Isolation and Imperialism* (Washington: Gibson Bros., 1898).

————. *The President's Policy: War and Conquest Abroad, Degradation of Labor at Home* (Liberty Tract, No. 7) (Chicago: American Anti-Imperialist League, 1900).

————. *Problems Raised by the War* (Washington: Anti-Imperialist League, 1898).

————. *Reminiscences of Sixty Years in Public Affairs,* 2 vols. (New York: Harper & Co., 1912).

————. *Republic or Empire* (Boston: New England Anti-Imperialist League, 1900).

Brooks, Francis A. *An Arraignment of President McKinley's Policy of Extending by Force the Sovereignty of the United States over the Philippine Islands* (Boston: Alfred Mudge & Son, 1899).

————. *An Examination of the Scheme for Engrafting the Colonial*

System of Government upon the Constitution of the United States (Boston: George H. Ellis, 1900).

————. *Objections to the President's Proposed Subjugation of the Filipinos* (Boston: Alfred Mudge & Son, 1899).

————. *The Unauthorized and Unlawful Subjugation of Filipinos in the Island of Luzon by President McKinley* (Cambridge: Caustic and Claflin, 1900).

Brown, Seth W. *Speech in House of Representatives, February 9, 1901* (New York: Anti-Imperialist League of New York, 1901).

Bruce, Henry Addington. *The Romance of American Expansion* (New York: Moffat, Yard, and Co., 1909).

Bryan, William Jennings, and Bryan, Mary Baird. *The Memoirs of William Jennings Bryan* (Philadelphia: John C. Winston Co., 1925).

Bryan, William Jennings, *et al. Republic or Empire* (Chicago: The Independence Co., 1899).

Bryan, William Jennings. *Speeches of William Jennings Bryan*, 2 vols. (New York: Funk and Wagnalls and Co., 1909).

Carnegie, Andrew. *Autobiography of Andrew Carnegie* (Boston: Houghton, Mifflin Co., 1920).

————. *The Opportunity of the United States* (New York: Anti-Imperialist League of New York, 1902).

Carpenter, Edmund J. *The American Advance* (New York: John Lane, 1903).

Chadwick, John White. *The Present Distress: A Sermon upon Our Oriental War* (New York: William Green, 1899).

Chamberlain, D. H. *Open Letter to Andrew D. White* (Anti-Imperialist Broadside No. 12) (Boston: New England Anti-Imperialist League, N.d., but probably September, 1900).

Chamberlain, Fred C. *The Blow from Behind, or Some Features of the Anti-Imperialist Movement Attending the War with Spain* (Boston: Lee and Shepard, 1903).

Chetwood, John. *Manila or Monroe Doctrine* (New York: Robert Lewis Weed Co., 1898).

Clews, Henry. *The Wall Street Point of View* (New York: Silver Co., 1900).

Cockran, W. Bourke. *Address Delivered in Faneuil Hall, Boston, February 23, 1900* (Boston: New England Anti-Imperialist League, 1900).

Codman, Charles R.; Hardon, Henry W.; and Parker, Alton B. *Anti-Imperialism—The Great Issue* (Boston: New England Anti-Imperialist League, 1904).

Cromer, The Earl of. *Ancient and Modern Imperialism* (London: John Murray, 1910).

Crooker, Joseph Henry. *The Menace to America* (Liberty Tract No. 12) (Chicago: American Anti-Imperialist League, 1900).

Crosby. Ernest. *Swords and Plowshares* (New York: Fink and Co.. 1902).

Curry, J. L. M. *Address before the Alabama Polytechnic Institute, June 14, 1899* (Auburn, Alabama: Alabama Polytechnic Institute, 1899).

Dunne, Finley Peter. *Observations by Mr. Dooley* (New York: Harper and Bros., 1902).

————. *Mr. Dooley in Peace and War* (Boston: Small, Maynard and Co., 1899).

————. *Mr. Dooley's Opinions* (New York: Harper and Bros., 1900).

————. *Mr. Dooley's Philosophy* (New York: Harper and Bros., 1906).

Fernald, James C. *The Imperial Republic* (New York: Funk and Wagnalls, 1898).

Egleston, George W. *Is A Limited Policy of Imperialism Justified?* (N.p., 1898).

Fiske, John. *American Political Ideas Viewed from the Standpoint of Universal History* (New York: Harper and Bros., 1885).

Fleming, William Henry. *A Question of National Honor* (Boston: Anti-Imperialist League, 1899).

Forbes, W. Cameron. *The Philippine Islands,* 2 vols. (Boston: Houghton Mifflin Co., 1928).

Foreman, John. *Will the United States Withdraw from the Philippines?* (Liberty Tract No. 14) (Chicago: American Anti-Imperialist League, 1900).

Foster, John W. *American Diplomacy in the Orient* (Boston: Houghton Co., 1903).

Gage, Norris L. *National Growth versus Foreign Conquest* (N.C.: Wilson-Clark Co., 1899).

Gardiner, Charles A. *Our Right to Acquire and Hold Foreign Territory* (New York: G. P. Putnam's Sons, 1899).

Garrison, William Lloyd. *Imperialism,* Address at the Annual Meeting of the Progressive Friends, Longwood, Pa., June 10, 1899 (N.p., N.d., but probably Anti-Imperialist League, and definitely June or July, 1899).

————. *The Root of Imperialism* (N.p., Copy in *United States Imperialism: Broadsides and Circulars,* Widener Library, Harvard University).

Giddings, Franklin Henry. *Democracy and Empire* (New York: Macmillan Co., 1901).

Gompers, Samuel. *Seventy Years of Life and Labor: An Autobiography,* 2 vols. (New York: E. P. Dutton, 1925).

Gookin, Frederick W. *A Liberty Catechism* (Liberty Tract No. 3) (Chicago: American Anti-Imperialist League, 1899).

Griffis, William Elliot. *America in the East* (New York: A. S. Barnes and Co., 1899).

Halstead, Murat. *America's New Possessions* (Chicago: The Dominion Co., 1899).

Hardon, Henry Winthrop. *The Philippine Case* (New York: Evening Post Job Printing House, 1899).

Harrison, Francis Burton. *The Cornerstone of Philippine Independence* (New York: The Century Co., 1922).

Harrison, Frederic. *National and Social Problems* (New York: Macmillan Co., 1908).

Hay, John. *Addresses of John Hay* (New York: The Century Co., 1906).

Hoar, George F. *Autobiography of Seventy Years,* 2 vols. (New York: Macmillan Co., 1903).

————. *Letter of Senator George F. Hoar to His Constituents* (Anti-Imperialist Broadside No. 10) (Boston: Anti-Imperialist League, N.d., but probably January, 1900).

————. *No Constitutional Power to Conquer Foreign Nations and Hold Their People in Subjection Against Their Will* (Boston: Dana Estes and Co., 1899).

————. *Speech in United States Senate, February 27, 1901* (Anti-Imperialist Broadside No. 13) (Boston: New England Anti-Imperialist League, N.d., but probably March, 1901).

Huffcut, Ernest W. *The Philippine Problem in the Light of American International Policy* (Utica, New York: Oneida Historical Society, 1902).

Irwin, Wallace. *Random Rhymes and Odd Numbers* (New York: Macmillan Co., 1906).

Janes, Lewis C. *The Doctrine of 'the Survival of the Fittest' No Warrant for Forcible Assimilation* (Anti-Imperialist Leaflet No. 26) (Boston: Anti-Imperialist League, N.d.).

Johnson, Alfred S. (ed.). *The Cyclopedic Review of Current History* Vols. 3 and 4, Columbian Annual, 1893 and 1894 (Buffalo: Garretson, Cox and Co., New York, Vol. 3, 1894; Vol. 4, 1895).

Johnson, Willis Fletcher, *A Century of Expansion* (New York: Macmillan Co., 1903).

Jordan, David Starr. *The Days of a Man,* 2 vols. (New York: World Book Co., 1922).

————. *Imperial Democracy* (New York: D. Appleton & Co., 1899).

Kimball, John C. *Uncensored Manila News* (Cambridge: The Co-operative Press, 1899).

Latane, John Holladay. *America as a World Power* (New York: Harper & Brothers, 1907).

Laughlin, J. Laurence. *Patriotism and Imperialism* (Liberty Tract No. 2) (Chicago: Central Anti-Imperialist League, 1899).

LeRoy, James A. *The Americans in the Philippines,* 2 vols. (Boston: Houghton Mifflin, 1914).

Lodge, Henry Cabot (ed.). *Selections from the Correspondence of Theodore Roosevelt and Henry Cabot Lodge,* 2 vols. (New York: Charles Scribner, 1925).

Lomax, Tennant. *An Imperial Colonial Policy: Opposition to It the Supreme Duty of Patriotism* (Montgomery, Alabama: N.p., 1898).

Magoon, Charles E. *Report on the Legal Status of the Territory and Inhabitants of the Islands Acquired by the United States During the War with Spain* (United States Government Printing Office, Washington, 1900).

Mahan, Alfred Thayer. *From Sail to Steam: Recollections of Naval Life* (New York: Harper and Bros., 1907).

————. *The Influence of Sea Power upon History, 1660-1783* Boston: Little, Brown, & Co., 1890).

————.*The Interest of America in International Conditions* (Boston: Little, Brown & Co., 1910).

————. *The Interest of America in Sea Power* (Boston: Little, Brown & Co., 1898).

————. *The Problem of Asia and Its Effect Upon International Conditions* (Boston: Little, Brown & Co., 1907).

Masters, Edgar Lee. *The New Star Chamber and Other Essays* (Chicago: The Hammersmark Publishing Co., 1904).

Mead, Edwin D. *The Duty of the American People* (Boston: Anti-Imperialist League, 1899).

————. *Governor Roosevelt's 'Exact Parallels'* (Boston: Peace Crusade Committee, N.d., but undoubtedly 1900).

————. *The Present Crisis* (Boston: George H. Ellis, 1899).

Miles, Nelson Appleton. *Serving the Republic* (New York: Harper Co., 1911).

Morgan, H. Wayne (ed.). *Making Peace with Spain: The Diary of Whitelaw Reid September-December, 1898* (Austin: University of Texas Press, 1965).

Morison, Elting E. (ed.). *The Letters of Theodore Roosevelt* (Cambridge: Harvard University Press, 1951).

Morris, Charles. *Our Island Empire* (Philadelphia: Lippincott, 1899).

Mowry, William A. *The Territorial Growth of the United States* (New York: Silver, Burdett and Co., 1902).

Nevins, Allan (ed.). *Letters of Grover Cleveland: 1850-1908* (Boston: Houghton Mifflin Co., 1933).

New England Anti-Imperialist League. *Free America, Free Cuba, Free Philippines* (Boston: New England Anti-Imperialist League, 1901).

―――――. *To The American People* (Boston: New England Anti-Imperialist League, 1901).

Parker, George F. (ed.) *The Writings and Speeches of Grover Cleveland* (New York: Cassell Publishing Co., 1892).

Parkhurst, Charles H. *Our Fight with Tammany* (New York, 1895).

Patterson, Thomas M. *The Fruits of Imperialism* (Boston: George H. Ellis Co., 1902).

Pettigrew, R. F. *The Course of Empire* (New York: Boni and Liveright, 1920).

―――――. *Imperial Washington* (Chicago: Charles H. Kerr and Co. Co-operative, 1922).

Philippine Information Society. *Our Relations With the Insurgents Prior to the Fall of Manila* (Boston: Philippine Information Society, 1901).

―――――. *The Parting of the Ways* (Boston: Philippine Information Society, 1901).

Randolph, Carman F. *The Law and Policy of Annexation* (New York: Longmans, Green and Co., 1901).

Reid, Whitelaw. *Problems of Expansion* (New York: The Century Co., 1900).

Reinsch, Paul S. *World Politics* (New York: Macmillan Co., 1900).

Roosevelt, Theodore. *The Strenuous Life* (New York: The Century Co., 1905).

Root, Elihu. *Military and Colonial Policy of the United States* (Cambridge: Harvard University Press, 1916).

Shafroth, John F. *Are the Filipinos Capable of Self-Government?* (Anti-Imperialist Leaflet No. 16) (Boston: New England Anti-Imperialist League, 1901).

Sherman, John. *Recollections of Forty Years in the House, Senate and Cabinet* (Chicago: The Werner Co., 1895).

Smith, Edwin Burritt. *Republic or Empire: With Glimpses of 'Criminal Aggression'* (Liberty Tract No. 9) (Chicago: American Anti-Imperialist League, 1900).

―――――. *Shall the United States Have Colonies?* (Anti-Imperialist Broadside No. 14) (Boston: New England Anti-Imperialist League, N.d.).

Snow, Alpheus Henry. *Colony or Free State, Dependence or Just Connection, Empire or Union?* (Washington: N.p., 1907).

Storey, Moorfield; Lichauco, M. P. *The Conquest of the Philippines by the United States, 1898-1925* (New York: Putnam, 1926).

———. *Is It Right?* (Liberty Tract No. 8) (Chicago: American Anti-Imperialist League, 1900).

———; Codman, Julian. *Marked Severities* (Boston: Ellis Co., 1902).

———. *The Recognition of Panama* (Boston: Ellis Co., 1904).

———. *Our New Department* (Boston: Ellis Co., 1901).

———. *What Shall We Do With Our Dependencies?* (Boston: N.p., 1903).

Stroever, Carl. *The Annexation Problem* (Chicago: Independence Co., 1898).

Strong, Josiah. *Expansion under New World Conditions* (New York: The Baker and Taylor Co., 1900).

———. *Our Country: Its Possible Future and Its Present Crisis* (New York: Baker, Taylor, Inc., 1885).

Sumner, William Graham. *The Conquest of the United States by Spain* (Boston: Dana Estes and Co., 1899).

Swift, Morrison I. *Advent of Empire* (Los Angeles: Ronbroke Press, 1900).

———. *Anti-Imperialism* (Los Angeles: Public Ownership Review, 1899).

———. *Human Submission* (N.p.: Philippine Liberty Press, 1905).

———. *Imperialism and Liberty* (Los Angeles: The Ronbroke Press, 1899).

Thurston, Lorrin A. *A Handbook on the Annexation of Hawaii* (St. Joseph, Michigan: A. B. Morse Co., N.d., but presumably 1897).

Towne, Charles A. *The Continental Republic: A Protest Against Colonialism* (Boston: New England Anti-Imperialist League, 1903).

Von Holst, Hermann. *The Annexation of Hawaii* (Chicago: Independence Co., 1898).

Warren, Winslow. *The White Man's Burden* (N.c.: Anti-Imperialist League, N.d., but probably February, 1899).

Welsh, Herbert. *By Way of Manila* (In Welsh Papers, Pennsylvania Historical Society, N.d.).

———. *The Other Man's Country* (Philadelphia: Lippincott, 1900).

———. *Stranger Than Fiction* (In Welsh Papers, Pennsylvania Historical Society, N.d.).

———. *To Lincoln's Plain People: Facts Regarding 'Benevolent*

Assimilation' in the Philippine Islands (Philadelphia: City and State, 1903).

Winslow, Erving. *Anti-Imperialist League: Apologia Pro Vita Sua* (Boston: Anti-Imperialist League, N.d., but presumably 1908).

Woolsey, Theodore S. *American Foreign Policy* (New York: The Century Co., 1898).

V MANUSCRIPT SOURCES

Anti-Imperialist Broadsides and Leaflets. Widener Library, Harvard University, Cambridge, Massachusetts; and among William Augustus Croffut Papers, Library of Congress, Washington, D.C.

Anti-Imperialist Speeches at Faneuil Hall. Widener Library, Harvard University, Cambridge, Mass.

Appel, John C. "The Relationship of Labor to United States Imperialism" (unpublished Ph.D. dissertation, University of Wisconsin, 1950).

Edward Atkinson Papers. Boston Athenaeum, Boston, Massachusetts; Massachusetts Historical Society, Boston, Mass.

George S. Boutwell Papers. Massachusetts Historical Society, Boston, Mass.

Gamaliel Bradford Papers. Massachusetts Historical Society, Boston, Mass.

Grover Cleveland Papers. Library of Congress, Washington, D.C.

William Augustus Croffut Papers. Library of Congress, Washington, D.C.

David Starr Jordan Papers. Stanford University Library and Hoover Institution Library, Stanford, Calif.

Kennedy, Philip W. "The Concept of Racial Superiority and United States Imperialism (unpublished Ph.D. dissertation, St. Louis, University, 1962).

Richard Olney Papers. Library of Congress, Washington, D.C.

Report of the Annual Meeting of the Anti-Imperialist League, 16 vols., 1905–1920 (Anti-Imperialist League, Boston), Widener Library, Harvard University, Cambridge, Massachusetts; and The Boston Athenaeum, Boston, Mass.

Report of the Annual Meeting of the New England Anti-Imperialist League, 6 vols., 1899–1904 (New England Anti-Imperialist League, Boston), Widener Library, Harvard University, Cambridge, Mass.

Carl Schurz Papers, Library of Congress, Washington, D.C.

Scrapbook (compiler unknown) containing broadsides, circulars, leaflets, and miscellaneous letters pertaining to anti-imperialism in the period 1898–1901, Widener Library, Harvard University, Cambridge, Mass.

Scrapbook (compiled by Mrs. William James) containing letters, newspaper and magazine clippings, etc., relating to anti-imperialism in the period 1898–1904, in Widener Library, Harvard University, Cambridge, Mass.

Moorfield Storey Papers, Library of Congress, Washington, D.C.

Herbert Welsh Papers, Pennsylvania Historical Society, Philadelphia, Pa.

United States Imperialism (pamphlet collection), 7 vols., Widener Library, Harvard University, Cambridge, Mass.

SECONDARY MATERIALS

I ARTICLES

Auxier, George W. "Middle Western Newspapers and the Spanish-American War," *Mississippi Valley Historical Review,* XXVI (March, 1940), 523-534.

———. "The Propaganda Activities of the Cuban Junta in Precipitating the Spanish-American War, 1895–1898," *Hispanic American Historical Review,* XIX (August, 1939), 286-305.

Bailey, Thomas A. "The United States and Hawaii during the Spanish American War," *American Historical Review,* XXXVI (April, 1931), 552-560.

———. "Was the Election of 1900 a Mandate on Imperialism?" *Mississippi Valley Historical Review,* XXIV (June, 1937), 43-52.

Baker, George W. "Benjamin Harrison and Hawaiian Annexation: A Reinterpretation," Pacific Historical Review, XXXIII (August, 1964), 295-309.

Bedichek, Roy (ed.). "Independence of the Philippines," *University of Texas Bulletin,* No. 2429 (August 1, 1924).

Blodgett, Geoffrey T. "The Mind of the Boston Mugwump," *The Mississippi Valley Historical Review,* XLVIII, No. 4 (March, 1962), 614-634.

Bradley, Harold Whitman. "Hawaii and the American Penetration of the Northeastern Pacific, 1800–1845," *The Pacific Historical Review,* XII, No. 3 (September, 1943), 277-286.

Coletta, Paolo. "Bryan, McKinley and the Treaty of Paris," *Pacific Historical Review,* XXVI (May, 1957), 131-146.

Dozer, Donald Marquand. "Anti-Expansionism during the Johnson Administration," *The Pacific Historical Review,* XII, No. 3 (September, 1943), 253-275.

Farrell, J. T. "Archbishop Ireland and Manifest Destiny," *Catholic Historical Review,* XXXIII (October, 1947), 269-301.

Gibson, William M. "Mark Twain and Howells: Anti-Imperialists," *New England Quarterly,* XX (December, 1947), 435-470.

Hacker, Louis M. "The Holy War of 1898," *American Mercury,* XXI (November, 1930), 216-326.

Hammond, Richard J. "Economic Imperialism: Sidelights on a Stereotype," *The Journal of Economic History,* XXI (December, 1961), 582-598.

Harrington, Fred H. "The Anti-Imperialist Movement in the United States, 1898–1900," *Mississippi Valley Historical Review,* XXII (September, 1935), 211-230.

————. "Literary Aspects of American Anti-Imperialism, 1898–1900," *New England Quarterly,* X (December, 1937), 650-667.

Hendrickson, Kenneth E. "Reluctant Expansionist: Jacob Gould Schurman and the Philippine Question," *Pacific Historical Review,* XXXVI (November, 1967), 405-421.

Holbo, Paul S. "Presidential Leadership in Foreign Affairs: William McKinley and the Turpie-Foraker Amendment," *American Historical Review,* LXXII (July, 1967), 1321-1335.

La Feber, Walter. "A Note on the 'Mercantilistic Imperialism' of Alfred Thayer Mahan," *Mississippi Valley Historical Review,* XLVIII (March, 1962), 674-685.

Lanzar, Maria Carpio. "The Anti-Imperialist League," *Philippine Social Science Review,* III, No. 1 (August, 1930), 7-41; No. 2 (November, 1930), 118-132; IV, No. 3 (July, 1932), 182-198; No. 4 (October, 1932), 239-254; V, No. 3 (July, 1933), 222-230; No. 4 (October, 1933), 248-279.

Lasch, Christopher. "The Anti-Imperialists, the Philippines, and the Inequality of Man," *The Journal of Southern History,* Vol. XXIV (August, 1958), 319-331.

Leuchtenburg, William E. "Progressivism and Imperialism: The Progressive Movement and American Foreign Policy, 1898–1916," *Mississippi Valley Historical Review,* XXXIX (December, 1952), 483-504.

Livermore, Seward W. "American Strategy Diplomacy in the South Pacific: 1890–1914," *Pacific Historical Review,* XII (March, 1943), 35-51.

Lodge, Henry Cabot, Jr. "Our Failure in the Philippines," *Harper's Magazine,* CLX (January, 1930), 209-218.

Loewenberg, Bert James. "Darwinism Comes to America, 1859–1900," *Mississippi Valley Historical Review,* XXVIII (December, 1941), 339-368.

Nichols, Jeannette P. "The United States Congress and Imperialism: 1861–1897," *The Journal of Economic History,* XXI (December, 1961), 526-538.

Niebuhr, Reinhold. "Awkward Imperialists," *Atlantic Monthly,* CXLV (May, 1930), 670-675.

Pratt, Julius W. "American Business and the Spanish American War," *Hispanic American Historical Review,* XIV (May, 1934), 163-201.

―――. "The Collapse of American Imperialism," *American Mercury,* XXXI (March, 1934), 269-278.

―――. "The Ideology of American Expansion," in *Essays in Honor of William E. Dodd,* Avery Craven, ed. (Chicago, 1935), 347-361.

―――. "The 'Large Policy' of 1898," *Mississippi Valley Historical Review,* XIX (September, 1932), 219-242.

Russ, William A., Jr. "The Role of Sugar in Hawaiian Annexation," *The Pacific Historical Review,* XII (December, 1943), 339-350.

Smith, Thomas C. "Expansion after the Civil War, 1865–1871," *Political Science Quarterly,* XVI (September, 1901), 412-436.

Stanley, Peter W. "William Cameron Forbes: Proconsul in the Philippines," *Pacific Historical Review,* XXXV (August, 1966), 285-302.

Tate, Merze. "Twisting the Lion's Tail over Hawaii," *Pacific Historical Review,* XXXVI (February, 1967), 27-46.

Tompkins, E. Berkeley. "Scylla and Charybdis: The Anti-Imperialist Dilemma in the Election of 1900," *Pacific Historical Review,* XXXVI (May, 1967), 143-161.

―――. "The Old Guard: A Study of the Anti-Imperialist Leadership," *The Historian,* XXX (May, 1968), 366-388.

Vevier, Charles. "American Continentalism: An Idea of Expansion, 1845–1910," *American Historical Review,* LXV (January, 1960), 323-335.

Welch, Richard E. "Senator George Frisbie Hoar and the Defeat of Anti-Imperialism, 1898–1900," *The Historian,* XXVI (May, 1964), 362-380.

―――. "Opponents and Colleagues: George Frisbie Hoar and Henry Cabot Lodge, 1898–1904," *New England Quarterly,* XXXIX (June, 1966), 182-209.

Whittaker, George William. "Samuel Gompers, Anti-Imperialist" (unpublished article in possession of author).

Williams, William A. "Brooks Adams and American Expansion," *New England Quarterly*, XXV (June, 1952), 217-232.

II BOOKS

Adams, Ephraim Douglass. *The Power of Ideals in American History* (New Haven: Yale University Press, 1913).

Alderson, Bernard. *Andrew Carnegie: The Man and His Work* (New York: Doubleday, Page and Co., 1909).

Bailey, Thomas A. *The Man in the Street* (New York: Macmillan Co., 1948).

Bancroft, Frederick. *The Life of William H. Seward,* 2 vols. (New York: Harper and Bros., 1900).

Barnes, James A. *John G. Carlisle: Financial Statesman* (New York, 1931).

Beale, Howard K. *Theodore Roosevelt and the Rise of America to World Power* (Baltimore: Johns Hopkins Press, 1956).

Beisner, Robert L. *Twelve Against Empire* (New York: McGraw Hill, 1968).

Bemis, Samuel Flagg. *The American Secretaries of State and Their Diplomacy,* Vols. VI, VII, and VIII (New York: Pageant Book Co., 1958).

Bicknell, Edward. *The Territorial Acquisitions of the United States, 1787–1913* (Boston: Small, Maynard & Co., 1913).

Billington, Ray A. *Westward Expansion* (New York: Macmillan Co., 1949).

Bodelsen, C. A. *Studies in Mid-Victorian Imperialism* (New York: Alfred A. Knopf, 1925).

Bowers, Claude G. *Beveridge and the Progressive Era* (Boston: Houghton-Mifflin Co., 1932).

Burns, Edward Mc N. *David Starr Jordan* (Stanford: Stanford University Press, 1953).

Callahan, J. M. *American Relations in the Pacific and the Far East: 1874–1900* (Baltimore: Johns Hopkins Press, 1901).

Chadwick, F. E. *The Relations of the United States and Spain* (New York, 1909).

Clark, Grover. *The Balance Sheets of Imperialism* (New York: Columbia University Press, 1936).

Coletta, Paolo. *William Jennings Bryan: Political Evangelist* (Lincoln: University of Nebraska Press, 1964).

Conroy, Hilary. *The Japanese Frontier in Hawaii, 1868–1898* (Berkeley: University of California Press, 1953).

Curti, Merle E. *Bryan and World Peace* in *Smith College Studies in History,* Vol. XVI (Northampton, 1931).

Dennett, Tyler. *Americans in Eastern Asia* (Barnes and Noble, Inc., New York, 1941).

Dennis, Alfred L. P. *Adventures in American Diplomacy: 1896–1906* (New York: E. P. Dutton and Co., 1928).

Dulebohn, George Roscoe. *Principles of Foreign Policy Under the Cleveland Administrations* (Philadelphia: University of Pennsylvania Press, 1941).

Dulles, Foster Rhea. *America in the Pacific: A Century of Expansion* (Boston: Houghton, Mifflin Co., 1932).

———. *The Imperial Years* (New York: Thomas Crowell, 1956.).

Dunn, Arthur W. *From Harrison to Harding,* 2 vols. (New York: Macmillan, 1922).

Fuess, Claude Moore. *Carl Schurz: Reformer* (New York: Dodd, Mead & Co., 1932).

Garraty, John A. *Henry Cabot Lodge* (New York: A. A. Knopf, 1953).

Gillett, Frederick H. *George Frisbie Hoar* (Boston: Houghton, Mifflin Co., 1934).

Glad, Paul W. *The Trumpet Soundeth: William Jennings Bryan and His Democracy, 1896–1912* (Lincoln: University of Nebraska Press, 1960).

Gresham, Matilda. *The Life of Walter Quintin Gresham,* 2 vols. (Chicago: Rand Co., 1919).

Grimes, Alan P. *The Political Liberalism of the New York Nation* Chapel Hill: University of North Carolina Press, 1953).

Grunder, Garel A. and Livezey, William E. *The Philippines and the United States* (Norman: University of Oklahoma Press, 1951).

Haas, William H. (ed.). *The American Empire* (Chicago: University of Chicago Press, 1940).

Harbaugh, William Henry. *Power and Responsibility: The Life and Times of Theodore Roosevelt* (New York: Farrar, Strauss, and Cudahy, 1961).

Hendrick, Burton J. *The Life of Andrew Carnegie,* 2 vols. (New York: Doubleday, Doran, and Co., 1932).

Hibben, Paxton. *The Peerless Leader: William Jennings Bryan* (New York: Farrar and Rinehart, 1929).

Higginson, Mary Thatcher. *Thomas Wentworth Higginson: The Story of His Life* (Boston: Houghton Mifflin Co., 1914).

Hobson, John Atkinson, *Imperialism* (London: Allen and Unwin Ltd., 1938).

Hofstadter, Richard, *Social Darwinism in American Thought* (Boston: Beacon Press, 1955).

Holt, W. Stull. *Treaties Defeated by the Senate* (Baltimore: Johns Hopkins Press, 1933).

Howe, M. A. DeWolfe, *Moorfield Storey: Portrait of an Independent* (Boston, New York: Houghton Mifflin Co., 1932).

James, Henry, *Richard Olney and His Public Service* (Boston: Houghton Co., 1923).

La Feber, Walter. *The New Empire: An Interpretation of American Imperialism, 1860-1898* (Ithaca: Cornell University Press, 1963).

Langer, William L. *The Diplomacy of Imperialism,* 2 vols. (New York: Alfred A. Knopf, 1935).

Leech, Margaret. *In the Days of McKinley* (New York: Harper & Brothers, 1959).

Livezey, William E. *Mahan on Sea Power* (Norman: University of Oklahoma Press, 1947).

Long, J. C. *Bryan, The Great Commoner* (New York: Appleton and Co., 1928).

Lynch, Denis Tilden. *Grover Cleveland: A Man Four-Square* (New York: Horace Liveright, Inc., 1932).

May, Ernest R. *Imperial Democracy: The Emergence of America as a Great Power* (New York: Harcourt, Brace & World, Inc., 1961).

———. *American Imperialism: A Speculative Essay* (New York: Atheneum, 1968).

Millis, Walter. *The Martial Spirit* (Boston: Houghton Mifflin Co., 1931).

Moon, Parker Thomas. *Imperialism and World Politics* (New York: The Macmillan Co., 1926).

Morgan, H. Wayne. *William McKinley and His America* (Syracuse: Syracuse University Press, 1963).

Moore, John Bassett. *Four Phases of American Development* (Baltimore: Johns Hopkins Press, 1912).

Nevins, Allan. *Grover Cleveland: A Study in Courage* (New York: Dodd, Mead and Co., 1934).

Niebuhr, Reinhold. *The Structure of Nations and Empires* (New York: Charles Scribner's Sons, 1959).

Olcott, Charles S. *The Life of William McKinley,* 2 vols. (Boston: Houghton Co., 1916).

Osgood, Robert Endicott. *Ideals and Self-Interest in America's Foreign Relations* (Chicago: University of Chicago Press, 1953).

Page, Kirby. *Imperialism and Nationalism* (New York: George H. Doran Co., 1925).

Parker, George F. *Recollections of Grover Cleveland* (New York: The Century Co., 1911).

Pratt, Julius W. *America's Colonial Experiment* (New York: Prentice-Hall, Inc., 1950).

———. *Expansionists of 1898* (Baltimore: Johns Hopkins Press, 1936).

Pringle, Henry F. *Theodore Roosevelt: A Biography* (New York: Harcourt, Brace & Co., 1931).

Puleston, W. D. *Mahan: The Life and Work of Captain Alfred Thayer Mahan* (New Haven: Yale University Press, 1939).

Rauch, Basil. *American Interest in Cuba: 1848-1855* (New York: Columbia University Press, 1948).

Rhodes, James Ford. *The McKinley and Roosevelt Administrations* (New York: The Macmillan Co., 1922).

Russ, William Adam, Jr. *The Hawaiian Republic (1894-1898),* (Selinsgrove, Pa.: Susquehanna University Press, 1961).

———. *The Hawaiian Revolution, 1893-94* (Selinsgrove, Pa.: Susquehanna University Press, 1959).

Ryden, George Herbert. *The Foreign Policy of the United States in Relation to Samoa* (New Haven: Yale University Press, 1933).

Samonte, Jose Vedasto. *The American System of Colonial Administration* (Iowa City: The State University of Iowa, 1925).

Sanchez, Ramiro Guerra y. *La Expansion Territorial de los Estados Unidos* (Habana: Cultura, S. A., 1935).

Schumpeter, Joseph. *Imperialism* (New York: Meridian Books, 1955).

Seeley, J. R. *Expansion of England* (Boston: Roberts Brothers, 1883).

Stanwood, Edward. *A History of the Presidency from 1897 to 1909* (Boston: Houghton Mifflin Co., 1912).

Stevens, Sylvester Kirby. *American Expansion in Hawaii: 1842-1898* (Harrisburg: Archives Publishing Co., 1945).

Sullivan, Mark. *Our Times: The United States, 1900-1925,* Vol. I (New York: Charles Scribner's Sons, 1936).

Thayer, William R. *The Life and Letters of John Hay,* 2 vols. (Boston: Houghton Co., 1915).

Turner, Frederick Jackson. *The Frontier in American History* (New York: Henry Holt and Co., 1920).

Viallate, Achille. *Economic Imperialism and International Relations during the Last Fifty Years* (New York: Macmillan Co., 1923).

Weinberg, Alfred K. *Manifest Destiny* (Baltimore: Johns Hopkins Press, 1935).

Werner, M. R. *Bryan* (New York: Harcourt, Brace, and Co., 1929).

Wilkerson, Marcus. *Public Opinion and the Spanish-American War* (Baton Rouge: Louisiana State University Press, 1932).

Williams, Mary Wilhelmine. *Anglo-American Isthmian Diplomacy, 1815-1915* (Washington: American Historical Association, 1916).

Williams, Wayne C. *William Jennings Bryan* (New York: G. P. Putnam's Sons, 1936).

Williamson, Harold Francis. *Edward Atkinson: The Biography of an American Liberal* (Boston: Old Corner Book Store, Inc., 1934).

Winkler, John K. *Incredible Carnegie* (New York: The Vanguard Press, 1931).

—————. *W. R. Hearst: An American Phenomenon* (New York: Simon and Schuster, 1928).

Winslow, E. M. *The Pattern of Imperialism* (New York: Columbia University Press, 1948).

Wisan, Joseph. *The Cuban Crisis as Reflected in the New York Press, 1895-1898* (New York: Columbia University Press, 1934).

Wolff, Leon, *Little Brown Brother* (London: Longmans, Green & Co., 1961).

Index

Rogers, Henry Wade, 128, 141, 143, 204
Roman, Rhett, 27
Roosevelt, Theodore, 7, 21, 26, 50, 82, 85, 90, 100, 101, 104, 121, 148, 158-59, 174, 178, 194, 253, 263, 292; Administration, 257, 260-61; criticizes anti-imperialists, 141; corollary to Monroe Doctrine, 26, 265, 271-72; criticizes free trade advocates, 148-49; and Dominican Republic, 271-72; election of (1900) 225, (1904) 263-68, (1912) 283; and John Hay, 164; on McKinley, 89; and Mahan, 14, 100n, 141, 148, 159; on need for a modern navy, 14, 82; New York gubernatorial campaign, 170-71; and overseas expansion, 85, 100-01, 121; and Panama, 257-65; and the Philippines, 263, 272, 275; and Spanish-American War, 91, 104; and "the strenuous life", 21, 25n, 79, 170, 265; urges Hawaiian annexation, 100-01; and war, 21, 25n, 91, 104; dies, 292
Root, Elihu, 252

St. Louis Westliche Post, 142
Samoa, 1, 72, 225, 226n, 291; annexation, 23; Cleveland Administration and, 63-65; Treaty of 1889, 22; tripartite condominium, 22-24, 34
Sanford, Henry S., 19
San Francisco Newsletter, 38-39
Santo Domingo, 3, 23, 285
Schade, Louis, 138
Schouler, James, 48, 58
Schurman, Jacob G., 207
Schurz, Carl, 9, 23, 51, 99, 132, 149, 154n, 158, 222-24, 265; Anti-Imperialist League Vice-President, 9n, 127, 143, 147-48; and Carnegie, 164, 253; on cruelty in Philippines, 253; effect of imperialism on domestic life, 164; on election of 1900, 215, 232-35; on election of 1904, 263-65; on Hawaii, 40; interest in re-

form, 155-56; to McKinley on Spanish-American War, 92, 96, 104, 122, 161, 168-69; on maintaining the peace, 82-83; on Manifest Destiny, 9, 52-53, 169-70; as "mugwump", 151, 153, 211; officer of American Anti-Imperialist League, 9n, 134; officer of New York Anti-Imperialist League, 9n, 135; opposes annexation of Spanish colonies, 70, 161, 169, 211-13; opposes Roosevelt in New York gubernatorial campaign, 171; opposes Spanish-American War, 90, 93, 120, 122; on Panama, 265; on Samoa, 23; on Santo Domingo, 23; Saratoga speech, 163-64, 168; and E. B. Smith, 228, 230, 235; and Moorfield Storey, 230-31, 270-71; on third party movement, 217, 223-24, 228-31; University of Chicago speech, 183-84; war preparedness, 81; and Erving Winslow, 223, 264, 273
Seeley, John R., 8
Senate, U.S., approves Turpie Resolution, 61; and Hawaii (1893) 34, 37, 38, 39, 41, 42, (1897-98) 97, 102, 104-12, 115-18; Hawaiian coup d'état of 1895, 68; Morgan Report, 59; and Panama canal treaty, 257; and Samoa, 22, 23; Treaty of Paris, 176-79, 181, 183-95, 197, 201
Seward, William H., 3, 29, 56
Sewell, Henry M., 95
Shadwell, Bertrand, 251
Shaw, Albert, 16, 26, 159
Shepard Edward M., 232
Sherman, John, 132, 133, 158-59, 209, 263; Anti-Imperialist League Vice-President, 27, 145; anti-imperialist views, 72-73, 85, 97; memoirs, 72; as Republican opposed to imperialism, 150; Secretary of State, 72, 85n, 95-96, 154n; dies, 269
Skerrett, J. S., Rear Admiral, 30
Slayden, James L., 279
Smith, Adam, 148